STORM OVER THE BAY

Number Sixteen:
GULF COAST STUDIES

SPONSORED BY

Texas A&M University–Corpus Christi
John W. Tunnell Jr., General Editor

STORM OVER THE BAY

The People of Corpus Christi and Their Port

Mary Jo O'Rear

TEXAS A&M UNIVERSITY PRESS

COLLEGE STATION

This paper meets the requirements of ANSI/NISO Z39.48-1992
(Permanence of Paper).
Binding materials have been chosen for durability.

Library of Congress Cataloging-in-Publication Data
O'Rear, Mary Jo Holoubek, 1943–
  Storm over the bay : the people of Corpus Christi and their
port / by Mary Jo O'Rear.—1st ed.
      p. cm. — (Gulf Coast studies ; no. 16)
  Includes bibliographical references and index.
  ISBN-13: 978-1-60344-088-2(cloth:alk.paper)
  ISBN-13: 978-1-62349-550-3(pbk)
  1. Corpus Christi (Tex.)—History. 2. Corpus Christi
(Tex.)—Politics and government. 3. Corpus Christi Bay
(Tex.)—History. 4. Harbors—Texas—Corpus Christi.
5. Hurricanes—Texas—Corpus Christi Bay. 6. Disaster
relief—Texas—Corpus Christi—Citizen participation.
I. Title. II. Series.
  F394.C78.O74 2009
  976.4'113—dc22
                    2008042786

To Jim,

who brought me to this bay,

and to Jessica, Marc, Leyla, and Kenna,

who live on the edge of another one.

Contents

Illustrations and Maps

Acknowledgments

Less than a city history per se, more than a disaster account, this narrative of Corpus Christi's drive for a deep seaport had many progenitors. They include the following historians of Corpus Christi: Dan Kilgore, Anita Eisenhauer, Michael Ellis, Diana Fernández, Murphy Givens, Edna Jordan, Richard Laune, Alan Lessoff, Coleman McCampbell, Harry Plomarity, Frank Wagner, Bill and Marjorie Walraven, and Harvey Weil. Their writings about the city, the 1919 hurricane, and the port underpinned my research.

Vital as well were archivists whose inspired searches made each visit to their facilities a treat. They include Donaly Brice, Grace Charles, Sister Francisca Eiken, Allison Erlich, Beverly Hadley, Nancy Hebluetzel, Cecilia Hunter, David Kessler, Brother Edward Loch, Gerlinda Riojas, and most especially, Ceil Venable and Jan Weaver. Their counterparts in record keeping, librarians, were founts of patience, including Herb Canales and Laura Garcia of Corpus Christi Public Library and the staff of Jernigan Library, Texas A&M–Kingsville.

Also notably supportive have been editors at Texas A&M University Press, most especially Mary Lenn Dixon and her staff. Interested, involved, and informative, they have welcomed a novice writer.

Nothing could have been accomplished, however, without the contributions of devotees like Joe Fulton, Murphy Givens, Msgr. Michael Howell, Jim Moloney, Dale Miller Jr., and Geraldine McGloin. They shared private collections and personal memories that brought the story of early Corpus Christi to life.

Matching their enthusiasm with practical experience were advisors Larry Knight, Les Hunter, Tom Kreneck, Alan Lessoff, and Marshall Schott. Of particular help were Jim Maroney and the late Terry Barragy and Beth Baker Russell, all of whom read earlier versions of this work. They and Steve Schiwetz, who proofed and vetted this version, were especially generous with time and expertise. The errors remaining are my own.

Additional thanks goes to the Texas History Mafia and the Victoria Secrets. Participating in your excitement for all things historical has been a joy.

Above and beyond everything, the soul of this study rests on the interviewees. The hours spent with Alex and Genevieve Cox, Marian and John

Crutchfield, and Alclair Mays Pleasant were the highlight of my work. Their spirit, mirrored in the taped memories of Ramón Sánchez and J. R. Bluntzer, reaffirmed the strength and resilience of turn-of-the-century South Texans. They opened pathways for the rest of us.

Finally, I want to give special thanks to my friends and my family, who resolutely kept their eyes from glazing over while I rhapsodized about research, and to my husband, Jim. His grin, when I received the degree from Texas A&M–Kingsville, lit up the whole gymnasium.

STORM OVER THE BAY

Prologue *View from the Bluff*

A chance to redeem their souls was not given many scam-artists of the late 1830s, especially to such a profligate scoundrel as Henry Kinney. Fleeing from a canal scheme gone bad in Illinois, and, as he would tell it, a botched romance with Daniel Webster's daughter, he had escaped to Texas, the one nation least likely to extradite him to the United States. Even there he dodged civilized centers, opting instead to make final headquarters along the notorious Nueces River, a strip of land so contested by both Mexico and the Republic that few but outlaws and degenerates inhabited it.[1]

Gathering adventurers and gunhands for his own militia, he rode the river eastward until he crested its bluff, where he saw stretching below him a body of water iridescently aqua, glimmering past barrier isles into the distant Gulf of Mexico. Henry Kinney made Corpus Christi Bay his lodestone that day, and even though he died far away, its development and its people became the center of his existence.

In the seventy years following Kinney's arrival, the bay remained the center of South Texans' existence, a nexus of regional maritime trade. By the 1920s, however, locals were expanding their sights. They needed an international economy, and to achieve that, they wanted the federal government to designate their bay as the home of a deepwater port. Alone neither in their quest nor in their history, Kinney's successors were prepared to do battle with the entire Gulf Coast for the port. Like residents of Matagorda Island and Port Isabel, they had weathered Civil War blockades and Reconstruction turmoil. As had citizens of Mobile and Charleston, they had battled postwar apathy and financial panic. Less successfully than leaders of Houston and Galveston, they had lobbied for harbor dredging and jetty building. As eagerly as entrepreneurs in Brownsville and New Orleans, they had financed railroad expansion and business investment.

In their struggle for a deepwater port, however, Corpus Christians had four advantages their contemporaries lacked. One was the topography of the bay itself. While its sister inlets Matagorda, San Antonio, Aransas, and Baffin also fronted a string of barrier islands separating them from the gulf, only Corpus Christi Bay backed onto a rugged, towering outcropping. Elevated enough to provide dwellers balmy breezes as well as protection from floods, the bluff gave Kinney's settlers and their descendents a decided edge over counterparts at sea level.

A second advantage was the bay's indomitable inhabitants. Too far south of San Antonio and Austin to attract Central Texans and too far north of the Rio Grande to be easily accessible from the border, Corpus Christi accumulated a distinctive blend of ethnicities (approximately 10 percent African American, 30 percent Mexican American, and 60 percent Anglo American) drawn to waterfront life.[2] Even into the new century's Jim Crow restraints, long-time families like the Cox/Garcia/Mays, the Hickey/Dodsons, and the Mora/Sanchezes continued to assert their value to the community, bringing a spirited and active populace to the fight for a port.

A third advantage in Corpus Christi's deep water competition lay not in the city but in its hinterlands: the crop and cattle ranges that encompassed Nueces and adjacent counties. Land still meant power in the early years of South Texas settlement, and *ranchero* owners upon whose acreage farmers planted and *vaqueros* galloped wielded an inordinate amount of influence. Not least of these was Robert J. Kleberg, manager of the vast King estate lying south of the city. But unlike political bosses nearby (Archie Parr, Manuel Guerra) or up east (William Tweed), Kleberg did more than collect votes and amass privilege. His was an energetic and dynamic intelligence that developed a preventative for tick fever, founded the state's first Livestock Sanitary Commission, and perfected a method of irrigating scrubland desert. Having his patronage and expertise in lobbying the government for deep water was one of the greatest assets Corpus Christi could possess.[3]

The leadership of Kleberg's protégé, Roy Miller, created the city's fourth advantage. Handsome, vibrant, charismatic, industrious, and meticulous, Miller had secured the trust of most of the business community and citizenry not long after his arrival in 1904. Six years later he was well on his way to a prominent role in local politics. Committed to the cause of deep water, he, more than any elected civic, county, or state leader, spearheaded the fight for a port.

It was singularly appropriate, then, that a telegram from Congressman John Garner, reporting the almost certain designation of Corpus Christi as site for a new deep water port, was directed to him one January day in 1909. "[Rivers and Harbors] Committee has just agreed to report survey for twenty-five foot channel," it read. "Congratulations."[4]

The exultation in the newspaper the next day, "Corpus Christi's future as a deep water port will be assured. . . . [I]t is a great victory . . . the greatest in her history," came too soon.[5] Garner had neglected to warn Miller that regional rivals were already planning to wrest the port from them. Neither had he taken into account the graft that government-funded projects tended to attract, nor the violent personality clashes that permeated local politics at that time. But most importantly, Congressman Garner had overlooked the rising demand for reform that was sweeping Texas into the second decade of the twentieth century. Before the next ten years ended, the Progressive movement would strip the state dry, gut its electorate, and plunge the little town founded by Henry Kinney into one of the most destructive political fights in its history. Then the bay itself would attack, blasting inhabitants with winds and drowning them with floods of unimaginable sweep. How the community recovered from both blows and still secured a deep water port was a testimony to its populace and leaders—and a culmination of the long circuitous process begun years earlier when a fleeing reprobate first saw Corpus Christi Bay.

PART ONE

The Place and the People

1 Barrier Isles and Bays

The bay Kinney discovered had not always been pristine. Formed over a long period of time, it began as raging waters released from melting ice caps in the continental interior and cutting southeastward from the Edwards Plateau through marsh-laden muck into the Gulf of Mexico. Powered with the vigor of newly spawned mountain streams, these tributaries tore sediment from highlands and cliffs and plunged it down toward the Gulf. So tumultuous was their passage that even as the rivers approached the ocean, they continued to abrade underwater shelves, melding their sand with sediment still in solution. Hitting offshore ocean currents head-on, the torrents abruptly slowed and deposited their collected rubble. As centuries went on, the particles that dropped along the ocean bottom began to form into shallow, underwater ridges. Then, around 3000 BC, these ridges gradually broke through the surface, and a chain of reefs emerged off the coast of what became known as South Texas. These isles—San José, Mustang, and Padre—grew steadily with the accumulation of grit supplied by the Nueces and other rivers until they coalesced into each other, forming a truncated island system that bordered the western Gulf Coast from Galveston Bay to the mouth of the Rio Grande.[1]

By the middle of the first millennium AD, the barrier islands were about five miles wide, not more than ten feet in elevation, and separated from each other by unstable tidal inlets. Composed primarily of sand, some layers still bearing the marks of the Pleistocene era, the barrier isles were well defined, with beaches fronting the open gulf, coppices and hummocks extending centrally to well-vegetated dunes, and grassy ramps sloping down westward shores. Adjacent to Mustang Island, and just across the pass that separated it from San José, rested a small, triangular-shaped landmass formed by tidal flows between the lagoons and the Gulf of Mexico. These isles and the delta combined to separate the bays and wetlands of the evolving Texas coast from the gulf, creating a vast channel of calm water, one hundred and twenty miles in length and from four to six miles in width, an estuary so basic to the existence of the region that early Spanish settlers christened it, "Laguna de la Madre."[2]

In the meantime, the mainland opposite had become solid shoreline. Still deep and crooked, the Nueces, Aransas, and Mission rivers had already dropped considerable alluvial debris onto the floodplain as they slowed in their seaward flow. At the same time, the submerged coast had drained during the previous Holocene era, leaving the western gulf "broken into several segments by . . . Corpus Christi and Nueces Bays . . . Copano Bay, and . . . Petronila, Oso, and Chiltipin Creeks." Each was fed by its own set of smaller streams, so that the buildup of deposits alongside the rivers combined with newly emerged shores to form broad areas of relatively flat coastal inland prairies. These low rolling plains, soon covered with grass, began to support "water-tolerant hardwood . . . willows . . . and huisache"[3] as well as an abundance of "game, wild geese, ducks, brents, cranes, jack snipe, quail, wild turkey and deer."[4] Even more basic was their soil, a black, stiff loam "of untold richness," which, in most areas along the coast, eased downward toward the gulf in a gentle three-foot-per-mile gradient.[5]

Gentle the gradient was, except along the western bayfront. This strip of land between Nueces Bay to the west and Corpus Christi Bay to the east was marked by a characteristic fairly unique to the area: an abrupt and very commanding bluff that rose upwards some forty to fifty feet, then dropped precipitously to a coarse sand and shell beach at its foot. Another legacy of ancient deposition, erosion, and shifting riverbeds, such a combination of bluff and beach was rarely matched in the coastal region. The beach, not more than three or four feet above sea level, was about three and one-half miles in length, widest where it extended northward onto a small peninsula jutting between the two bays and narrowest to the southeast as it followed the coastline curve. Midway between the two points, the shell shoreline grounded onto the bluff, which dominated not only the flat beach and rolling plains around it but also Corpus Christi Bay, just a few hundred feet away.[6]

This bluff is . . . [a] peculiarly beautiful and attractive . . . elevated plateau . . . a magnificent natural grandstand from which to view the broad expanse of the bay beneath, two thirds of which it encircles. One can see for miles to the north, east and south, till sky, water and shorelines seem to melt. Looking eastward no land is in sight—a broad expanse of water. Northward and southward—to the right and left the fluffy shores slope away to the horizon.[7]

Conjoined to the beach and the bluff were the bays.

Nueces Bay was the lesser, an elongated inlet, "some ten miles long and

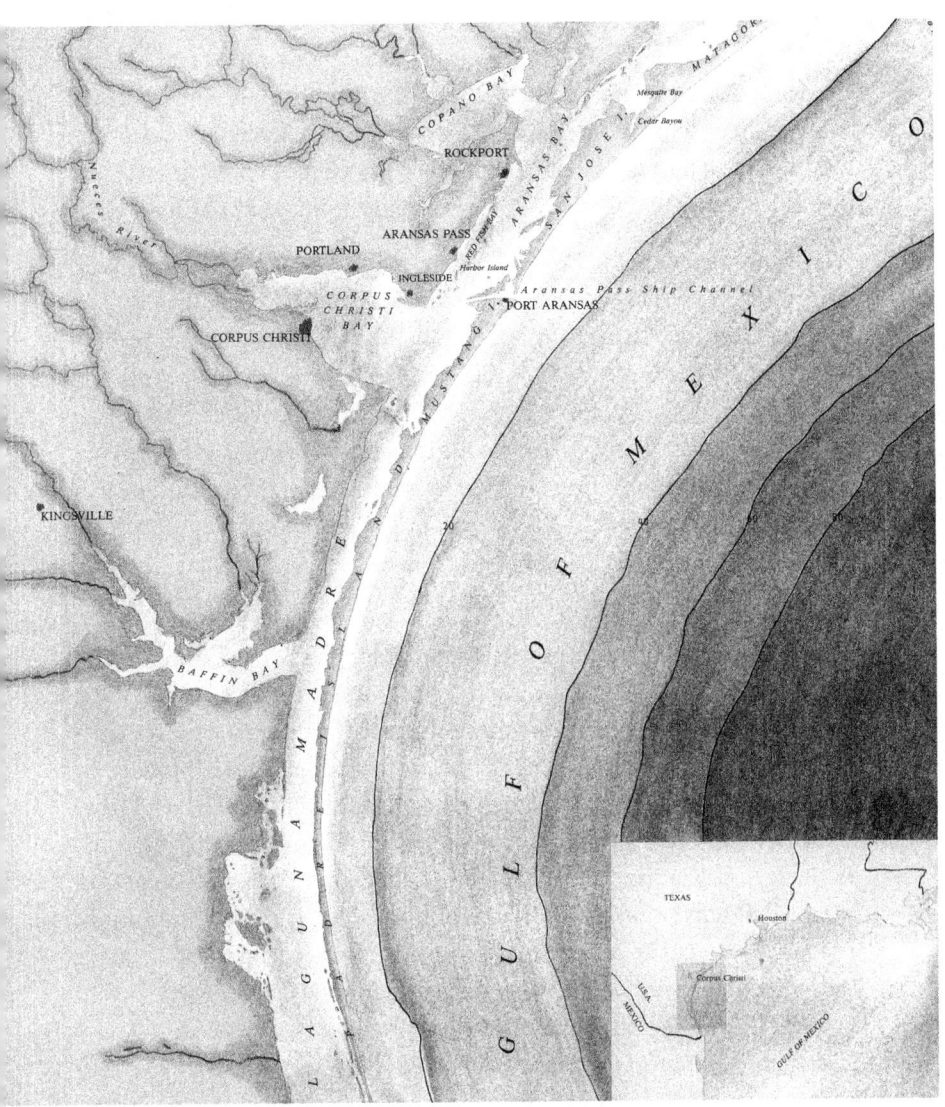

1. Gulf waters, lagoons, rivers, and inlets surrounding Corpus Christi Bay.
Courtesy the Institute of Marine Biology, Port Aransas, University of Texas.

six or eight wide containing many pretty little green Islands," into which the Nueces River flowed.[8] This smaller bay, in turn, flowed into Corpus Christi Bay, nearly a circle of about fifteen miles diameter, with a maximum depth of thirteen feet, which coursed finally into the Laguna Madre. It was Corpus Christi Bay that the mainland bluff embraced, closing in upon it in a sweeping curve, "hugging the bay close," determined to show it at its best.[9]

> [In] the mornings . . . the whole bay would be as one vast mirror, unruffled save by schools of fish seeking to escape a prowling porpoise. About eleven o'clock, a faint zephyr would . . . increase until it became a raging gale, when the whole bay would be converted into a seething, tumultuous waste of waters . . . long into the night. With the approach of . . . a near-full moon . . . the tumultuous waves . . . are as tens of millions of dancing miniature mirrors, and the tenor of the surf, near at hand, is accompanied by the deep boom of . . . the coast twenty miles distant.[10]

Integral to the barrier islands, beach, bluff, and bays were the winds, monsoonal and as much a part of the formation process as the water. Wind had always been a major force behind ocean currents, wave trains, tidal inlets, and dune displacement, with southeasterlies being the most prevalent in this area. The "delicious freshness of the atmosphere"[11] caused by "delightful . . . invigorating sea breezes . . . moderating the heat of [the] nearly tropical sun,"[12] were most common during the summer months. They helped create "probably one of the healthiest and pleasantest spots in the world. From the earliest dawn, refreshing breezes invigorate the body, dissipate the intensity of heat, and nerve the system to a healthful action. The cool nights invite weariness to repose, disturbed neither by the promenading flea, nor the buzzing mosquito."[13]

But just as important were the "strong offshore and longshore northerlies . . . of winter . . . nearly all of which are stormy and associated with the passage of a cold front." It was these winds and the storms they brought that one observer characterized as "perfectly awful—take your breath away and make you sit bolt upright in your chair, feet on the rung, as if your life depended on it."[14]

It was this take-your-breath-away, sit-bolt-upright quality—the sudden shock of danger in the midst of everyday life—that attracted certain people to the bay of Corpus Christi. Their ability to tolerate risk, both natural and man-made, started the area down its road to a deepwater port.

2 Castaways and Cattlemen

The area's first inhabitants knew nothing but risk. Chronically on the edge of starvation, early Native American nomads subsisted on the shellfish and roots of island wetlands, and, by AD 800, had left enough detritus to create considerable kitchen middens along the northern shore of Corpus Christi Bay.[1] Their more organized cousins, the Karankawas, moved in by the 1500s and raided the area's wildlife for their nourishment.

> In the fall they camped on the offshore islands catching fish in cane weirs and eating the roots of certain underwater plants. . . . Until April they subsisted mainly on oysters that were found in abundance along the mainland shores. As summer approached the coastal dwellers moved inland to harvest the fruit of various cacti, principally tunas and the prickly pears.[2]

Inured to nature, these gatherers inadvertently opened their domain to human enemies when they captured, then carried with them, the survivors of a 1528 Spanish flotilla. Wrecked upon the Florida coast and further decimated when their flimsy rafts shattered on Texas islands, the remaining Europeans roamed with their captors over the Nueces River valley for years until finally able to escape. Their long trek home ended in northwestern Mexico in 1536.[3]

Eager to tell their tales to fascinated government officials, the castaways relished the New Spain haciendas their survival won. But it was their writings, and those particularly of their leader, Álvar Núñez Cabeza de Vaca, that most affected the coastal gulf plains. Quite possibly one of the first non-natives to stand upon the great chalk bluff and view Corpus Christi Bay, Cabeza de Vaca diverted colonial attention to the New Mexico highlands with his reports of precious metals, then petitioned to colonize South Texas himself. Unsuccessful in his attempt and eventually recalled to Spain, the old soldier never saw the Gulf Coast again.[4]

But others did, attracted by his descriptions of sheltered bays and secretive inlets. Eager to exploit waters too distant from missions and towns to secure, smugglers began to headquarter on the barrier islands. There they "lightered," offloading illicit cargo onto shallow-bottomed skiffs, then sailing across Corpus Christ Bay to the mainland, where warehouses held the goods until transfer across the Rio Grande. The malfeasance grew so blatant that by 1830, the military commander of the Provinces of the East urged Mexico's government to restrict even legitimate trade in the area.[5]

But revolution moved too quickly, Texas won its independence, and the next few years saw the contrabandists' resort along the bay gain even more ill repute. By 1839 the estuary system of Corpus Christi, lying within a contested borderland of two enemy republics, had become a haven of "outlaws, thieves and murderers."[6]

It was the new home of Henry Kinney as well. The fugitive grifter took little time to cut himself into the illicit trade, soon controlling the only viable marketing post in the region. Nor did he demur at counterespionage, convincing both republic officials and Mexican authorities of their need for his spy services. But it was the bay that awoke in Kinney a surprising sense of duty, showing itself partially in a dogged determination to turn his bluffside property into a thriving city. Soon he and his agents had plastered the eastern seaboard and Europe with broadsides advertising a settlement with unlimited opportunity.[7] Some adventurers moved in, but his most spectacular success came in 1845 when President James K. Polk ordered an entire army under the command of Zachary Taylor to the south bank of the Nueces River in a conscious attempt to provoke Mexico into an act of war. Corpus Christi's population ballooned from one hundred persons in July 1845 to two thousand by January 1, 1846, and included unfamiliar types like lawyers, business agents, hairdressers, photographers, and sutlers. But the stay was not permanent, and when Polk sent Taylor downriver nine months later to arouse the Mexicans along the Rio Grande, a shrunken Corpus Christi resumed its place as "the most murderous, thieving, gambling, cut-throat, God-forsaken hole in the 'Lone Star State.'"[8]

This sentiment did not stop new settlers from coming, chief among them a newlywed couple from Prussia, Felix and Maria von Blücher. Already acquainted with Kinney from his service in the U.S. Army during Taylor's occupation, Felix relinquished a constricted future in Germany for a freer one in Texas and persuaded his sweetheart to join him. Educated, elitist, and eager for change, Maria joined other European settlers swayed by Kinney's blandishments, and within a few years, Corpus Christi had assumed the somewhat respectable status of an up-and-coming coastal town. By 1852, despite the fact that it was using the same "lightering" process to unload cargo that smugglers had thirty years earlier, the bayside settlement had been incorporated by the state legislature. Within a year it elected its first mayor and sent Henry Kinney to the State Senate for four terms.[9]

But national tensions were overtaking local concerns, and the secession crisis in 1861 stopped the nascent seaport dead in its tracks. Distraught by the statewide vote for dissolution, Kinney followed Sam Houston in resigning his post, then fled to Mexico, eventually to die in a gunfight in Matamoros. Corpus Christi, in the meantime, struggled for survival, its early wartime boom in contraband shipping brought abruptly to a halt by Union gunboats in 1862. By the time Texas troops straggled back from the last formal surrender of the Civil War, Corpus Christi was almost deserted, "a dilapidated town with no business doing whatever."[10]

The aftermath of rebellion, however, brought new life to Corpus Christi—and old faces willing to take new risks. Slavery had never been as extensive in South Texas as it had in the eastern part of the state, although it carried its own horror. One of those most affected was Malvina Britton Moore, brought from Virginia in 1849 and traded to a new master to offset a debt. Adjusting to unfamiliar climate and conditions, she hired her time out, accumulated savings, and by the time of emancipation, was in a position, with her husband Sam, to make decisions never allowed her forebears. One of those decisions was where to live, and together the couple chose to remain in Corpus Christi, willing to face the barely suppressed rage of an unrepentant white majority in order to provide a better life for their daughter.[11]

Also choosing to stay was Mariah Cox, whose weapon of survival in the coastal town was real estate. Determined to own rather than ever again be property, she cooked, ironed, and washed enough clothes to secure unclaimed lots on the bluff behind the bay. Amid land so scraggly "you couldn't pay a white man" to go there, she cleared brush, built homes for herself and her daughter, Sally Garcia, set up her son-in-law Florentino as manager of other holdings, and lived long enough to see her scrubland become neighborhoods.[12]

Guarding these neighborhoods and the rights of their residents were another set of fighters, the 10th Virginia Regiment. Stationed in Corpus Christi to preserve the newly won liberty of black Americans, these Negro troopers patrolled mud streets, set up the first Congregational church, and helped ease the town into a grudging acceptance of freedmen. When demobilized, some stayed, seeking work as "blacksmiths, wagon drivers, carpenters, cistern makers and fishermen"—and found themselves jostling for space, and jobs, with a very different kind of Texan.[13]

These were *Tejanos* or Mexican Texans, whose ancestors had hazarded their lives in the area long before *norteamericano* settlers and slaves intruded. Some, like Juan José Cisneros and his wife, María Antonia, had been part of José de Escandón's original Nuevo Santander settlement in 1757; through the years their descendents had gradually moved their *ranchos* farther north of the Rio Grande to be closer to the gulf. The first fifty years of the next century saw other *Latinos* move into the Coastal Bend: *rancheros* like Juan José Montemayor, who settled along the Nueces River, *empresarios* like Martín de León, who secured land along the Rio Guadalupe, and *federales* like Captain Enrique Villarreal, who owned a grant to the area between Nueces and Corpus Christi bays. It was upon Villarreal's property that Colonel Kinney had "squatted" in 1841, eventually closing the deal for it years later. Sensitive to Tejanos around him, the adventurer warned them about bandit incursions, worked with them on sheep and cattle holdings, and rode with them in his own private militia, a requisite for survival in the tumultuous Nueces Strip.[14]

Time and the Treaty of Guadalupe-Hidalgo made changes, however. Aggressive Anglo domination brought little but trouble to Texas-born *Mexicanos*, and many began to gravitate from rural plains along the rivers to larger enclaves near the coast. Some of the dislocation was forced, involving descendants of the first Tejanos displaced from their ranchos by skilled lawyers, family partitions, and market fluctuations. Carrying well-honed skills as *vaqueros* but reluctant to work for interlopers, many saw hope in the horse-driven economy of the towns.[15]

And it was hoof power—the combined resources of burros, oxen, and mules pulling huge two-wheeled carts—that kept Corpus Christ alive in the postwar pall of the late 1860s. This *carreta* trade, noted for its slow, two-mile-an-hour passages across desert, linked the bayside community to outposts like Laredo, San Antonio, and Chihuahua City. But it was the cargo of hides and wool that brought to the city two young opportunists who would change it forever.[16]

Never as debt-ridden as Kinney, and far shrewder, Mifflin Kenedy and Richard King operated steamships on the Rio Grande during the Mexican and Civil wars, converting their assets into unclaimed pasturage between hostilities. As eager to monopolize land as they had the river, the two established ranches up and down the Wild Horse Desert south of Corpus

Christi, eventually encompassing several counties and nearly over one million acres. However, owning and profiting off the barren scrublands were two different things, and it was not until the boatmen began pasturing sheep that they saw some return to their enterprise.[17]

But it was feral cattle roaming the plains that provided the real future to King and Kenedy—and to Corpus Christi. At first too far away, and too tough, to entice eastern meatpackers, the herds' only value lay in the refuse of their carcasses. Accordingly, by 1869 Richard King and his fellow ranchers had begun to utilize the myriad hide-and-tallow factories dotting the coast from Corpus Christi to Rockport. There, skinned, boiled, and rendered, the remains of Texas longhorns were bundled into stacks of wet hides or siphoned into tightly-fastened lard barrels, ready to join sackloads of wool and cotton on the long carreta trail to Mexico. For King, Kenedy, and the other ranchers of the Nueces Valley region, Corpus Christi was becoming the shipping headquarters of their livelihood.[18]

The abandonment of tallow factories for cattle drives did not diminish the cowmen's interest in the small town. Impatient with erratic mail delivery and inconsistent wagon transport in the 1870s, King set up his own stage line and centered it in Corpus Christi. At about the same time, he helped establish a local newspaper, donated land for local public schools, and brought to the city its first ice-making plant. Three years later he put one of the town's newest lawyers on permanent retainer. When it became evident that railroad competition from surrounding areas had cost Corpus Christi merchants over 30 percent of their trade to northern Mexico, King and Kenedy stepped in with local businessmen to build a rail line to the city.[19]

Their decision was not ill judged. In the nearly three-hundred-mile span that separated South Texas' two largest cities, Brownsville and San Antonio, from each other, Corpus Christi lay roughly in the middle—and less than fifty miles away from King's and Kenedy's headquarters. As political seat of Nueces County, with an already established sheriff, post office, and jail, the little town had survived frontierhood, thrown off Reconstruction ennui, and, by the 1870s, was eager to accept ranchero patronage in order to become the commercial center of South Texas.[20]

So King and Kenedy combined with local citizens Perry Doddridge, David Hirsh, and Uriah Lott to create the Corpus Christi, San Diego and Rio Grand Narrow Gauge Rail Road. Dedicating the railroad's depot in November 1876, the investors saw its crew start west and, in less than five years, lay tracks from Corpus Christi through San Diego to Realitos. Although bought out by the Texas-Mexican Railway in 1881, the line continued on to its final destination in Laredo, providing Corpus Christi, and shippers like Richard King and Mifflin Kenedy, with rail access to Mexico. Five years later a new line, the San Antonio and Aransas Pass, connected Corpus Christi northward to the Alamo City. The coastal city was on its way to becoming a hub of overland transportation.[21]

Outlets and Immigrants

But why overland only? What of the bay, Corpus Christi's natural outlet to the gulf that had kept Kinney in contraband and Confederates in cotton until the Union blocked it down? What about the long lagoon in front of the city that all but promised businessmen easy access to piers and wharves? Technology happened, and by the late 1800s steam-powered freighters of the day had found it so difficult to enter Corpus Christi Bay that the little port could sustain only the most accommodating ocean-going trade.[1]

One reason for the impediment lay in the two outlets to the gulf that governed access to the bay: Aransas Pass, between Mustang Island and San José Island twenty-five miles northeast of the city, and Corpus Christi Pass, between Mustang and Padre islands eighteen miles to the southeast. Although deep enough themselves, with natural channels dredged daily by tides ebbing and flooding between bay and gulf, the passes were blocked by mounds of sediment deposited when outward flows collided with strong ocean currents. Growing denser and higher every day, these sandbars taxed the ingenuity of topographical experts and military engineers alike. Assigned to the coast as part of the U.S. Army's survey of river and harbor works in 1853, an officer, Captain W. G. Freeman, summarized the problem: "Accounts vary materially as to the depth of water that can be carried at high tide over the bars of the two passes, but from the best information within my reach I do not think it would be prudent to risk more than 7 ½ feet over Aransas, and 5 ½ over Corpus Christi bar." Brevet Captain George McClelland, of later Civil War fame, was even more damning in his appraisal: "[G]overnment stores should never be sent to Corpus Christi Pass in vessels drawing more than 5 ½ to 6 feet scant—and in no event when it is possible to send them to Aransas, bad as the latter is."[2]

Nor were obstructed passes between the gulf and Laguna Madre the only obstacle shippers faced. The naturally worn tidal channels between the passes vanished as the sea floor rose abruptly toward the mainland, and as a result, water levels of the bay were both shallow and unpredictable, with depths rising and falling as much as nine feet from one year to the next. Charts drawn from 1875 to 1887 indicated an additional problem:

the logical passageway from Aransas Pass southeast between Harbor Island and Mustang Island, where one would have to sail in order to cross Laguna Madre and Corpus Christi Bay in order to get to city wharves, was even more unstable. Always subject to storm and wave action, the levels in this strait could range from five and a half feet in one year to two feet the following year, but at no time were they deep enough for the ocean-going vessels of the day.[3]

As a result, shippers to Corpus Christi were using the same "lightering" process employed by smugglers a century earlier; stevedores on the gulf side of Mustang and St. Joseph islands would unload cargo from large gulf steamers, transfer it to shallow-drafted barges and skiffs, then sail across the bay to the docks fronting the city. There it would be wharfed until entrained south to Falfurrias or Premont or west to Kenedy or San Antonio. Compared to more open coastal ports like Galveston and New Orleans, Corpus Christi was at severe disadvantage.[4]

But it was not dead, and thwarted plans to make bay waters navigable soon cluttered city and county files. The earliest came, not surprisingly, from Henry Kinney, who persuaded slave owner John M. Moore to dig a deepwater channel across the bay in the 1850s. "He worked Negro slaves and white men in a dredging boat for two years before the Civil War but he did not succeed."[5]

A more impressive attempt coincided with the building of the Texas-Mexican rail line from Corpus Christi to Laredo in the 1870s. Contracting with the most aggressive shipping firm of the gulf, Morgan Lines, local businessmen persuaded Richard King to extend his transportation interests to the sea. Within three years of his investment, the Corpus Christi Navigation Company had dredged part of the bay to a depth of eight feet, then worked with the city to extend the railroad pier all the way out to the new channel. When the freighter *Gussie* docked at Central Wharf in 1874, three thousand people and a town full of eager shippers greeted it. For over ten years trains chugged out to the bay at pier's end to offload and take on cargo. Then the channel silted over, the steamers began dragging too much bottom, and Morgan Lines abandoned Corpus Christi altogether. A further attempt seven years later also ended in despair. What good was a harbor that could only float ships with draughts of not more than six feet?[6]

Such failures—and the Morgan Line debacle—led to a kind of mental shake-up among shippers like King, politicos like Mayor D. C. Heath, and newspapermen like W. P. Caruthers. Private dredging was out; leaders' only hope lay in fully funded government channeling of the gulf.[7]

The federal government reciprocated by establishing a Corps of Engineers' headquarters in Galveston Bay in 1880, the first step to streamlining gulf access. Initial efforts heralded hope: the Rivers and Harbors Committee in the U.S. Congress authorized creating a jetty between the two islands leading into Aransas and Corpus Christi bays, and by the late 1880s the problem of sandbars impeding ships from the gulf had significantly diminished. The next step, to improve Aransas Bay itself, was logical and quickly taken. But the final act, to dredge Corpus Christi Bay to a depth respectable enough to allow deep sea shipping, never came. Corpus Christi had been eclipsed by upcoast rival Galveston.[8]

Perched on the east side of a barrier island, Galveston directly fronted the gulf and backed onto a natural harbor, making it the most accessible cotton port in the country. By 1889 the federal government had designated the Island City as the deepwater harbor to be developed on the Texas Coast, best suited to accommodate "the ocean-going vessels and naval necessities" of the Trans-Mississippi West. Consequently, throughout the rest of the century Galveston monopolized major appropriations that could have gone to Corpus Christi or other developing ports.[9]

Nor were Galvestonians particularly humble in their achievements. An early 1900 article in the *Galveston Daily News* snidely described its sister city's feeble attempts at trade:

> The Corpus Christi people have been trying for many months to get a steamer service to their port from Galveston. Not being able to induce outside people to take a line to them, they . . . took steps to have a line of their very own. They held meetings, subscribed money . . . [and] on Wednesday the *Cumberland* sailed to Corpus Christi for the first time. . . . As the matter is almost as vital to the people of Corpus Christi as is the local school election, it may have been the occasion for a public ovation.[10]

In return, Corpus Christi newspapers could only rejoice in the Island City's occasional missteps—"It was Galveston's own . . . fault that it did not get an appropriation [from last year's bill.] The city said $1,700,000 or nothing, [so] it was nothing"[11]—emphasize Galveston's horrific vulnerability—"Take it all in all, . . . the conclusion is reasonable that some time or other, a tidal wave, driven by some howling tempest . . . swift and terrible . . . may yet engulf Galveston Island"[12]—and disparage accusations of envy—"The *News* can gain nothing by giving expression to such suspicions. It surely does not judge others by itself."[13]

In the meantime Galveston forged ahead and by the turn of the century had formulated such a widely approved plan to deepen its channel that acceptance from the Rivers and Harbors Committee was practically a given. Faced with the loss of even more funding, Corpus Christi leaders temporarily turned their backs to the bay; hope for growth would have to come inland—with a bigger city and better politicians.[14]

Making the city bigger had already begun with the arrival of the San Antonio and Aransas Pass Railway in 1886. Now straddling two railroad lines, civic leaders saw potential in tourism and made a desperate attempt to embellish natural resources. First to be reinvented was the old artesian well, dug by Taylor's troops forty years earlier. Now assuming health-giving properties, its "wretched-tasting" waters drew hundreds eager to join the national craze for taking the "cure."[15]

Next to boost were the beaches, both mainland and barrier isles. Despite its "distance of a day or two's extent," Padre Island promised sports fishing, while the beach north of the city was termed "most excellent [for] bathing." "As a summer resort for Mexicans and Texans . . . [with a] climate tempered by healthful and refreshing sea breezes," Corpus Christi was becoming an advertiser's dream.

The city council mandated repairs to downtown streets and sidewalks, set speed limits "no faster than a slow trot," and passed laws "regulating the sale of liquor to minors, Habitual Drunks, and insane persons." Ten years after Bell's great invention hit the Centennial Exposition in 1876, aldermen contracted with Erie Telephone and Telegraph Company to wire Corpus Christi.

In the meantime, people were coming. From the shrunken antebellum settlement of less than a thousand, Corpus Christi's population quadrupled by 1890. Part of the reason lay in its commercial freighting. Jobs for experienced draymen and bull-whackers to drive the wagons between Corpus Christi and destinations north, south, and west had always been available. Even as tracks began to displace trails, saddlers, stablemen, horse "doctors," and drovers remained necessary to the area's mobility, as did carters and *carreteros*, carpenters, blacksmiths, and harness makers. The wharves, piers, and passes offered their own opportunities ranging from pilots and helmsmen to longshoremen and stevedores. Ferrymen and bargemen competed for hire, and at night, scavengers waded the bayfront, collecting from the debris and refuse of the waters some kind of valuable they could trade in on a meal—or a drink—the next day. The entry of two major railroads into Corpus Christi by the mid-1880s increased the job pool. Many of those who had driven the spikes and laid the ties stayed behind to maintain the yards, repair the engines, and in some cases, drive the locomotives.[16]

Agricultural diversity also increased the population. With the foremost industry on the prairies in 1877 being sheep and cattle ranching, Corpus Christi had become one of the "principal marketing centers of livestock and livestock products from Nueces and neighboring counties." By the 1890s, the city was still exporting animals and their by-products, "including 500 carloads of cattle, 1,500,000 pounds of wool, [and] 250,000 pounds of hides." Although cotton production on the plains soon outstripped that of livestock, Corpus Christi maintained its position as dominant exporter in the region, and jobs flourished—meat packing, cattle shipping, cotton picking, market trading.[17]

In the meantime, other forms of harvest were taking place in the waterways, particularly that of the green sea turtle.

> Beginning in the 1880's, turtles . . . were shipped . . . upside down and trussed to wholesale dealers especially in Galveston and Corpus Christi. . . . In 1884, at least two [local] . . . facilities . . . canned sea turtles. . . . [One] plant handled twenty thousand pounds of turtle valued at $800.00 between August 1, 1895, to August 1, 1896.[18]

In 1897, with Corpus Christi handling 53 percent of state turtle catches, its canners had joined watermen, packers, pickers, planters, ranchers, vaqueros, and sheepmen to bring city population close to the highwater mark of five thousand. Well on its way to economic soundness, the old town was shunting its nefarious origins aside to embrace respectability.[19]

But it still enticed risk-takers. One of these was teenager Nicamor Mora, willing to chance a better life across a hostile border than endure the inequities of Porfirio Díaz's Mexico. Slipping across the Rio Grande in the early 1890s, he trekked through dry wastelands, dodged mounted patrols, and crossed cotton fields, seeking a job that would match his mechanical abilities. His eventual arrival in the city was a godsend to George Blücher, youngest son of early settlers Felix and Maria Blücher and owner of the icehouse there. After fifteen years, old methods of cold preservation—

keeping shiploads of frozen snow in pits lined with straw—had been supplanted by steam-powered, ammonia-cooled refrigeration units; Blücher had revamped his entire plant to maintain the technique. But the change to electrical power and the incessant struggle to keep gulf humidity from corroding the cylinders, pistons, and pipes taxed even Blücher's ingenuity, and in Nicamor Mora he found a technical soul mate. Together, often working twenty-hour shifts, the two kept Lone Star Ice Factory in operation, providing refrigeration services for restaurants and hotels and foot-high ice blocks for housewives and bodega operators. By the turn of the century, Nicamor Mora was assistant engineer of the company, had married, and was raising a family on Water Street.[20]

Living on the bluff above was another immigrant who had taken the same chance on Corpus Christi, albeit much earlier. Educated but unable to advance in the fratricidal tumult of 1850s Ireland, Thomas Hickey crossed the Atlantic only to arrive in the United States on the eve of its own civil war. Joining the Confederacy, he fought until Appomattox, survived a bout of malaria, then headed for South Texas where he fell in love with a girl as devoutly Catholic as himself. The two started married life in the city, and within thirty years, Hickey had become head cashier of the Corpus Christi National Bank and a member of its Board of Directors.

By 1900, a widower twice over and father of seven, Hickey lived atop the bluff in a large and spacious home, just a few doors down from the town mansions of ranchers Mifflin Kenedy and Richard King.[21]

Within walking distance of Mora's icehouse and Hickey's downtown bank sat the establishment of another adventurer, one whose gifts lay not in machinery or money but in words. Leaving San Francisco for a bayside city considerably smaller, Silas Gunst saw in Corpus Christi a thirst for knowledge, and in 1902 he chanced family and fortune to set up a bookstore there. Stocking it with almanacs, law tomes, home remedy and recipe books—and the occasional novel—he augmented his merchandise with typewriters, ink, fountain pens, and paper. By 1910, the Corpus Christi Book and Stationery Store had become an integral part of Chaparral Street, part of the combination of shops, saloons, restaurants, and dry goods emporiums attracting customers from city and country alike.[22]

The irony that many of the country customers spoke neither English nor Spanish was the legacy of two other gamblers in South Texas, Stanley Kostoryz and John Hoelscher. Taking advantage of the late-century need of many ranchers to increase their cash flow, these speculators purchased

2. Corpus Christi National Bank in the late 1800s, where Tom Hickey started as a cashier. *Courtesy Corpus Christi Public Library.*

huge lots of rangeland, then divided them into subplots for individual farmers. Setting moderate prices and plastering America and Europe with handbills and advertisements, Kostoryz and Hoelscher started a mini land rush of Czechs, Germans, and Midwesterners to Nueces County and its environs.[23]

But the newcomers found themselves dislodging those most directly associated with livestock raising, the vaqueros for whom the large ranchos had become a refuge after the Mexican War. Now these artisans of the range discovered that riding, horse-breaking, and bull-dogging skills were irrelevant to the Eastern Europeans who replaced rancheros. Tejano identity meant nothing to farmers who derided all Spanish-speakers as *Meskins*, and the amount of crops a worker's children could harvest carried far more value than their health or education. Many rural Latinos who hadn't moved to the city earlier soon faced few choices: to become sharecroppers on land their ancestors may have once owned or to become migrant workers, "Mexican laborers," who would clear the land and tend the crops, then move on to the next harvest.[24]

Their simmering hostility would soon explode, with painful national and international effects on both sides, but for others the new fields were a haven. Laborers in Mexico earning, at best, fifty-seven cents for a full day of picking cotton, noted that Nueces Valley farmers were paying up to six times that amount. Just as wary of abuse as had been Nick Mora, they flocked across the border anyway and, between 1890 to 1910, more than doubled the number of Mexicanos in the state. As desperate as their earlier counterparts to succeed in South Texas, these immigrants risked their lives to work.[25]

However, the farms they worked—whether owned by Czechs or Germans or Midwesterners or Tejanos—could never be totally self-sufficient and profitable without market access, and the market was still on the coast. Therefore, caliche-and-shell-layered roads emerged, crisscrossing the region to hub at Corpus Christi. Produce wagons and trucks rumbled over them into town. Back streets curved off from them, leading to warehouses and depots, and overall-clad drivers climbed down from cramped seats to stretch their legs on them before trudging off to do business with clerks and stationmasters. On market days, wives and children rode in with their men, eager to savor "big city" amenities: dry-goods emporiums, where a seasoned seamstress could peruse shirtwaist patterns while her husband bought seeds; medical offices, where the doctor could lance one child's boil and cure another's colic; and Gunst's stationery store, where a young reader could hide amid inkpots and bookshelves to sneak a peek in *The Call of the Wild*.[26]

Then, at day's end, after families had been sent home or bunked with local kin, old Corpus Christi came alive again. Drunks lurched out of alleyway outhouses, bumping into sailors and stevedores crowding smoke-filled saloons. Gambling dens and brothels (two within walking distance) seduced visitors and "townies" alike, and live music—ragtime, blues, *conjunto*—blasted the night, ricocheting across the bay into the slumbering settlements of Portland and White's Point, to be silenced only by the coming dawn.[27]

Promises
and
Potential

Meanwhile, civic leaders struggling for a way to bring sea dominancy to Corpus Christi finally discovered the solution in their own geography. What did Corpus Christi have that made it more suitable for deepwater facilities than any other town of the coast? Not its enviable rail service; Brownsville's was almost equivalent. Nor were its banking facilities that extraordinary; Freeport had good banks too. Cattlemen and cotton farmers traded in Corpus Christi, but they traded in Rockport and Aransas Pass as well. The one thing that graced this area above all others was its own personal gift from nature, city fathers decided: Corpus Christi was immune to hurricanes.

Not that anyone called them hurricanes at the time. No, up until the end of the nineteenth century, the late-summer blasts that did so much damage were simply called "overflows," "storms," or, in extreme cases, "equinoxial storms." Nor had more than a handful of early-twentieth-century meteorologists begun to realize that such disturbances were not simply strong winds of extraordinary velocity. Rather than cloud-contained masses of violent air that moved straight across land, hurricanes were radically different: core-centered, spiraling bands of thunderstorms, fueled by equatorial ocean heat and formed when this heat combined with humid air above it, then mixed with surface and upper-air winds blowing from the same direction. The result, a "huge . . . heat engine . . . that convert[ed] the warmth of the tropical ocean and atmosphere into wind and waves," released energy equivalent to an atomic bomb exploding every ten seconds. Such power and might were only partially understood in the early twentieth century.[1]

Yet everyone knew that a hurricane's greatest danger was not the wind itself, but the accompanying storm surge. When the converging winds, hot air, and humidity first began coalescing on the surface of equatorial seas, the resulting pressures would push the waters below the core upward. As the hurricane gained in intensity, so also would the mounding of the seas beneath it, the piling up relieved only by deeper ocean currents that siphoned off a greater part of the waters even as they built. So long as the hurricane stayed in open sea, the surge below its center could remain loose. But when the hurricane headed toward a coastal area that mirrored its own low barometric pressure, the once deep ocean floor became more shallow, thus cutting off the currents that had dissipated the waters at their core. The closer the hurricane got to the shore, the shallower the floor became and the closer to the surface the waters would rise. In places where the sea floor sloped gradually, like the Gulf of Mexico, the resulting mound simply had more time to build, gaining in power. The result, anticipating the actual landfall of the hurricane, was an abnormally high tide that swiftly eroded beaches and undercut any dunes or buildings in the vicinity.[2]

As the hurricane hit, this abrupt rise in water level was accompanied by waves riding the top of the storm surge and crashing with a force of sixty-four pounds per cubic foot. Such waves became battering rams, tearing homes off their foundations, wresting trees from their roots, or ripping tracks from their trestles. Yet the mayhem never stopped with the waves. The storm surge could inundate an entire region with twelve to fifteen feet of water, then push into the adjacent rivers and bays and flood areas far inland. It was the kind of catastrophe that people who had never experienced it could not begin to imagine.[3]

The people of "storm-proof" Corpus Christi had indeed experienced such havoc—and not too far back in their own past. The 1880s were a "hurricane-rich" period, partially because of what scientists call a "Multi-decadal Mode," a cycle when sea surfaces become unusually warm before turning cool. Seven hurricanes affected the South Texas coast from 1885 to 1888, with three hitting the area in the year 1886 alone, including one that wiped out the upper coastal town of Indianola.[4] Just twelve years earlier occurred

the worst storm [to strike] Corpus Christi since the city was named Kinney's Rancho. A gale accompanied by rain increased in intensity towards the evening of September 4. Bathhouses and wharves were beaten by the waves back into lumber. Waves "mountainous high" rolled onshore. Heavy winds and rains continued until 3 P.M. on the fifth when the eye passed overhead. Soon after, winds became southerly and were at their worst. Schooners were shoved inland, ramming houses and trees on their way. Water Street was no longer in existence. . . . The Brazos Santiago lighthouse, already rotting, was completely wrecked, and the light keeper's wife lost her life in the storm.[5]

The establishment of the Federal Weather Service in 1870 spurred scientific, and a certain amount of popular, interest in hurricanes, and the increasing use of the telegraph helped to give better warnings and collect more information. But well into the twentieth century, such knowledge was still spotty. As a result, all kinds of unfounded theories about hurricanes abounded, tending to downplay their destruction or minimize their impact. Shore communities desperate to entice economic investment especially embraced these pronouncements, advocated by the "experts" so highly regarded by pundits of the day, and it became almost a competition to see which weather authority could boost his town's safety the most.[6]

As always, Galveston won hands down, with no less an authority than its own chief of the Federal Weather Service, Isaac Cline, armed with a medical degree, a U.S. Army Signal Corps certificate, and seven years of meteorological service in Arkansas and West Texas. Determined to prove the virtual impossibility of a catastrophic storm striking his new city, Cline penned an article in July 1891 demonstrating the difference between "true types of West India hurricanes" and those of less intensity. Gulf Coast hurricanes were the less intense, he ruled, being simple "cyclonic disturbances," responsible for less property loss than "a single tornado in the central states." Using charts and wind flow data, he pronounced the Texas coast "exempt from . . . severe meteorological disturbances," except for those few, like the ones that hit Indianola, that were caused by occasional accidental forces. He concluded with a rebuff to regional critics: "The opinion held by some . . . that Galveston will at some time be seriously damaged by some such disturbance, is simply an absurd delusion. . . . It would be impossible for any cyclone to create a storm which could materially injure the city."[7] Anchored in such certainty, the *Galveston News* indignantly accused ports like Corpus Christi of "petty jealousy . . . because [their newspapers] warn the good people of the Island City of their perilous position in the cyclone period."[8]

Ironically, just ten days before Cline's article was published, the Island City had been hit by another hurricane, this one classified as "extreme," meaning its winds were more than 136 miles per hour. But the occurrence did not lessen the weather chief's authority, any more than the worst hurricane of the century, which hit Galveston on September 8, 1900. With a population close to forty thousand by that time, a considerable number had evacuated before landfall. Yet many stayed, and by the time they became aware of danger, a steamer had broken free of its moorings, destroying all three railroad routes to the mainland and wrecking the only wagon bridge. Winds, "veering constantly, calming for a second and then coming with awful, terrible jerks," gusted over 130 miles per hour as waters, swelling nearly twenty feet high, raged inland.[9] By sunrise the next morning, six thousand people had died. Yet Cline maintained his prominence, admitting merely that "no one ever dreamed that the water would reach the height" it did; he received a commendation and a promotion within a year.[10] Meteorology was an unformed subject, scientists were important men, and competing coastal cities needed their assurances.

Not the least of these was Corpus Christi, rich with sympathy for its broken rival. "A Hurricane's Awful Work: Over 500 Lives Lost. . . . The injured and almost heart-broken people suffered for food and drinking water for several days before the outside world could render them any assistance," the paper reported. The publication was quick to report local aid, "Hon. Jeff McLemore and a party of Corpus Christi boys [were] the first relief party to reach Galveston Monday evening."[11] But the *Caller* also seized the opportunity to remind its readers that their own city had remained untouched. "'No storm at Corpus Christi. All safe and well here.'"[12]

Even the paper's description of a boat trip to the Laguna Madre on the evening the hurricane hit, to take advantage of "fish . . . by the millions . . . trying to escape the threatened storm," took on the appearance of a chamber of commerce ad, contrasting the relative calmness of the lagoon with the "threatening weather [and] rough seas breaking outside in the gulf a few miles away."[13] The coup de grâce was an untitled editorial in the same issue, compassionate and condescending at the same time: "The editor of the *Caller* has, ever since Indianola was destroyed by a storm from the gulf, been among those who were afraid for Galveston every equinox, located as it is on a sand island in the gulf, exposed to the storms of the sea. Now the expected has appeared, it is to be hoped . . . that precautions are taken to ward off any such awful calamity in the future by the building of a strong and high sea wall."[14]

But why not a sea wall for Corpus Christi? What made it so different from its Galveston Bay rival that what was considered a precaution for one city was deemed unnecessary for the other? The answer—and ultimately, city fathers reasoned, the key to a port—lay in two things that made Corpus Christi unique along the gulf: its barrier islands and its bluff. In the event that a hurricane such as Galveston's threatened, authorities promised, the barrier islands, Padre and particularly Mustang, would act as natural shields, blocking the surging tides and waves from even approaching the mainland. The bluff, in the meantime, would keep townspeople and buildings above the reach of any water that did mange to pour through. The *Caller* expressed the idea best in its 1900 editorial bemoaning the Galveston disaster: "The *Caller* feels it a duty . . . to say that such a disaster could not possibly befall Corpus Christi, the bay being protected from the gulf by Mustang Island, some twenty miles long and about two miles wide, while the land nearly all around the bay . . . rises forty feet high from the water's edge—a combination of desirable natural conditions not to be found on the coast within a thousand miles from here, and in but few places on the globe."[15]

Such an assumption seemed warranted, according to letters received by the local paper. As early as 1886, a San Antonio citizen had put it bluntly to the people of Corpus Christi: "With your high bluff you need have no fears of tidal waves or storms." The *Fort Worth Gazette* added its own opinion: "Nueces County, being high, renders it exceptionally attractive and free from the fearful consequences of living on low ground, as experienced by Indianola and Galveston," and a month later got even more specific about the city's location, "so much more elevated and protected from storms than any other point on the Texas coast." An advertising brochure for the Texas-Mexican National Railroad described the city as "built upon a bluff that rises fifty feet above low water mark, and thus is the only coast city of the Gulf of Mexico, between Vera Cruz and Florida, that is absolutely secure against inundation." Finally, even the opera critic of Galveston got into the act, "Here, although the bay may be lashed at times to fury, little apprehension is felt by the inhabitants, who feel perfect security in the high bluff at hand to offer a safe protection."[16]

A northern paper, concerned about the losses in Indianola and Galveston, had dared to suggest *all* coastal cities were in danger: "The overwhelming disasters which within a short time have completely obliterated . . . important towns upon the Texas coast are almost without parallel. The storms which have swept away these places were more than local hurricanes. . . . The similarity of the fate . . . indicates very clearly that the entire Gulf Coast of Texas and even Louisiana lies too low to furnish safe sites for any considerable towns unless a great deal of money is spent in dyking and building sea walls to serve as a protection against the Gulf storms."[17] But the *Caller* editor quickly set the record straight. "The above is from the *Philadelphia Times.* Our esteemed contemporary overlooked Corpus Christi standing on its bluff of forty feet."[18]

It was this belief, then, that Corpus Christi was impervious to harm because of built-in defenses provided by nature, which allowed city residents to concentrate all their energies on making a living, rather than on protecting themselves from the sea. Breakwaters or sea walls, especially of the type finally built by Galveston after the 1900 disaster, seemed cumbersome, expensive, and extraneous. And lest any skeptic claim that such sentiments were simply the wishful thinking of civic leaders so eager to get federal approval for a deep sea port that they would distort the truth, even the requisite scientific expert got into the act. In a 1900 *Corpus Christi Caller* article eerily reminiscent of Isaac Cline's essay nine years earlier, George Reeder, government meteorologist and bureau chief of the local U.S. Weather Observatory, extolled the safety of the city. "Topographically the site of Corpus Christi can not be equaled. . . . Its location is fortunate from a health standpoint, on account of its natural drainage systems; from a safety point, during the tropical storm season, because of its high bluff, and from a point of beauty because of its picturesque surroundings." Then he fixed upon the two protective aspects of the area, the "magnificent bluff, from thirty-five to forty feet in height . . . the highest point of land anywhere along the coast from Florida to the Rio Grande . . . and . . . the safest for our wives and children to visit during the summer months," and the barrier islands. "If . . . a storm should ever approach this immediate coast, Mustang Island, a 'waif of the sea' . . . directly in front of Corpus Christi, about fifteen miles to the eastward, and . . . parallel with the coast, [will be] Nature's Wall, placed there to receive and break the force of the mighty water that runs ahead of the storm."[19]

Finally, to further reassure his residents, Reeder brought in one more advantage: "Another point in favor of Corpus Christi [is that] there is no water back of the city, i.e. *to the west*; nothing but good, hard solid prairie land. . . . [In most cases], should the center of the storm (where the barometer reaches the lowest) pass near or directly over a place . . . then . . . move off, the wind shifts abruptly to the northwest, soon reaching a gale as the barometer rises, sweeping everything out to sea. This could not occur at this point on the coast." Reeder then added one more consideration: Nueces Bay, which, he maintained, lay northward, would be an extra advantage. It could be a receptacle for "the great volume of water which would [pull out from] Corpus Christi Bay" if there were ever a significant storm surge. The meteorologist concluded with this observation: "Compared with the rest of the coast country, one cannot help but notice the fact that Nature has been lavish with her gifts to this section."[20]

The scientist had spoken. Any qualms Corpus Christians may have felt about living on a hurricane-prone coastline had been edited into a manageable reality, a reality reiterated by the *Caller* a few years later. "Corpus Christi has never known a bad storm. . . . The contour of the coastline is such that we are situated outside the hurricane belt. The big blows originate in the West Indies and sweep northwestward toward Galveston, leaving Corpus Christi in a cup-like eddy off [to] the left. Besides, the islands which lie between our harbor and the gulf effectively bar out tidal waves or sudden rises." So, the editor concluded triumphantly, "Such a tidal wave and destruction of life and property as occurred at Galveston September 8, 1900, is an utter impossibility."[21]

With such words to live by, Corpus Christians could strive unencumbered toward the population growth and political pull needed to achieve a deepwater port—and they were succeeding. Between 1900 and 1910, the city doubled its size and was on its way to doubling again by the end of the next decade. Besides the birth rate, factors such as economics and public education drove the expansion and increased the city's diversity. African American citizens now comprised nearly 10 percent of the population and a comparable amount of the workforce,[22] but an increasingly hostile Jim Crow climate, along with the de facto segregation that marked most Southern culture at that time, had constrained them into fairly rigid neighborhoods. "The black part of town in the 1910s was roughly triangular" and about sixteen blocks at its widest, encompassing the far northside height as it sloped downward toward Nueces Bay. "With few exceptions, it was bounded by Leopard Street on the south and West Broadway on the north. Kenedy Avenue, as a general rule, was the western cutoff. To the east, no blacks appear to have lived downtown, or even on much of the bluff."[23]

But some did. One was Sally Cox Garcia's daughter Annie, who had married a black Irish-American, James Mifflin Mays, and moved with him down to Irishtown, an area along the beach slightly north of the business district. Annie and James built a small house behind his parents,' and there she gave birth to two little girls. But the marriage did not last, and, by the time the oldest, Alclair, was five, Annie had moved back to Sally's home on Tancahua Street. Her work as a maid in the Nueces Hotel caught the attention of its owner, W. W. Jones, who hired her to cook in his mansion on the bluff's North Broadway street.

"The Jones' were fancy and had to be served in style," so Annie always donned a large white apron before serving the elaborate breakfasts,

3. The W. W. Jones mansion on Broadway Street, where Annie Mays worked, raising her daughters in a small building at the back. *Courtesy Corpus Christi Public Library.*

lunches, and dinners expected by her employers. But a little two-story building on the back of the lot came with the job, and here she raised Alclair and Anita, the three of them often walking back down Tancahua in the evenings to visit with Sally.

Like many of her peers, Annie was determined that her daughters get the education denied her. When they were little she took them to day school at the Congregational parsonage and later paid Malvina Moore's granddaughter to instruct the girls in piano. But by the time Alclair turned twelve, she, Anita, and their cousin Juanita had become members of Holy Cross Catholic church, so they started attending the parish school that the nuns operated.[24]

Many of their friends, however, still walked to the Public Free Colored School on Winnebago Street, the second building used to educate African American children in the city. Solomon Coles, dynamic preacher and educator, had aroused the black community's interest in education in 1877, and before long 67 percent of the area's youth were enrolled in the elementary school he converted from a broom factory. As the new century brought with it a fervid racism, education was one of the few avenues of advancement left for black Corpus Christians—that and economic enterprise.[25] "Just on the other side of . . . Bayview Cemetery . . . and a block or so from the . . . school lived a barber named Henry Larkin whose home was also his shop. Larkin was one of the few black barbers in Corpus Christi in 1919. But his customers did not have to travel far for a haircut. The other black-owned businesses were close at hand, too, such as the Etkin Johnson Restaurant . . . Tom Blackshear's Billiards on nearby Media Street and the SAP Café just a skip away, on Aubrey Street. And there was Mrs. Coatin Young, who sewed dresses and sold them out of her home at 1217 Oso Street."[26]

Those that did not sew, barber, sweep, or manage a business worked as housemaids, cooks, hackmen, and carpenters. What they could not get out of life would drive the dreams of their children.

Far more numerous than African Americans, Mexican Americans also were targeted by the Jim Crowism of the early century. With the exception of a few professionals and entrepreneurs who had fled the old country during the early days of the Mexican Revolution, most Tejanos in Corpus Christi lived in segregated areas, the primary one being The Hill, an area on the bluff directly behind the affluent rich.[27]

The finer homes were on the bluff, but behind them was "The Hill," a term synonymous with its Mexican American residents and their culture.

The Hill included the area from Leopard Street east to Tancahua extending south across the railroad tracks to Agnes.[28]

But again, the rigid boundaries did not encompass all, most especially Nick Mora. The able Mexican mechanic, still almost indispensable to the Blüchers, was in his forties now and lived in a one-story home on the beachfront next to Lone Star Ice Factory. The plant had expanded since his arrival, its two large ice tanks virtually taking over an entire block of North Water and necessitating a full-time watchman, at least during the winter. The advantage of job proximity was intensified when Lorenza, Nick's only daughter, moved with her husband into the Water Street home of her parents. Like his father-in-law a refugee from Mexico and long-time Blücher employee, Manuel Sánchez also shared worksite responsibilities with Mora. The bluff beckoned, however, and an available lot on Artesian Street soon passed into the family's hands.[29]

But property did not preclude prejudice, and Mexican American children like Lorenza had not been welcomed in the city's two "white" schools. By the late 1880s, the citizens of The Hill began to push for their own public school, and finally in 1896, "a room was rented for Mexican children who wished to attend . . . school;" it opened with an enrollment of eighty students. Others pursuing economic success on the bluff included the Grand family, who built the first large business building there; J. J. Gonzales, who opened the community's main furniture store; and Juan Galvan, who operated his shrimp fleet from there. It was also on The Hill that Vicente Lozano began buying up property, eventually accumulating more than one hundred lots.[30]

Other groups also moved to the bluff, Lebanese like Anton Sammons and his family, who set up a general store on Leopard Street in 1916, and Greeks like George Demotsis and Andrew Lymberry, who opened a café. Immigrants had already proven their value to Corpus Christi in these first decades of the century, including John Mircovich from Serbia who built a fishing schooner in 1884, opened the Bay Saloon and Restaurant in 1899, and was offering macaroni soup and Italian beans in his Bay Grocery on Water Street in 1919.[31]

Not restricted to living on The Hill, but experiencing an unvoiced discrimination all the same, were descendants of the Irish who had settled the Coastal Bend after the Civil War. Attracted by glowing reports of the potential of Texas and encouraged by letters from Confederate veterans like Thomas Hickey, whole families of Gallaghers, Dunnes, Clearys, and

O'Doughertys left Ireland for the Gulf Coast. Many, like Hickey's two brothers, spread into the neighboring towns of Laredo and San Diego, while others, like Annie Mays's in-laws, settled into Corpus Christi's Irishtown, just north of the business section. Some fortunate few moved onto Upper Broadway, where Hickey's widow still lived, sharing her husband's mansion with her son Tom and a stepdaughter, Nelly. But more common was the growing ability of second-generation Irish to buy into middle-class neighborhoods like that of Hillcrest, on the northwest side of the bluff overlooking Nueces Bay. It was there that Marian Dodson, Hickey's fifth child, purchased a home with her young husband Samuel in 1916, and there they started their family.[32]

Blatant anti-Catholicism of the nineteenth century, however, followed Texas Irish into the twentieth. Consequently, those in Corpus Christi worked doubly hard to demonstrate their Americanism, electing over twenty-five countrymen to city and county office by the first new decade. Fiercely competitive, they had their own bucket-and-brigade firefighting unit, the Shamrock Hose Company, and even their own baseball team, which competed against the one fielded by German Americans south of town.[33] But prejudice continued to haunt the Irish of Corpus Christi, as it did, far more viciously, the Mexicans and blacks of the city. Dealing with it complicated lives already filled with the problems of earning a living and raising a family; one could only hope that as the city grew, so would its capacity for change.

For Corpus Christi had grown. By 1910, its census topped eight thousand, justly meriting the designation of "city." Three major railroad lines now stationed there, with another on the way. A causeway connecting the peninsulas between North Beach and Portland was being planned, along with a brand-new county courthouse to serve the increasing amount of litigation. With a highly developed labor force and strong retail and transportation interests, Corpus Christi had achieved its goal of growth. It was time for civic leaders to secure the goal of a deepwater port, and in Washington, D.C., they had just the politician to do that.[34]

PART TWO

Politicians and the Port

5 Populists and Patrónes

Any less impressive a figure than District Fifteen's newly elected representative to Congress could hardly have been found in Washington in the early years of the new century. Short, bushy-browed, and ruddy-cheeked, John Nance Garner wore clothes as casually as he drank his liquor, exuding a bonhomie to friend and foe alike.

But the outer geniality masked sharp intelligence, ruthless ambition, and a superb gift of manipulation. These traits brought the young lawyer to the Nueces Valley town of Uvalde in 1893 and propelled him into a county judgeship his first year there. Maneuvering between vying factions honed his talents for diplomacy, and it took Garner less than three years to gain a state seat. Six years later, running in a region he had created himself as a member of the House redistricting committee, "Cactus Jack"[1] became the first U.S. representative from the 15th Congressional District of South Texas—with voters' orders to secure a "direct [deep water] channel from Corpus Christi to Aransas Pass."[2]

But Garner had to secure himself in Congress first, and that was not easy in a Republican-dominated Capitol. The date of his arrival, 1903, marked Theodore Roosevelt's second full year as president, and the New Yorker's acclaimed handling of the anthracite coal miners' strike, along with the antics of his young and irrepressible family, had already assured a GOP hold on the presidency for the next five years. Moreover, Congress itself was in the thralls of Joe Cannon, so dominant a Speaker of the House that "Cannonism" became synonymous with parliamentary despotism. "Cannon controlled the house in its entirety and was able to make the House subservient to his will. No bill could be considered without his advance permission. He [personally] appointed all committee members and controlled all avenues of promotion."[3]

Such an unimpressive character as Cactus Jack, "just another cow thief from Texas," would merit little or no consideration from so august a potentate, and sure enough, Garner's first assignment was to the defunct Railways and Canals Committee. Since it would take time for the Uvaldean to put himself into prominence, "for the first few years," he remembered,

4. "Cactus Jack" (John Nance) Garner, elected to Congress in 1902 and a prime mover in securing a port for South Texas. *Portrait of John Nance Garner, DI 01349, Sam Rayburn Papers, 1906–1990, Center for American History, University of Texas at Austin.*

"[he] just answered roll calls, looked after chores for [his] constituents, studied, played poker, and got acquainted." But time, close observation, and a strong hand at cards pushed Garner into the position of assistant minority whip, and by 1909 the conservative leanings of the Taft administration had fragmented the GOP. Within a year, House Speaker Joe Cannon would lose his power in a St. Patrick's Day legislative coup, and a hugely empowered Ways and Means Committee would start setting House agenda, with seniority now the key to important committee chairmanships.[4]

The shift from cronyism to longevity as a basis for power augured well for John Nance Garner, having already won election to the House three times straight. It also played well for the Democratic Party, whose Solid South constituency came to dominate Congressional legislation for the next fifty years. But for certain, the power shift in Congress during the last years of Taft's presidency benefited South Texans. It was their scruffy, bantamweight representative, now after six years of intense study and manipulation, who was now in one of the most powerful party positions in Washington. What better man to secure a deepwater port?

And secure it he did—at least that is what Roy Miller read into the triumphant congratulatory telegram Garner sent to the Corpus Christi Commercial Club that cold January day of 1909. But it did not happen. Ten years would pass, and there would still be no port. In spite of the efforts of the Commercial Club, the energy of Roy Miller, and the machinations of John Nance Garner, no government-sponsored dredger came near Corpus Christi Bay for the next decade. The reasons were many and varied, some having little to do with the city itself, others originating deep in its past.

The economic downslide of the 1890s was one factor. Still reeling from the severe summers and deadly winters of 1887–88, rancheros in the South Texas plains received a body blow when sheep and cattle prices tumbled five years later. At the same time, small-spread farmers attempting to recover from drought found it almost impossible to extend their mortgages, much less pay them off. The limited amount of money in circulation created a creditor's market, lenders favored more cost-efficient clients, and soon large operations, often foreign-owned, began to absorb small farms and ranches. As the century waned, many Anglo landowners found themselves in the same situation of earlier Tejanos: evicted from their land and forced to work as tenants, sharecroppers, or migrant harvesters.

Resentment was fierce—as was the landsmen's determination to resist, a resistance that took the form of organized political action. Finding the only viable agrarian faction at that time, the state grange, unwilling to "antagonize merchants or railroads," angry farmers formed the Texas Farmers' Alliance and began to support any candidate favoring inflation, federal loans, and railroad regulation. Desperate to maintain dominance after years of Reconstruction impotence, Texas Democrats found themselves embracing Alliance aims, including the creation of a state railroad commission, in order to keep the party intact. But the old guard seethed when agrarian issues split the 1892 state convention anyway, and the courting of African American votes, both by the Alliance and its offspring the Populist Party, further antagonized die-hard secessionists. The loss of the national election in 1896, in spite of a ticket headed by fusion candidate William Jennings Bryan, exacerbated Democrats' anger, and the collapse of Alliance and populist power by 1900 justified an end to state agrarian reform—and a determination to punish those who had shaken party stability.[5]

This determination threatened even Corpus Christi's hinterland, rural South Texas, a region remaining relatively calm during the political upheavals of the previous decades. Tejanos, the majority there, had weathered five governments, three wars, and numerous shifts in land policy since 1830, along with the same natural disasters, market declines, and credit crunches now experienced by their Anglo counterparts. Many had watched entire estates disappear, while others, having owned nothing when they came, still held nothing more than the dirt-floored *jacales* and roofless cooking huts granted by their landlords.[6]

Whether *hacendado* (landowner), or *campesino* (peasant), however, they shared the same Spanish-Indio heritage that helped them survive the desert scrublands of trans-Nueces Texas. Key to this heritage was the custom of *peónes acasillados*, or the relationship between the *patron* and the *peón*. Arising in late-sixteenth-century Mexico as a response to the ever-growing labor shortage, plantation owners began to provide housing, wages, medical care, and personal garden plots to their workers in exchange for lifetime commitment, a commitment cemented by the growing debt into which each worker fell. Of obvious benefit to the hacendado, the arrangement also helped the campesinos, most of who were dispossessed Indios otherwise doomed to scrubland subsistence farms, back-crushing mine work, or prison-like sweatshop labor.[7] In addition, the peónes acasillados system provided an intangible advantage: protection. "The hacendado, if wise, became the defender of his Indians, looking after them in emergencies.

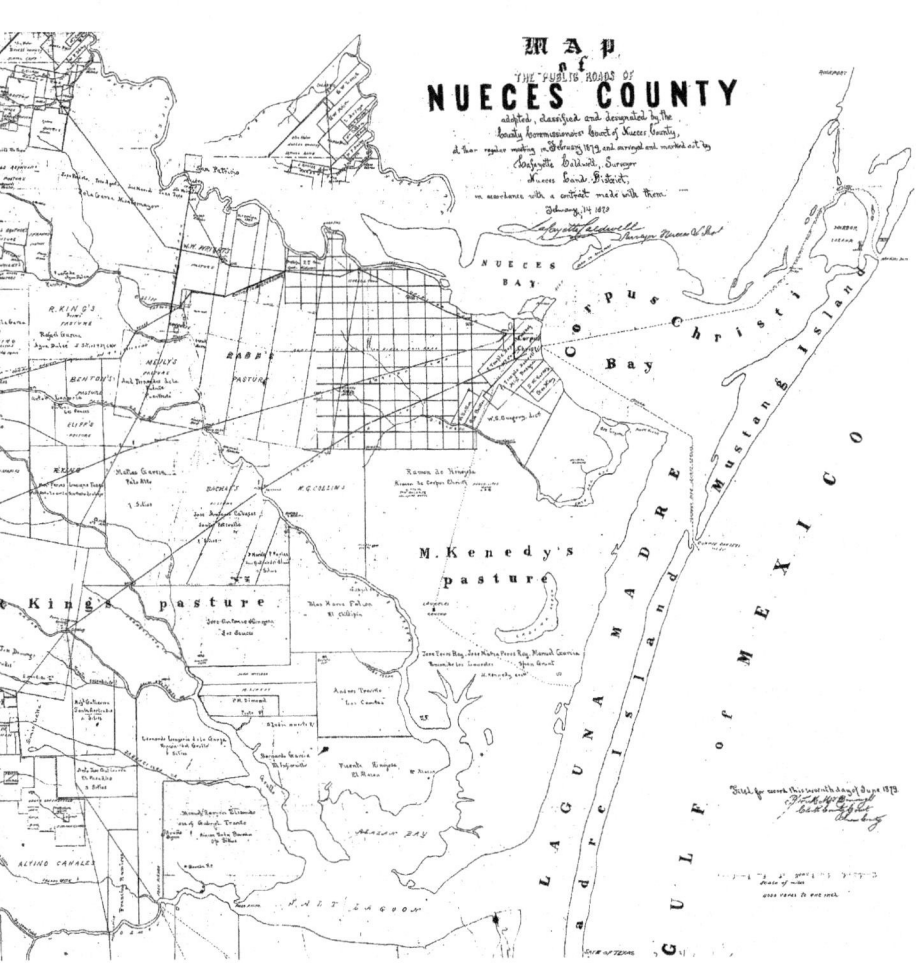

5. Ranches, farms, and pastures around Corpus Christi in 1879. *Courtesy Corpus Christi Public Libraries.*

He kept at bay voracious labor contractors and saw to it that his workers had food, clothing, shelter, and a priest to baptize their young, marry their offspring, and bury their dead."[8] The same system of patronage accompanied José de Escandón in his 1747 colonization of the Rio Grande valley of South Texas, and as population in the region increased, so did the power of hacendados.[9]

> Since the *peón* received very small remuneration for his work he was always in debt to the ranchman. In case of necessity, or sickness or death, the master always furnished the money. . . . Besides debts similar to these, the *peón* was cursed with . . . the food debt which accumulated year after year . . . [from] the . . . stores at the ranch where . . . all goods were sold on credit and at a very high price. . . . Since he had no means of transportation, [the *peón*] depended upon the master for the use of a wagon. . . . The same thing happened in time of sickness, no physician could be summoned without the master's advice. . . . If the son of a *peón* was to be married, the master was consulted about it; and if he sanctioned the engagement, he made it known by asking for the girl's hand. The father did not recognize the formal engagement until the master gave his sanction.[10]

Such power was addictive. It was also made to order for the enterprising Richard King and Mifflin Kenedy, who knew nothing about the pastures they had purchased after the Mexican War but everything about exploitation. Using means legal and otherwise, the two joined existing patrónes in amassing huge fiefdoms along the trans-Nueces strip, King actually transplanting his from the old country.[11] "In 1854, after King had bought the herds of a drought-stricken Mexican village, he extended an offer to the village: he would resettle the entire community on his ranch where they could have homes. . . . The village accepted the offer, and the resulting *entrada* consisted of more than a hundred men, women, and children with their belongings. The *vaqueros* and their families became . . . *Los Kineños*, the people of the King Ranch . . . known for their skill and loyalty to the King family," a loyalty as basic as land itself.[12]

By 1900 the patrón/peón system was an intrinsic part of economic and social life between the Nueces River and the Rio Grande—and of political life as well. As representative democracy was not part of the culture brought from Mexico, the rough-and-tumble of early Republic politics found most Mexicanos unmoved. Left to their own devices and mostly illiterate, ranch hands would never have flocked to the polls, but as dutiful peónes, they had to.[13]

"The Mexicans . . . rely on the people who hire them to tell them how to vote."[14]

"They know what they have to do."[15]

And that was to vote. Loose electoral standards of the nineteenth century made even noncitizens eligible, requiring one to have only "first papers," the official declaration of intent to become a citizen, as document enough for registration. Consequently, residents of only a few months joined with native Tejanos at the polls, waiting patiently while ranch overseers ticked off their names and showed them how to mark the ballots. Legends abounded of illiterate peónes being corralled into stockades days before an election and feted with *mescal* and barbecue to ensure their vote, but the harsh reality of losing one's livelihood and safety was reason enough to vote the patrón's ticket. Texas in the mid-1800s was no refuge for Spanish-speaking Americans still being scapegoated for the massacres at Alamo and Goliad and for the Cortina Wars, while the last years of the century were pockmarked with border uprisings, cattle raids, and unprovoked attacks upon isolated householders.[16] Tejanos needed the ranchero for protection; he needed them for votes. Bloc balloting along the border, therefore, existed for decades as a tolerated feature of state and local government. It was not until the end of Reconstruction that the peónes acasillados tradition became the well-oiled engine in a whole new apparatus: the South Texas political machine.[17]

This had its roots in the 1875 return of the Democratic Party to Austin. No matter how damaging to Republicans and freedmen, the Redemption did restore a certain amount of stability in the state, giving adventurous entrepreneurs a chance to rediscover trans-Nueces Texas. Soon its flat plains, easy access to Mexico, and vast herds of cattle attracted railroad tycoons, and merchants followed, eager to set up banks and stores in every cow town sprawled across the tracks. By the 1880s the business community had become a dominant force along the border, with the same potential for ballot control that ranchers had held for years. Quick to recognize the political implications was Stephen Powers, long-time litigator for Richard King and Mifflin Kenedy and prime agent in their ever-growing land acquisitions. Taking in a partner, the Brownsville lawyer spent the last years of his life educating his protégé in title procurement and border politics, and by 1883 young Jim Wells had launched a three-pronged takeover of county and town government. Supported by King, Kenedy, and like-minded ran-cheros, Wells took their votes, each guaranteed from loyal ranch hands, to local businessmen, who exerted their own control over workers and ten-ants. Coalescing the groups, he showed each how to get the most value from elected representatives. From the county he promised ranchers se-cure land-titles, low property taxes, and preferential real estate evaluations. From the towns he promised businessmen low municipal taxes, minimal utility fees, and large police forces. From the state, Wells advocated more railroad development and increased protection along the border, each vital by the end of the century. He would supply the candidates to achieve these aims; businessmen and ranchers would guarantee the votes.[18]

For the Tejanos whose ballots fueled this arrangement, there were some benefits. Many held jobs in Wells's organization. "The machine sometimes recruited laborers, small-time farmers and ranchers, or members of their families for the low-ranking jobs in the county and city governments and the party hierarchy."[19] Others counted on Wells for legal services. "The South Texas boss . . . defended *peónes* for minimal fees or for no charge at all, sometimes arranged their release from jail without the formality of a trial, and even used his influence with Texas governors to secure par-dons. . . . Wells and his organization stood as a buffer between the pop-ulace and an alien legal system, which they neither understood nor fully trusted."[20] But even more importantly, the *obreros* and vaqueros (the work-ers and horsemen) who worked his land and corralled his cattle bonded with Wells. "I was their friend and they could trust me," he affirmed. "I took no advantage of them. . . . I buried many a one of them with my money and married many a one of them. It wasn't [just] two or three days before the election, but through the years around, and they have always been true to me."[21]

During the devastating droughts of the 1880s and 90s, Wells organized county relief and gave unsparingly from personal funds to help members of his *familia*. Like Mifflin Kenedy, he married a Catholic and, again like the Kenedys, built a church where he worshiped with his people. Like the Kenedys and Kings, he established a ranch school, and like all the pa-trónes, maintained a vital interest in the health and activities of his workers and their children. "Every time my grandmother had a baby," one recalled, "Mrs. Kenedy would come to the house to see the baby and give my grand-mother some milk."[22]

Such concern led border boss Manuel Guerra to forge the same kind of link with his people. Eschewing a privileged Mexican education at the age of fourteen, the young man made his way to a Corpus Christi dry goods store and clerked just long enough to learn Texas politics. Ruthlessly ambitious and charismatic—"he became a political boss because the people were willing to follow him and wanted him to be one"—young Guerra returned to the valley and became, in short order, an American citizen, head of the local Democratic Party, and right hand man of Jim Wells.[23] "He accomplished his political control . . . through family relations . . . through financial aid, [and] . . . by giving the elect political positions. . . . All the landowners in Starr County were a branch of his family or were related through marriage; he afforded credit to the ranchmen at his stores and issued teacher's certificates to his favorites in exchange for votes. . . . His financial success, his magnetic personality and handsome appearance made Don Manuel Guerra a leader of his people."[24]

At the peak of their powers, rancheros like Guerra, jefe políticos like Wells, and old seamen like Richard King ruled domains like empires. "Their word was law and like feudal barons they [could] do and undo at will." For their campesinos, life was not materially better than that in the old country, but it was a secure and safer life, a life where toil, joy, and pain were generally shared by worker and boss alike. It seemed no obligation, then, to vote as the patrón wished—just the return of a favor.[25]

It was this bond, then, that kept South Texas voting Democrat amid the Alliance and populist upheavals of the 1890s, a bond that seemed impervious to change—until its own makers destroyed it and, in the process, skewered Corpus Christi's chance of deep water a decade later.

Protests and Progressives

Destroying the bond between worker and ranchero was the last thing Robert Kleberg had in mind when he and fourteen other investors, including Jim Wells, met in Corpus Christi in 1903 to set up the St. Louis, Brownsville, & Mexico Railway. Named administrator of King Ranch after the captain's death in 1885, and answerable to King's formidable widow Henrietta on a daily basis, the young Virginia-educated barrister mastered range life soon enough to merit his own Kineño nickname, El Abogado (The Lawyer). By 1900 he had paid the debts the old man left, consolidated and doubled ranch holdings, perfected a thriving mule and burro trade, and successfully sunk the first of numerous artesian wells.[1]

Excited by the immediate impact dependable water made on his own pastures, Kleberg envisioned even more. "The men wondered why I cried [when the first well came in]," he explained later. "But I knew that once a definite source of water was available I could induce railroad construction which in turn would lead to the development of South Texas." Kleberg's aim—and that of most landed gentry in the trans-Nueces region—was to turn the Wild Horse Desert into irrigated farmland, with fields of cabbages, onions, dates, citruses, and olives attracting farmers and developers from all over the nation. Bottomed-out beef prices and excessively arid summers had crippled the cattle ranchers; selling unused pastures in forty- to eighty-acre lots to Midwesterners and immigrants seemed a perfect solution. The 1904 completion of the St. Louis, Brownsville, & Mexico line south from Corpus Christi to the border was a major step forward, as was the creation of development companies like the Kleberg Town & Improvement Company, which converted scrub desert along the tracks into irrigated town and farm sites. With carloads of farmers soon to arrive, eager to buy land, equipment, seeds, and supplies from ranching benefactors like Kleberg, the region's future looked bright.[2]

But Kleberg had not reckoned on nature, neither Mother Nature nor the human kind. Early experiments with cabbages, onions, and olives near his main ranch house seemed promising, but within five years he had to admit defeat. In some areas, groundwater was too mineral-laden for benefit, but the main problem was quantity, not quality: artesian wells, even those dug as deeply as his, simply could not meet the needs of such water-intensive crops. In time, with the combination of the new railroad line and developer-dug canals, Rio Grande farmers would harvest the subtropical produce of which Robert Kleberg had dreamed. But his experiments in water had not been wasted. The artesian wells could produce enough moisture for consistent dry-land farming, and soon promised harvests of sorghum, corn, and "a-bale-to-an-acre" cotton attracted whole families. By 1909 the population of South Texas was on its way to doubling its previous count.[3]

As were the problems. Far from assuaging rancheros' economic ills by buying up unused land, the new farmers were adding whole new complications. Some were cultural. Many of the settlers were direct immigrants from Eastern Europe, most were migrants from the Midwest and the Northern Plains, but none felt the regard for Texas-Mexicans that the old landowners did. For the newcomers, vaqueros and obreros of the old ranches were valuable now only as seasonal harvesters, temporary cultivators, or occasional farm hands, and their families important only for the number of thirteen-year-olds who could plow a field or seven-year-olds who could pick cotton every day. Nor was schooling encouraged. "Illiterates make the best farm labor," a manager stated flatly.[4]

Even more personal was the trampling of Tejano identity. "All Mexicans regardless of their racial descent or political affiliations," stated a daughter of the border, "[were] essentially Catholic." Whether they were devotees decorating home altars with statues and pictures of saints, or agnostics delighting in infidelity and unbelief, the Roman church framed their lives.[5] "These . . . rabid hat[ing] . . . fallen-away Catholics[6] . . . might attack the church . . . because it was theirs to do or undo at their will, but woe to the Protestant who dared to slander it."[7]

Though slander it they did. Although some immigrants were Catholic themselves, seizing an opportunity to set up their own churches in unfamiliar land, most of the settlers on Texas ranges had been raised as strong antipapists. Years of Baptist and Methodist indoctrination, combined with prejudices absorbed from nativist kin, led many to brand the faithful as foreign invaders eager to take over American territory for Roman rule. Priests were devils' adjuncts who wore horns, and nuns were baby killers who beat themselves daily with steel-tipped whips. Even the piecemeal understanding that arrived after the Civil War, during which nursing sisters and Irish

American regiments convinced many that Catholics were truly patriotic, did not extend to rural areas. Riots, physical attacks, and arson marked southwest towns where priests and nuns set up chapels, and new "liberal intellectuals . . . who declared that the church was undemocratic and did not encourage its members to become autonomous individuals," created a special kind of bigotry.[8]

Traditional *Mexicano* Catholicism reinforced these images of a submissive populace, "poor . . . intellectually as well as spiritually." At best, Tejanos occasioned pity: "They're so ignorant and such staunch Catholics and don't seem to know any better."[9] At worse, they were the "listless . . . lowdown"[10] offspring of a "hybrid race . . . degraded, demoralized and priest-ridden."[11]

For regardless of religion, race played the trump card in newcomers' prejudice against Mexican Americans. Fed on a national racism dating back to the English colonists and encouraged by recent Supreme Court decisions endorsing Jim Crow laws in the South, Midwestern and European "whites" joined local "Anglos" in disparaging border *Mestizos* for the darkness of their skin.[12]

> The Mexican here is a servant class, a laborer, *peón*, slave. The white child looks on the Mexican as on the Negro before the war, to be cuffed about and used as an inferior people.[13]
>
> Inferior race, yes, they are.[14]
>
> They have an inferior intellect even if they become well educated.[15]
>
> Any other dark skinned, off-color race is not equal to us [whites]. I may be wrong and expect I am but I feel and the general public here feels that way. They are not as good as Americans.[16]

As a result, the new century found more and more Texas-Mexicans refused tables at restaurants, hustled out of hotel lobbies, and barred from serving on juries. Their children were punished for speaking Spanish on the playground, and neighborhoods began to covenant against them. Courting couples were pushed out of city parks, and prisoners denied due process.[17] "I asked . . . Doc Marsden . . . the old type deputy sheriff about the Mexicans who disappeared. He said some of them died of heart failure. He whips them."[18] Such hostility did not go unnoticed, although many Texas-Mexicans expressed their bitterness quietly. "We . . . of the Border, although we hold on to our tradition and are proud of our race, are loyal to the United States, in spite of the treatment we receive by some of the new

Americans. Before their arrival, there were no racial or social distinctions between us. Their children married ours, ours married theirs, and both were glad and proud of the fact. But since the coming of the "white trash" from the north and middle west we felt the change. They made us feel for the first time that we were Mexicans and that they considered themselves our superiors."[19]

Others showed poignant insight. "We were wholly unprepared, politically, educationally, and socially when the avalanche of Americans fell upon us. . . . Mexicans from across the river look down upon us and call us by what to them is the vilest epithet, *Texanos*, and the Americans do not consider us as such, although some of our Texas-Mexican families have lived here for generations. . . . We are going now through a very painful period of transition and like the white black bird do not know yet just what we are."[20] Still others were tempted to resist violently, and soon patrónes were caught in the middle, torn between reasserting their old protective habits or placating the new citizens in their valley. For farmers were threatening the economic well-being of rancheros as well.[21]

Far from appreciating the old landowners, new Texans had begun to resent them. Settlers could withstand the rigors of planting cotton and sinking wells in the windswept humidity of South Texas, and they were accustomed to loneliness on farm sites purchased from land development firms. But company-managed towns, company-owned stores, company-issued scrip in place of U.S. currency—these shocked Midwesters. As did the dearth of public services. Fed up with interminable, poorly maintained roads, deficient public schools, and nonexistent health facilities, the farmers turned to county officials for redress and were ignored. To improve such problems would create huge increases in property taxes, and since the large landowners owned most real estate, they would be paying the heaviest burden. It would be unfair to subject them to such "a punishing tax rate," county officials explained politely, by people "who would pay very little of the tax" themselves. Infuriated, farmers flocked to the polls, only to watch their candidates repeatedly lose to patrón-driven machines.[22]

Incensed and determined to change the politics and attitudes of their adopted state, newcomers joined a furious torrent of reform inundating the country, the Progressive movement. Spawned by post–Civil War technological advancements, fostered by an increasingly literate populace, and fed by newspaper and magazine publishers eager to increase their profits, progressivism by the early 1900s sheltered a wildly diverse group of activists under an ever-expanding umbrella. Eugenicists shared space with civil rights leaders like W. E. B. DuBois, and free-love proponents huddled next to Christian fundamentalists like William Jennings Bryan. Union leaders locked arms with New York society suffragists, and muckraking photographers elbowed socialist writers. War heroes like Theodore Roosevelt crowded pacifists like Jane Addams, and investigative reporters Idas Tarbell and Wells mingled with politicians "Pitchfork Ben" Tillman and "Golden Rule" Jones.[23]

What united such disparate leaders were progressivism's most commonly-held views: industrialism was good so long as it didn't abuse society; oppression, both personal and institutional, was bad and must be eradicated; and only effective government could make things right, a government infused with strongly Christian, mainly white, middle-class, Protestant virtues. This emphasis upon government's right to intrude upon American lives departed from early-nineteenth-century laissez-faire individualism, and it threatened the Gilded Age moguls and big city machines that had wielded power since the Civil War. Moreover, extremist drives to purge individuals of corruption, subsequently successful with the passage of the Eighteenth Amendment and states' sterilization of the ill-bred, reeked of Nietzschean elitism. But nuts-and-bolts reformers around the nation accomplished much. Meat-packing companies and pill manufacturers underwent federal inspection; government service applicants took qualification tests; senators campaigned for popular votes; and states set child labor limits. Parks and historic sites became national treasures, and legislatures passed initiative and referendum laws. Spurred on by technology and an innate sense of self-righteousness, America's middle class quite consciously remolded society into its own image.[24]

An image, however, that was slightly tarnished in the South. Like national Progressives, reformers in Dixie fostered increased industrialism, corporate regulation, and Prohibition. More inclined to trust state governments than federal, they dutifully endorsed initiative and referendum proposals and set up compulsory attendance laws for public school children.[25] But the Old Confederacy's advocates died hard, and hovering over most reform attempts was the ever-present "Negro question," the fear that integration and full justice for all citizens would bring miscegenation and mingling of the races. As a result, social reforms in the South took on a unique paternalistic character "in which whites would offer blacks help, guidance, and protection in exchange for . . . continued subservience." Docility, willingness to accept low pay, and wariness of overstepping legal barriers were the price blacks paid for a modicum of peace—that and the loss of their vote. For essential to gaining control of state governments after Reconstruction was the disfranchisement of Negro voters, a process white Southerners mastered.[26]

Texas Progressives were eager to learn. Building on measures cautiously enacted by Gov. James Hogg in the 1890s—creation of a railroad regulatory commission, restriction of corporate land holdings, reduction of county and municipal bond debts—twentieth-century activists were already setting controls over mental hospitals, renovating the state prison system, establishing river reclamation projects, and consolidating school districts. Operating as liberal Democrats in an increasingly one-party state, the reformers were as disparate and occasionally dysfunctional as their national kin. Women's Christian Temperance Union officials clashed with Prohibitionists over the efficacy of local option, and conservationists castigated state forestry officials for the continued deforestation of East Texas.[27]

But the one doctrine upon which most Texas Progressives agreed, over and above the need for drastic economic growth, was the necessity for voter disfranchisement. Joining hands with Old Guard Democrats still fuming over populist betrayals, political insurgents railing against border bosses, die-hard racists reliving Reconstruction, and disgruntled farmers fighting patrón machines, they targeted minorities and the poor in the name of electoral reform.[28]

Why not a white man's election? . . . No matter what state it may be there is a class of foreigners who claim American citizenship but who are as ignorant of things American as the mule . . . The white men and white women of Dimmit county must rise up and demand what is right, demand what is pure, and demand a white man's election.[29]

We want to get rid of the unnecessary and disgusting traffic in Mexican votes and put the electoral franchise in the hands of people who are capable of wielding it intelligently and with cleanness.[30]

Believing as we do that the public offices of this or any other county are . . . not purchase[able] as an article of commerce from an illiterate, irresponsible and non-tax paying people . . . we are here . . . as a band of law-abiding citizens . . . to devise ways and means by which [this county] can be taken and lifted from the low plain to which she has fallen morally.[31]

Their goal to eliminate "graft and corruption at the polls" had, as its method, the restriction of the ballot to the elite.[32]

> Editor Vinson . . . [of the] *Big Wells Record* . . . bewails the fact that [with disfranchisement] it will be possible for seventy per cent of the white voters to control the politics of the county. Bless his heart, that is exactly what we want.[33]
>
> All white voters and candidates for office regardless of party or political creed [can] participate in the election, the only restriction being against negroes' [sic] seeking nominations or voting in the primary.[34]
>
> Any discriminating person can see that the [disfranchising] amendment is in no sense intended to operate against the thrifty or deserving poor but only against the vagrant or quasi-vagrant class.[35]
>
> All this slush about manhood suffrage is idiotic.[36]

Texans studied the Deep South, which, over the years since Reconstruction, had perfected the art of electoral obfuscation. Forbidden by the Fifteenth Amendment to directly deny African Americans the right to vote, Southern states resorted to less obvious stratagems. Literacy tests demanded an ability to read and write which still eluded most freedmen's descendants, and secret ballots stopped boss-led voting en masse. Property restrictions disqualified sharecroppers, and limited registration periods rendered "roaming agricultural workers . . . voteless ones." "Grandfather clauses" allowed illiterates to vote only if older male relatives had registered during the years blacks could not. But the most universally used tools of disfranchisement were the poll tax and the "White Primary," and these Texas Progressives seized with a vengeance.[37]

The White Primary rested upon a 1905 act requiring a statewide direct-primary system for any political party polling over one hundred thousand votes. After years of back-room-boss selection of standard bearers, reformers now boasted of putting "the reins of power into the hands of the intelligent and incorruptible element of citizenry." But their actual objective was much grimmer. Claiming private membership privileges for public political institutions, Democrats reserved the right to choose those eligible to vote in primary elections. "We . . . cordially invite all white voters of the County . . . to participate in said Primary election," specified one county manifesto.[38]

Moreover, "white" depended upon each region's definition of the term. In East Texas it meant anyone not black. "Some institution had to be inaugurated to put an end for all time to . . . Negro votes in elections. For this purpose the Citizens White Primary was organized."[39] In parts of South Texas, the term became even more specific. "'White man' is defined by the constitution to be a Caucasian, Mexicans being barred, whether they possess white blood or not."[40] But the goal remained the same. "County Democratic leaders' widespread adoption of the white primary . . . denied most blacks the ballot in state contests."[41] "In southeastern Texas . . . along the Gulf and the Louisiana border . . . Negroes make up over a quarter of the population, and are as much out of the political picture as they are in the Delta country of Mississippi."[42] "Now we have a white man's primary that absolutely eliminate[s] the Mexican vote as a factor in nominating county candidates."[43] "Mexicans don't vote here. They would not try it more than once."[44]

Effective ballot "cleansing," however, had to extend beyond racial exclusion at the polls. In order for complete disfranchisement of all undesirables—the occasional African Americans passing as white, the border Mexican Americans considering themselves "Caucasian," the tenant farmers still demanding relief—Texas Progressives needed to make voting a financial burden, and they did it with the poll tax.[45]

Ironically, poll taxes, a small fee paid yearly by county voters that went to public school coffers, had already been part of Texan politics for decades. But collection had been haphazard at best and differed county to county. The drive to constitutionalize the fees, making them not only mandatory but also onerous enough to exclude the working poor, began in the early 1900s, spearheaded by one of Texas' most unregenerate ex-Confederates, Alexander W. Terrell. So incensed at the South's loss that he retreated into Mexico after Appomattox, Terrell later took up law in Houston during Reconstruction, then served in the state senate for four terms after Democrats regained power. A well-timed run for the state house in 1902 gave him the opportunity to effect electoral reform, and he preached the poll tax amendment with the anger and zeal of a backwoods evangelical.[46]

Bemoaning the monies lost by derelict payers—"The records of the comptroller's office reveal . . . that in the year 1900 there were 136,000 voters who failed to pay their poll tax of $1.50 each; one dollar of the amount due from each voter belongs to the school fund"—he waved the bloody flag: "White women and children—many of them widows and orphans of dead confederates—have picked cotton and hoed corn under a burning sun for a generation to raise school taxes for Negro children." He targeted blacks: "Thus we white people of Texas have worked and paid taxes through good and ill report to make the Negro capable of citizenship"; upbraided them: "Will he now requite us with ingratitude? Will he vote against the constitutional amendment that . . . help[s] us get rid of the vicious elements of his own race and of our race? Will he still follow the advice of the office seeker who has been riding into federal offices on his back, or will he co-operate with the white men of Texas who have educated them?"; and tried to intimidate them: "The future destiny of the Negro in Texas depends on how he will now vote. . . . If, with rank ingratitude, he will not help to relieve the tax [burden] . . . let him beware. For mark my word, six months will not pass, if that amendment is defeated, until Texas will make a black and white assessment roll. White children could no longer toil in the field and shop to educate Negroes, but would leave them to receive such education as the taxes paid by their black parents would afford. This is not a threat, but a prediction from one who believes that Negro capable of gratitude."[47]

Unfazed, African Americans, Mexican Americans, the white poor, labor leaders, and ex-populists turned out in droves to vote down the amendment, but to no avail. By a two to one majority, the poll tax amendment swept the state and carried 194 of the 221 counties. Within a year, Terrell became the new chair of the House Committee on Privileges and Elections, and the first of a series of laws designed to erode Texas' electoral base to one-third its pre-twentieth-century size appeared.[48]

Primary among its requirements was the $1.75 baseline fee, a combination of state and county poll assessments amounting to almost 1 percent of a farm family's annual income. An additional dollar added by some cities brought the total to $2.75. For propertied or salaried urbanites, the tax seemed payable; for hotel porters or railroad foremen, the outlay amounted to at least one-tenth of a week's salary, nearly all of a whole day's pay.[49]

Nor did the restrictions stop at fees. To pay, one had to appear at the county tax collector's office between October and the end of January with proof of local residence, then tuck the receipt in a back pocket until the next city or county election, almost a half year away. To men who followed the crops or worked on the rails, the four-month registration limit was almost as daunting as the tax itself.[50]

For the next two years, Terrell and the state legislature added to electoral laws until suffrage was as fragmented as a reflection in a funhouse. Persons officially denied the vote included natives of China, Hawaii, and Burma, military servicemen, county paupers, the feeble-minded, lunatics, women, and anyone who had "participated in a duel as principal or accessory." But the real disfranchised were the one hundred and forty-five thousand black Texans forbidden access to party primaries and the thousands of Mexican Americans, farmers, and working poor unable to pay registration fees. Within ten years after instigation of poll taxes and the white primary, participation in Texas' general elections dropped to 20 percent of the voting public, hovering around the same level for the next half century.[51]

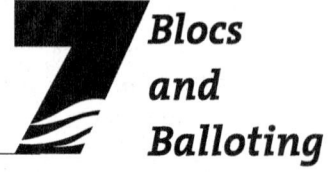

Blocs
and
Balloting

But what had Progressive voter restrictions to do with Corpus Christi's fight for a port? At first glance, nothing—until Nueces farmers, still gloating over disarming border bosses, found themselves affiliating with the shrewdest of them all. The boss was Robert J. Kleberg, the issue was deep water, and the problem was transportation. In the early days of coastal development, simple carretta trade, although slow, had been effective and cheap enough for producers to maintain trade with outlying towns both in the trans-Nueces and across the Rio Grande. This changed with the coming of railroads that promised speedy access to coastal and interior entrepôts, but their rapid monopolization by holding companies and shipping lines left local landsmen hamstrung. A supportive state railroad commission created in 1891 began to strip rail moguls of their powers, and successive Supreme Court and congressional acts in the next twenty years strengthened such reforms. But the aftermath found shippers still vulnerable to the machinations of city port authorities. For most of South Texas' newcomer farmers, that meant subjection to Galveston, notorious for rate manipulation and poor storage. Sure enough, in 1906, some of Kleberg's staunchest critics, eager to market cotton, sorghum, and corn, lost thousands of dollars when a freight blockade sidelined their crops along Island City wharves for weeks; two years later it happened again.[1] For the first time, rural planters looked at Kleberg not in anger but in pain, and he offered relief: deep water.

The technique was not new; the U.S. Army Corps of Engineers had been dredging channels to access deep-draught freighters for some time. But most seafloor digging had been done in already accessible ocean fronts. Now, for the first time, engineers developed dredgers that could go far within inlets and bays, and Houston had already contracted one to cut from Galveston Bay to the city itself. When completed, Houstonians could brag of a deepwater port whose very efficiency and depth would leave Galveston foundering. Officials in Beaumont, home of the Spindletop oil gusher, were planning the same. If Beaumont, so close to Houston they shared the same fog, could secure deepwater channeling from the federal government, why not Corpus Christi, Kleberg reasoned?

His logic was flawless, but more important to farmers who were willing to ignore ballot corruption in the face of economic ruin, Kleberg had connections: ties to cabinet officials, national representatives, state senators, and U.S. attorneys; and most important, a friendship with the Grand Old Jefe of Border Bosses, James Wells. Already working with Wells and friendly legislators in Austin, Kleberg had preserved patrón powers with a little-noticed amendment to the Terrell Election Law. Now he turned his attention to bringing South Texas a deepwater seaport.[2]

The first part of his plan necessitated redistricting the area and electing young Garner as congressman from the Coastal Bend. Once comfortable in Washington, the tyro representative got busy. "His services included . . . [erecting] a new system of jetties at Aransas Pass, . . . sponsoring legislation for the construction of an international railroad bridge at Brownsville, lobbying for the retention of troops at Fort Brown, securing a federal soil survey for South Texas, arranging the location of a federal experimental farm just outside Brownsville . . . [and] promoting the construction of post offices in the new towns of the Valley."[3] It soon became evident, however, that persuading the U.S. Army Corps of Engineers to dredge a channel across the Laguna Madre to Corpus Christi was going to take more influence than even poker-playing Cactus Jack could engender on his own, and in 1904, Robert Kleberg discovered Roy Miller.

Bright, industrious, and enthusiastic, Miller was an extroverted embodiment of the older man's ambitions. Born in Kansas in 1884 but taken to Texas early by his parents, the youngster hawked newspapers on the streets of Houston, earned a business degree from the University of Chicago, and served as railroad editor for the Houston Post, all before he was twenty. But his real opportunity came when Sunset Central Railway, headquartered in the Bayou City, hired him as advertising agent. His natural ebullience, persuasive sales pitches, and personal attention to detail quickly brought Sunset Central success and Miller the attention of King Ranch Enterprises.[4] The unabashed optimism and energy of the youth, together with his determined advocacy of economic growth, secured him a job with Kleberg—and a new home in Corpus Christi.

Significantly smaller in population and decidedly more limited in vision than Houston (which had already completed the first phase of dredging for

6. Robert J. Kleberg and Roy Miller on the bottom steps of the King Ranch "Big House," with relatives and in-laws, including Richard King's widow, Henrietta, behind them. *Courtesy Murphy Givens.*

its ship channel), Corpus Christi seemed to have little to offer Miller when he arrived in late September 1904. Its streets still turned to mud during heavy rains, and its bluff, so touted for invigorating breezes and healthy climate, had become entangled with weeds and refuse blown from the bay. But the little town was bustling all the same; the first Monday in November was just a few weeks away, and, to a degree almost unparalleled along the coast, Corpus Christians loved elections.

The love was deep and crossed ethnic lines. "In Corpus Christi, Mexicans vote," a rancher commented. "In Corpus Christi they are proud of their political power."[5]

It was Latinos' understanding of popular democracy that Henry Kinney extolled during the 1845 Texas Constitutional Convention: "Most of the population, or at least a large proportion of that of the place where I reside, is Mexican. They have come as much to sustain the interests of the whole country as the American population; they have been always as willing to pay their proportion towards the support of government as the Americans; as ready to go into the field and fight against a people of their own race for the preservation of our independence."[6] Kinney defended their right to vote during a debate to limit the franchise to Anglo American males only: "To me it is a matter of little consequence what a man's name or complexion may be. . . . If a certain population have equal rights with us, secured to them by the laws of the country, then I look upon them as citizens, equally with ourselves."[7] With their efforts, Kinney and his supporters not only prevented "white" from becoming a requirement for suffrage, they kept Hispanics within the sphere of the official state electorate.

Nor did Texas-Mexicans of Corpus Christi waste their franchise. Constrained to live separately from Anglo neighbors and co-workers, mostly on top of the city's famous bluff, they used their votes to gain attention from precinct-elected officials. "[Today's] election was probably the hardest contested one ever held in this city . . . The main battle ground occurred on the Hill, where the Mexican vote predominated," wrote the *Weekly Corpus Christi Caller* of April 8, 1892. An article in the same paper from April 7, 1911 observed, "By far the greatest interest of the day was centered about the political place on the hill, located over the old Grande saloon. It is possible that the fate of more city elections have been decided in the old structure, built by Pancho Grande over a quarter of a century ago . . . than any of the other polling places in the city. And the condition holds good today."

In their desire to vote "for the Americans who protect and help them better their conditions," Tejanos were no different from early Irish settlers who had elected representatives to virtually every city and county commission since 1854. Like the Irish, the bloc ballots cast by Hispanics worked to their advantage. Street improvements benefited neighborhoods, while jobs on county road crews augmented income. Positions as county deputies and court clerks offered advancement, and a growing middle class applauded the occasional election of a fellow Mexicano to city government. Spanish-language newspapers pushed political agendas, and the number of Spanish-surnamed children attending city public schools gradually increased.[8]

But there was a dark side to Hill politics. As the century began, accounts of ballot-brokering by bribery and coercion intensified, and an old saying, "As the money goes, so goes the Hill and as the Hill goes, so goes the election," gained more and more credibility. Fueled by images of patrón-peón politics in the hinterland and stoked by growing violence along the border, Anglo antagonism hardened as more Mexican nationals sought refuge on The Hill.

For restaurateur Ben Garza, the suspicions were frustrating. "About 90 percent of the Mexicans [here] are native-born. We are handicapped by the steady flow of immigration of the laboring *peón* class. . . . We have American ways and think like Americans. We have not been able to convince some people that there is a difference between us. To the average American we are just Mexicans."[9] For activist and publisher Pedro Ochoa, it was tragic. "People here have no reason for worry or thought other than of the best in regard to the feelings of the Mexicans in this country. We are Texans, and though we deplore the conditions of strife and turmoil in our native land . . . we are just as true to this country as though native born. . . . You may say that Pedro Ochoa . . . American citizen . . . is preaching peace amongst his Mexican people."[10]

Peace-loving but just as threatened were Corpus Christi's African Americans, whose 10 percent population count came nowhere near reflecting their actual political impact. Restricted, like Sallie Cox Garcia, to the north side of The Hill, city blacks formed a strong element of Ward Five, supporting usually the Republican ticket or the occasional Independent slate. Their influence elicited grumbles from business advocates, who in the *Weekly Corpus Christi Caller* of April 7, 1911, stated that they, along with Mexican Americans in Ward Four, constituted "the most irresponsible vote in the city, the most easily gotten out of the beaten track, and the easiest to turn either way."[11]

But bloc balloting paid off, and local blacks held office in both county and city governments up to the 1890s. Then the conservative "lily-white movement" struck the state, and, like the Progressives of the Democratic Party, the Texas GOP began to publicly support white supremacy. By 1902 Nueces County Republicans had maneuvered African Americans out of party delegations and chosen rabid racist, John C. Scott, to run for the newly formed Fifteenth Congressional District seat. That he lost to John Garner was not nearly so significant to black Corpus Christians as the fact that Scott carried the city. His tallies, and the accompanying approval of the constitutional amendment for a mandatory poll tax, created anxiety among partisan allies. "Lily Whiteism . . . [is] a movement that seeks the overthrow of the Negro. . . . The Negro element is a very potent factor in politics, and without it the Republican Party can never hope for success in this State. No people have ever been truer to Republican principles than the Negroes. . . . To [their] elimination . . . [we are] opposed," wrote the *Corpus Christi Caller* on October 31, 1902.

But disfranchisement fears seemed baseless in the immediate aftermath of Terrell Law enactment. Nueces County was slow to enact an official "whites only" primary, and poll tax collection proved anticlimactic, since the county had been requiring such fees for over ten years. In fact, Nueces's registration revenue, arcing to 10 percent of its total state remittance in 1898, maintained a consistent 7 percent rate well into the first decade of Progressivism. Prominent African American businessmen like D. N. Leathers continued paying their poll taxes—and voting—long after the amendment went into effect, and younger leaders like R. L. Moore and Dave Pruitt did the same as they gained stature on The Hill. Even Annie Mays's husband Mifflin registered in 1910, replacing his deceased father on the rolls. Stricken from Republican Party councils and eyed askance at Democratic primaries, black Corpus Christians were proving that their voices could still resonate in city, county, and national elections.[12]

As were Mexican-Americans with even greater effect. Well after disenfranchisement gutted the Hispanic votes in other counties, Corpus Christi Tejanos remained the deciding factor in most major elections. Candidates rented huge assembly halls to address them, and government officials waited to speak until introduced by them. Newspapers extolled them and editors exhorted them. The *Corpus Christi Caller and Daily Herald* (April 3, 1915) said, "Considerable abuse has been heaped upon Mexican citizens. They have been libeled and scoffed at, held up as straw men and beaten to pieces. . . .

[This] systematic defamation has been engaged in without warrant. We have known Mexicans . . . to be men of their own mind. . . . The *Caller* does believe that many Corpus Christi Mexicans are men of integrity, not to be thwarted in their convictions by intimidation, slanders or dollars."

Thus poll lists grew. Long-time voter Manuel Sánchez persuaded his father-in-law, Nick Mora, to register for the first time in 1904, two years after the tax became constitutional, and Florentino Garcia, Sallie Cox's husband, continued to renew his voting rights long after Progressives left Austin. Publisher and activist Pedro Ochoa faithfully paid his poll fees as did Ben Garza. Forming a significant percentage of the populace and forced by de facto segregation into two pivotal precincts, they and other city Tejanos wielded an ironic electoral sway.[13] "The Mexicans control the balance of power politically here," admitted one worker.[14] "The Mexicans stand together and . . . vote in a bloc," affirmed a businessman.[15] "All day Tuesday business was practically at a standstill in the city. . . . The all prevailing idea was . . . How will 'the hill' go?" the *Weekly Caller* reported on April 7, 1911. And how The Hill would go—along with wards one, two, and three—became prime topics of conversation as campaigns approached their climax.

For elections in Corpus Christi were wild, raucous, bawdy—and tremendously entertaining. In 1900 forty-seven hundred people lived in the city proper, and over twelve hundred showed up at the November polls that year, more than 60 percent of eligible turnout.[16] The appeal cut through all classes. Lebanese and Serbian-born restaurateurs crowded precinct stations alongside Civil War survivors. Mexican-born nationals lined up with commercial fishermen and their crews. Grizzled, care-worn farmers queued behind retired military veterans, while nervous first-timers waited, clutching wrinkled receipts in their hands. Candidates canvassed streets to offer stragglers free rides to the polls, and marching bands led supporters down into Irishtown, then up The Hill, alternating John Philip Sousa with *corridos* and ragtime. As the election judges scanned naturalization papers, swatted flies, and spat tobacco, ward bosses checked names and clipped chits to be redeemed later at party-controlled bars and *tabernas*.

The geography of the city helped maintain the centrality of events, with the bluff overlooking courthouse square on the beach. It took little time to tally a partial ballot count, then to send reinforcements to mobilize a recalcitrant ward. Victory and the spoils that accompanied it were to be won at whatever cost.

For elections cost a lot. Neighborhood rallies in city parks featured bands, barbeques, and beer; county office seekers hired whole trainloads of liquor, music, and food for their constituents. Candidates purchased newspaper space, printed posters, and distributed brochures while campaign managers buttonholed supporters in back alleys and cafés. Musicians practiced marches and *polkitas* for weeks,[17] and seamstresses sewed flags for victory parades down Chaparral Street. Newspaper publishers thrived when parties competed for votes as did liquor dealers, hotel managers, saloonkeepers, bordello operators, cigar makers, and short-order cooks. Nor were revenues dependent upon a general election every four years. Corpus Christi held its mayoral election every other year, a practice guaranteed to keep interest flowing. "After such a contest was decided, three or four hundred of the victorious voters, with the Mexican flag waving above, paraded the town in a body, while '*Qui viva Lovenkiold!*' and '*Este es el resultado de cinco de Mayo!*' rent the air from afar and near and mingled with the discordant notes of the brass band and the yelling of boys, producing a strange sound of confusion and rejoicing," reported the *Corpus Christi Weekly Caller* (April 8, 1892).

Such enthusiasm was warranted. By 1909 winning a local election meant gaining a municipal seat and a chance to run the city. Winning a county election meant power. Of all forms of government in the United States at the beginning of the twentieth century, county governments, headed by an elected judge and composed of commissioners, justices of the peace, a sheriff, and constables, had the greatest impact upon individuals. Charged with assessing property taxes as well as collecting them, county officials recorded land sales, awarded road contracts, set up and maintained jails, distributed relief to designated poor, hired and fired teachers, authorized bond proposals, and supervised their own elections. Such power was virtually unlimited, and in most cases overshadowed urban enclaves. "City governments . . . were . . . less important to citizens than the county. The boundary of the city government . . . was restricted to the central market town and excluded all the local settlements. The bulk of the population only came under the city jurisdiction during shopping and social visits. Although it dealt with many more people and the potential problems of large clusters of people, the city was a poor institution with a make-shift leadership and a few underpaid technicians."[18]

Most of these bureaucrats were controlled by the county judge, chief arbitrator and enforcer of state laws on a day-to-day basis. Head of the commissioners' court, which was the actual business board of the county, the justice also presided over his own judicial chambers, exercising jurisdiction in probate and eminent domain issues, in civil suits up to $500, and in criminal cases punishable by fine, jail, or chain-gang time. Such near-absolute authority made many South Texas towns virtual pawns in the hands of boss magistrates along the border and their officials.

But not Corpus Christi. Born out of lawlessness and nurtured in opportunism, the city embodied self-interest. Smart enough to understand the power of the ballot and shrewd enough to manipulate it, its people had long ago staked out their independence from county rule; as soon as the state extended legislative sway to towns with over five thousand people, they applied for and were granted a special governing charter. Pivotal in Nueces elections, the town would not be controlled. Influenced often by rancher entrepreneurs, incited occasionally by rabble-rousers—but never managed, Corpus Christi was a tiger to be ridden with care by the astute county politician.

Walter Francis Timon was one such politician. Educated in city schools and earning business and law degrees up east, he had returned early in the century to represent South Texas in the state house. Four years later, his ambitions unsated, he turned to local power. Adroit in the legerdemain of practical politics, he courted the city's Hill and business wards with financial pledges, and just as effectively, won over the rural and outlying districts with bravado. "Timon took cognizance of the threats that have been made against the Negro and Mexican voters . . . and said, 'If any man tells you [how] to vote . . . you come to me. Law and order prevails . . . in Nueces County, and I am ready to handle single-handedly any man or net of men that makes such a threat.'"[19] Personally armed himself and never one to avoid hostile confrontations, Timon knew his voters, and, once he became Nueces county judge in 1906, he made sure they knew him. By the middle of nine years of service, he had created a farm road system superior to most urban streets, an active public health department, and a huge building project packed with jobs for Corpus Christi laborers. Most importantly, he kept a discerning eye on the party purse, understanding that generous support of city officials could benefit the entire county in unimagined ways. It was with a certain amount of interest, therefore, that Timon viewed Roy Miller when the young man swept into the judge's beloved "Bluff City."

Targets
and
Trials

A veritable whirlwind, the young dynamo that was Roy Miller seemed to whisk over the shell-layered streets rather than walk them his first few years in town. Advertising and immigration agent for Robert Kleberg's St. Louis, Brownsville, & Mexico railroad, Miller immediately initiated "Blackland Specials," custom packaged trips to promote unused pasturelands. Before long, designated trains were running through the city every two weeks, crammed with prospective buyers eager to view the prize acreage down south. Within two years he was also running another King Ranch enterprise, the *Corpus Christi Caller*, bringing back the coastal promotion and civic boosterism that had characterized the newspaper in its early years. A year later he became a director of the Rivers and Harbors Congress and secretary of the Interstate Inland Waterway League, lobbying for a continuous canal connecting ports and harbors along the gulf. A year after that, he was in Washington, D.C., persuading John Garner to crash Speaker Cannon's impromptu poker party in order to include Corpus Christi on the 1909 Rivers and Harbors survey bill.

Nor was Miller inactive locally. Acting as his own agent, he bought up land along railroad access, then developed and sold it, alone and sometimes with partners. Perceiving the city's stagnant business base, he rejuvenated the Commercial Club and brought new entrepreneurs into its fold. Innately Progressive in outlook, he unashamedly cribbed Old Guard techniques and became a Democratic regular at socials, *baíles*, and barbeques.

His hard work paid off when he fell in love with Maud, the daughter of the city's esteemed physician, Alfred Heaney. The day they were married in the local Episcopal church, the couple were given a reception hosted by none other than County Judge Timon. Bereft of living offspring, Timon, like Kleberg, may have seen something of himself in the young, charismatic groom. Certainly, he saw a future for the region as Miller acquired stature and credibility nationwide. For the first time since Garner's fight for a government-funded port had started, South Texas politicians had a totally dedicated point man joining them in the fray. Bringing the city a deepwater channel suddenly seemed a certainty.

Then rampant factionalism intervened in the form of another ambitious newcomer to Corpus Christi, Walter Elmer Pope. Already a successful state district attorney with headquarters in Madisonville, Pope collected bankruptcy judgments, prosecuted divorce suits, initiated property claims, and juggled two law offices before resigning his public post in 1908 and relocating permanently to the Coastal Bend. There he became partners with, and son-in-law to, G. R. Scott, another prominent lawyer and realty specialist. Riding the crest of urban growth that ushered in the new century, Pope began a systematic land grab, scooping up forfeited plots on the bluff, laying title to unoccupied areas by the beach, and purchasing entire city blocks along the bayfront, either in his name or in the name of one of his companies. Before the decade ended, Pope was not only one of the most powerful property owners in the city, he was also a divisive political force as well.[1]

No optimist and possessed of a dry, acerbic wit that could leave plaintiff's attorneys speechless, Pope considered Kleberg's holdings in the town of eight thousand—two major railroads, two large banks, the longest-established law firm in the county, a land development office, property holdings on bluff and beach acreage, and the local newspaper—controlling, if not monopolistic. Preaching less single-family influence, he allied himself with a small group of financiers and businessmen to fight the King Ranch and its principal spokesman, Roy Miller.

The maverick's first break came in 1910 when, after all the maneuverings, last-minute rescues, and triumphant telegrams from Congressman Garner, the U.S. Army Corps of Engineers ultimately by-passed a deepwater channel to Corpus Christi Bay in favor of a cheaper outlet at Aransas Pass. In spite of their best efforts, which included concentrated publicity barrages and influence offensives in Washington, the politicians had been outmaneuvered by lobbyists for Aransas Bay.[2]

Seizing their opportunity, Pope's insurgents put up their own ticket for city office in 1911, with banker Clark Pease as mayoral candidate. Opponents fought back with a ticket headed by long-time Democrat Hugh Sutherland and, running for the first time, Roy Miller. A bitter campaign climaxed with another controversy; Miller won his council spot decisively but Sutherland's mayoral count was in question. By the time lawsuits, counter lawsuits, and appeals were done, city attorney Pope had secured the mayor's seat for Pease, incurred the lasting enmity of Miller—and gained a new ally: Archie Parr.

7. Archie Parr (in later years) and Walter Pope, allies in the struggle for
the Port of Corpus Christi. Parr picture © 1933, *courtesy* Corpus Christi
Caller-Times, *Pope picture courtesy W. E. Pope Papers, Special Collections and
Archives, Mary and Jeff Bell Library, Texas A&M University–Corpus Christi.*

Third-grade drop-out, sometime horse wrangler, and occasional trail boss, Archie Parr was as different from merchant politicians like Walter Pope as he was from law school gentrymen like Robert Kleberg. Forced from school at the age of nine, he worked the range in scrub territory west of Corpus Christi, finally acquiring a ranch near the town he would grow to love, Benavides. Along the way, he learned the language and culture of the Texas-Mexicans who rode with him. By the turn of the century, Parr had gained their trust and that of small-time farmers and stockmen in Duval County. Driven to excel and voracious in his ambitions, Parr lusted for dominance, and the chance assassination of a tax assessor in 1907 so weakened the reigning political system that he was able to grab control of the county a year later. From that point on, the Duval rancher did everything other bosses did, but he did it openly, shamelessly, and occasionally brutally, as boastful of his power as others were of their pedigree. Nor was Parr satisfied with reasonable victories. He had to be seen in control of everyone's votes, and tallies from his precincts became known for their one-sided landslides. Consequently, reports mixed with rumors began to circulate throughout the state, and before long, Duval became synonymous with voter fraud, bribery, kickbacks, and corruption. An election day gunfight culminating in three deaths in 1912 did nothing to enhance the county's image.

In the meantime, other border bosses were fighting battles of their own. Long-delayed reaction to the 1903 election law that allowed surrogate payment of poll taxes sent another surge of landsmen to Austin, and this time indignant farmers demanded partition: total separation of farm acreage from ranch lands. Their success was virtually absolute. By 1913, state divisions had reduced Jim Wells to only a third of his original territory, Manuel Guerra to barely a half, and Robert Kleberg's fabled King Ranch was facing property taxes in five different counties.

Determined to preserve his own domain, Parr persuaded friends in the legislature to create a county around Benavides. Many hearings and petitions later, the attempt was squelched, but not before drawing Progressive attention to Duval doings, including a courthouse fire a year earlier that abruptly ended a judicial-ordered audit. As cries arose demanding another investigation, Parr took the offensive, called in old favors, and declared himself candidate for South Texas' state senate seat.[3]

At this point, James Wells's carefully constructed political machine began to crack apart. Already economically damaged by the 1903 Terrell voting laws and strained further by a last-ditch drive to stop Prohibition, the apparatus shuddered to a stall with Parr's announcement. Incensed at the rancher's blatant corruption and worried about the notice he was drawing to the region, South Texas political leaders, including Roy Miller, Walter Timon, and Robert J. Kleberg, organized en masse to fight his nomination. Only a last minute save by Jim Wells pasted together a coalition that preserved "a measure of Democratic unity." As the party mechanism lumbered to life once more, Parr won the senate seat and a doubling of his power. "As a matter of senatorial courtesy, the upper chamber would automatically pass his proposals on local questions. Similarly, he could effectively counter . . . [any] bills designed to undermine the Duval County machine."[4]

Prideful and obdurate, the one time hired-hand gloried in his admission to the elite. Congressman John Nance Garner courted him; fellow senators hobnobbed with him; local officials catered to him; Roy Miller corresponded with him. Even an aging Wells extolled Parr, more than half-believing the senator's claim that Kleberg and his friends wanted "to kill you off and . . . take your place in this country."[5]

But not all kowtowed. Invigorated by Prohibition's near-win in 1911 and sensing fissures in Wells's previously impregnable organization, Progressives of all stripes—Anglo dissidents, disgruntled rancheros, fundamentalist teetotalers, reformed socialists—prevailed upon the State of Texas and the Justice Department to investigate Duval politics. The state prosecution went nowhere, with cronyism and biased grand jurors limiting what effective testimony existed. But the federal inquiry also accomplished little. Preoccupied with German aggression in Europe and beset with border violence at home, President Wilson had little inclination to tamper with South Texas politics in 1915.[6] Although he countenanced an eventual investigation, administration lawyers were admonished to limit inquiries only to matters influencing the election of federal officials. Here Parr lucked out. Although the grand jury found plentiful evidence of voter intimidation, suborned judges, and distorted tallies, these had little or no impact upon federal races. It would not be long before the charges against him, as usual, were dropped.[7] Discouraged and disheartened, their best attempts drifting into the dust of Duval County politics, reformers looked eastward for targets, figuring to have better luck in Nueces County.

The years after the acrimonious Pease-Sutherland race of 1911 had not been dull in Corpus Christi. Riding triumphantly upon his record and impassioned criticisms of fellow council members, Roy Miller won a resounding victory in local elections two years later, this time as mayor. Determined to restore the port as a municipal priority, he set about modernizing the city and, by the end of his first term, had initiated a trolley line, improved the water and sewage systems, beautified the eastern edge of the bluff, and extended street paving begun during the Pease administration.

He also strengthened his own position within the Democratic Party by creating the Young Men's Democrats Club. Its ostensible purpose, to organize rallies and set up committees during election campaigns, belied a more likely goal: to put a little distance between his own Progressivism and the Old Guard Democrats dominating the county. His popularity was intense, and by the time he ran for re-election in 1915, the "Boy Mayor" had gained the support of businessmen across party lines, including that of Gordon Boone, Pope's law partner. Miller's resounding victory carried his whole ticket with him, opening the way for a renewal of the deepwater port proposal.

But the 1915 mayoral results were overshadowed by the specter of the general election a year earlier. Ignominiously defeated by the Miller/Kleberg party in his run for re-election, Clark Pease and his supporters had mounted a strong fight for county office a year later, pitting their candidate, T. C. Brannon, against the wily Nueces veteran, County Judge Walter Timon. Blasted by a November 4, 1914 *Corpus Christi Caller* editorial as "nondescripts . . . who band together for no other purpose than to make a scramble for a few county offices," Brannon and his cohorts were doomed to defeat; but this time they took the loss and turned it inside out. On May 25, 1915, the *Caller* reported they had persuaded the federal prosecutor in Houston to open another investigation in South Texas.

Concerned about the allegations and wary of possible retribution, U.S. attorney John E. Green for the Southern District of Texas petitioned Washington for armed back-up. "Corpus Christi presents a condition worse than any other place in this District. . . . The people . . . will very much resent federal interference in what they are disposed to regard as their affairs. . . . [Their] reputation is bad. We should have ten or fifteen deputy marshals there."[8] Allotted three, Green set up his jury room in Corpus Christi anyway. By June 1915, over two hundred members of the Nueces County Democratic Party had been subpoenaed to testify about "alleged corruptions of the ballot."[9]

Rumors abounded on the first day of the hearing, and enough citizens shared sidewalk space with witnesses in front of the federal courthouse to

8. Corpus Christi by early 1919, modernized and beautified
into a viable home for a port. *Courtesy Jim Moloney.*

occasion comment by the *Caller and Daily Herald* (May 27, 1915): "In Corpus Christi political affairs for years have proved a most engrossing topic of conversation and one to draw the closest attention of a majority of voters. The present inquiry is developing the greatest amount of interest . . . and on streets, in stores and residences is the principal topic of conversation for about nine-tenths of the city." Nor were locals the only ones interested in the proceedings, according to the paper, which were "also proving a live news item for newspapers of the state, appearing on the front pages of most Texas dailies each day."

After five days of closed sessions, people's curiosity had reached fever point—and prosecuting attorney Green did not let them down. On June 5, 1915, the federal grand jury returned indictments against forty-two Nueces County citizens on grounds of conspiring to corrupt an election. Included among them were Judge W. R. Hopkins of the 28th District Court, Judge Timon, nine other county employees, five city officials, three merchants, three saloonkeepers, two ranchers, and the principal of a local elementary school. Nor were Anglos the only ones indicted; seven Mexican Americans and five African Americans made the list. All the old charges lodged against Archie Parr were trotted out along with some new ones: "using the machinery of the courts for prosecutions not warranted by law . . . depriving citizens of their liberty without due process . . . voting a large number of persons who had been convicted of felonies and who had not had their civil rights restored."[10] By the time the indictments were read out, the city was in shock, and the surprises had not ended. Appearing to make bond for all defendants were three of the leading attorneys in the state—and Walter E. Pope. Desperate for party support in his upcoming race for state representative, Pope seemed to have abandoned his old associates to work for the county.

His work was cut out for him. Before the next day dawned, one indictee had stormed The Hill, threatened witnesses, and shot a bystander in the head. Getting the malcontent removed to Galveston under bond would be the least of the challenges facing the defense. Securing a sympathetic venue, selecting a friendly jury, and discounting documented evidence would take all the expertise in law and human nature Nueces County could afford.

The resulting trial starting in September was a study of vignettes: women spectators being forced to leave the courtroom to avoid hearing testimony deemed "vile and indecent," a star witness contradicting his grand jury testimony because he "had been drunk for three years . . . but

[was] sober today;" a first-time candidate recounting his trip to The Hill on election day "with fifty dollars in bills which he dropped in Judge Timon's coat pocket," the *Caller and Daily Herald* reported on September 11, 1915.

Some of the testimony was riveting. One witness stated that a friend asked Judge Timon, "How much will it take for the Hill?" Timon's reply was that it would take from $2,500 to $3,000 "as the other side will spend money like water." Some was disarmingly honest. On the 11th, the paper recorded that "Mr. Acebo admitted that he voted Democratic ticket in the primary and general election but kept Independent signs in his saloon until the general election . . . 'because the Independents' money looked good to me.'" Some was unconsciously ironic. "Tom Ross, who is interpreting, is said to be one of the best in the country and his familiarity with the language and idioms of the Mexicans soon caused the Mexican witnesses to lose their self-consciousness and nervousness." The September 10th *Caller* added, "Mr. Ross was for many years a captain in the Ranger service."[11] One testifier, included in the Justice Department transcript, brought in an all-too-familiar name—Matt Dunn: "I stopped and asked [Tom] Dunn if he was helping. He said, 'I am' . . . and was there to help . . . Archie Parr. . . . Tom Dunn told me he got uneasy about Parr, and bought twenty-five votes at $50.00."[12] Another employed an unimpeachable source as character witness: "Judge Timon's . . . voice is deep, each . . . answer . . . given with strong emphasis. . . . 'I have lived in Nueces county for many years and as God is my judge I can say that never has it been necessary to buy a single vote in order to keep Nueces county in the Democratic column'" (*Caller and Daily Herald*, September 16, 1915).

Throughout it all, images of Walter Pope conferring with big-name attorneys, Roy Miller protesting a prosecutor's insinuations, and "Cactus Jack" Garner hopping off a train to proclaim the innocence of all added to the drama of the event.

Finally, the verdict came in, almost as twisted as the testimony itself. Of the original forty-two indicted for corrupting an election, five were convicted—three sentenced to the federal penitentiary for over a year, two to the county jail for six months. But the ringleader of the misdeeds, the man with the currency-laden coat pockets and the plan to "carry the Hill," was freed by a mistrial, the jurors apparently unable to agree on Judge Walter Timon's guilt. Also freed were the subjects of the bribes for which August Uehlinger, Lee Riggs, Tom Dunn, Henry Stevens, and Ed Castleberry were convicted; none of the remaining defendants were considered culpable. Thus had leaders of the Nueces Democratic Party, in the midst of the most humiliating exposé of voting practices they had ever undergone, secured the protection of their mighty and of their minions. In addition, those found guilty had special advantages; all were leading citizens of the city and four were over sixty years old. It took little foresight to realize their chances of ever seeing a cell in Leavenworth were practically nil.[13]

Frustrated, certain that jurors had been suborned, but doubting "that much good would be accomplished" by pursuing another trial against Timon, Green recommended in January of the next year to Attorney General Tom Gregory against further prosecution. "I feel that the chances of conviction on the second trial are not as good as they were on the first . . . and I know that the hard feeling which has been engendered in Nueces County as a result of these prosecutions will be increased by further pressing the charges."[14] The attorney general concurred, painfully aware of the blows the party was already receiving from angry Old Guarders incensed at the government's attack. "But what amazes us most about the Nueces County affair," ranted one, "[is] the determination of Attorney General Gregory to destroy, if possible, a Democratic organization which has always had to fight to maintain Democratic superiority. . . . When the great Department of Justice, presided over by a supposed Democrat, will resort to such low means in its persecution of good citizens . . . then it is high time for Texas Democrats to put on their thinking caps and wonder what the end will be!"[15] For Texas Progressives, however, the end was triumphantly clear. The prosecution of Nueces politicians, although not totally successful, had drawn blood; in the next few years they planned to destroy the highest official in the state.

James Ferguson, elected governor of Texas in 1914, was almost certainly an anomaly: he was an antisuffragist, liquor-supporting political neophyte who won his office with the votes of the oppressed. As aware as any that the financial strength of the state still rested on small stockmen and growers, he directly appealed to those that had been sidelined by the Terrell Laws of 1903, promising to limit the economic control landowners exercised over tenants. Nor was he any more subtle about the ax-wielding, tavern-destroying temperance movement sweeping the South. His vow to veto any liquor law the moment it hit his desk secured the gratitude of the thousands of Eastern Europeans who had settled Texas in the past decade—and a significant amount of their cash. Ferguson's real advantage, however, came from his own opponent. When Progressive Thomas Ball demanded the removal of Hispanic illiterates from the electorate and anticipated the day that "liquor and Mexicans will go from Texas simultaneously and rest together forever in death," he galvanized the trans-Nueces valley and put South Texas bosses, notably Archie Parr, squarely on the side of "Farmer Jim."[16]

The new chief of state came to the region's aid just as generously the next year when increasing violence between Mexicans and Texans coalesced into several major raids and an attack by Pancho Villa upon Columbus, New Mexico. Going further than simply dispersing state militia and Texas Rangers, Ferguson helped persuade President Wilson to deploy the entire National Guard along the border, with as many as thirty thousand men in the lower Rio Grande Valley alone. This earned him the undying gratitude of rancheros and farmers alike, along with merchants who had watched their markets disappear as each new attack led to more people leaving. "The mayors of the major towns were so concerned that the exodus would affect the economy that they issued a joint statement designed to allay the fears of the fleeing group, but as long as the raids continued . . . the mass migration continued. . . . Before normal conditions returned, more than half the Valley's population had left, and most of the farms were temporarily abandoned; the economy . . . practically ruined."[17] The presence of the guardsmen, many from as far away as New York, had an extra bonus. They spent money freely and that, along with requisitions from the military, helped keep the South Texas economy afloat, along with the fortunes of Jim Ferguson.[18]

By 1916 the governor needed all the help he could get to be re-elected. Steeper ad valorem taxes, necessary to pay for increased aid to education, had angered property owners and county officials, and the state attorney's refusal to enforce rent limits on landlords frustrated tenant farmers. A general backlash against foreigners of any type, fostered by the border troubles as well as reports of German atrocities in Belgium, strengthened nativism within the state, and reputed irregularities within the administration added to negative publicity. But the Progressives scuttled their chances again by choosing a Prohibitionist nonentity to lead the opposition, and Farmer Jim won a second term, this time with the new representative from Corpus Christi, Walter E. Pope, riding his coat tails.[19]

Within a number of weeks, Pope was striding the aisles of the House as commandingly as he had paced before juries, his voice ringing loudly enough "to shake the newspaper out of [colleagues'] hands" and his arguments convincing enough to merit respect from even his enemies. "I've got to leave," one muttered before Pope began speaking. "If I stay here, he'll sway me over to his side even though I know he's wrong."[20]

Strong in his knowledge of the position—he had studied the politics of his state as assiduously as those of his home city—he knew which legislators to ignore and which to cultivate, but Archie Parr was a whole separate category. A client since 1905, the Duval County man had primed Pope for the post for years, anticipating Pat Dunn's retirement and his own need for a colleague in the House he could trust. Indeed, almost immediately he put his protégé to the test: membership on the committee to investigate the acts and conduct of Gov. James E. Ferguson.

Disregarding the enmity of his opponents, Ferguson had bulldozed ahead in his second term, pushing through the state's first highway commission and vowing to stymie women's suffrage along with Prohibition, if the issues ever passed a floor vote. Determined to oust him one way or another, Progressives revived the old rumors of financial mismanagement, their clamor to investigate leading to the committee upon which Pope sat. Its final conclusion, that Ferguson's files showed no grounds for impeachment, came as a relief to the many rural residents who appreciated him. But a territorial fight over control of the University of Texas reignited his enemies' fire, and soon Ferguson was facing impeachment proceedings in a special session he himself had called.

Siding with him were his old ally Parr and as many South Texas legislators as he and Pope could secure. But their battlements were shaky. The United States had already plunged into war with Germany, Mexico was under suspicion for even receiving Zimmerman's suggestion to attack the Southwest, and anyone who publicly spoke German, Spanish, or Czech was considered a traitor. The federal Committee on Public Information had flooded the country with propaganda, and soon Lutheran ministers were being horsewhipped for preaching in their native tongue while elementary principals were urging their students to kill hybrid Americans. It was not a good time to support a governor who had taken loans from German-Texan brewmeisters.[21]

Nor could Pope count for support within his home city. Mayor Roy Miller, riding the crest of an unopposed third election to city hall, was successfully propelling a new attempt to persuade the Rivers and Harbors Committee to reconsider Corpus Christi as the site for a deepwater port.

But a necessary measure, getting the state to allocate ad valorem taxes for a bayfront improvement plan, had stalled when Pope included a provision that benefited his own interests. A series of irate messages from Miller and his council forced the representative to amend his proposal, but the enmity between the two intensified, as did prohibitionist sentiment within the county. There would be no help for Ferguson in Corpus Christi.[22]

Even Robert Kleberg, one generation away from Germany himself, would not support the governor. His financial investors encompassed far more than stockmen and sodbusters now. He had ties with bankers, businessmen, breeders, land developers, scientists, and university regents as well as town- and county-leaders throughout South Texas. Backing a politician who had drawn so much unfavorable publicity during this time of war would endanger all that, as well as the prospects of the deepwater port he had desired for so long. Besides, the sixty-three-year-old patriarch had just been stricken with palsy. Coming to grips with the limitations the condition imposed, keeping King Ranch Enterprises afloat, and securing his immediate and Kineño families from harm's way were the priorities demanding his attention in 1917.

So Farmer Jim went down—actually resigning the day before his conviction became public, and prohibitionist Will Hobby became Texas' new governor. But the Progressives were not done. Other legislators had opposed impeachment of Ferguson, but their sights were leveled on just one: Archie Parr.

Payback and Portents

The last great confrontation between Parr and the Progressives ignited during a district senatorial race, roared to a peak in the state house in Austin, and ended with a scorched-earth showdown in Corpus Christi that all but doomed deep water forever. It started with Parr's decision to run again for his state office in 1918, a decision that enraged regional Progressives. Before long, they persuaded McAllen businessman and Hobby supporter D. W. Glasscock to declare for the office. Desperate to win, both sides mounted illegal campaigns, taking advantage of confusion in the wake of the newly enacted Dean Laws, another legislative attempt to "purify" the electorate.[1] Parr's people tried to block women, able for the first time to vote in primaries, from going to the polls, while Texas Rangers supporting Glasscock spread rumors that any illiterate Hispanic even attempting to vote would be jailed.[2]

The resulting vote was inconclusive. Unofficial tallies gave the McAllen man enough votes to claim the nomination at the district convocation a month later, but they were incomplete. Parr had held the Duval count back, waited until the morning of the meeting, then announced his tally: over one thousand votes for himself, less than twenty-five for Glasscock. Even his supporters seemed embarrassed. "Democrats of other sections of the state wonder why and how such a small and sparsely settled county as Duval can give any candidate a majority of 1,162 votes, especially when at least one of the principal polling places was closed," the *Corpus Christi Caller* reported on August 4, 1918. But the new tally furnished Parr the number he needed to top his rival, and he strode into the convention assured of the nomination, having earlier changed the time of the gathering just to make sure his partisans outnumbered those of Glasscock.[3]

Upstaged but not discouraged, the Progressives held their own district nomination convention for senator, chose Glasscock, then easily prevailed upon state Democrats to second their candidate. Parr's name was stricken from the ballot—momentarily.[4]

Parr sued, secured a friendly judge, then won his case. "On the narrow grounds that the Glasscock convention failed to conform to the requirements of the Terrell Election Law, the judge certified Parr as the legal nominee of the Democratic Party and issued an injunction that compelled the county officials to delete Glasscock's name from the ballots and insert Parr's."[5]

All that remained was for Parr to coast through the general election of November. Valiant attempts to salvage Glasscock's candidacy were made by the Hobby Democrats of the 23rd District, included a well-publicized write-in effort sponsored by such leaders as Corpus Christi lawyer Edward Kleberg and local rancher Richard Mifflin King. "Assert your Americanism. Show the boys 'over there' that you are not more afraid than they to crush the thrones of Kings and Kaisers. . . . Scratch A. Parr, Write in the name of D. W. Glasscock. Do that and be a regular, unbossed Democrat," urged an advertisement in the November 5, 1918 *Caller.*

But the crown jewel of the Progressive onslaught was Roy Miller, and using his newspaper as a bully pulpit, he let the invectives fly. Duval County was a "a carnival of corruption and fraud," he wrote on November 3, 1918, where "men and women, not citizens of the United States . . . who could neither read nor write . . . were used by the . . . machine to pile up the fictitious majority necessary to give Mr. Parr the votes he needed." The convention that endorsed Parr was "packed at the eleventh hour by Aztec henchmen from the Rio Grande," and supporters of Parr, who included the area's representative in the House, Walter E. Pope, were purveyors "of booze and vice, of purchased governors, of salaried brewery lawyers, of corruptionists of every hue and kind who, for years, have not hesitated to traffic in the very bodies and souls of men and women." No matter that Miller's strongest ally, Robert Kleberg, had manipulated the votes of his workers for years, nor that Miller himself testified for the defense in the electoral fraud trial three years earlier. The chase was on, and the mayor, redolent with virtue and secure in his own "dictates of conscience," was leading the pack.

Watching from afar was Walter Pope. Stymied already by the city in his attempt to profit from bayfront development, rebuffed by Miller's council when he proposed competitive bids for the job, and all but ignored in the *Caller*'s write-up of election wins, the conflict between the mayor and himself had become personal. But it would have to wait; first, Parr needed to secure his senate seat.

And he did. By the time the votes were counted in the general election, Parr had carried the 23rd District with a majority vote of 624. Desperate, Progressives took their battle to the senate, and for six long weeks in early

1919, the entire membership listened to testimony and affidavits castigating the corrupt county leader. But Parr was not inactive. Hiring the same attorney who defended the Nueces County Forty-Two in 1915, he and Pope conducted their own investigation of the challenger and his supporters. By the time his turn before the senate came, Marshal Hicks had a full portfolio of abuses and frauds ready to unleash against the plaintiff, along with the testimony of Mission, Texas, residents, so disgusted with Glasscock's business practices they were the only Anglos in the valley to vote overwhelmingly for Parr.[6]

In the end, Parr kept his seat, saved not so much by his integrity as by the dishonesty of his adversary. In a replay of the old adage, "Better the devil you know," the senate voted sixteen to fourteen to keep their colleague. The Progressives retired in defeat; it was a time to rest for a while and regroup.[7]

Battles in Corpus Christi, however, were just beginning. Enraged by the polemics in Miller's editorials, Walter Pope had become even more incensed by a February 15, 1919 *Caller* article that virtually accused the representative of attempting to profit from bayfront development. "The proposed bill of Mr. Pope does not provide for an adjustment of [property] claims that would be equitable. . . . [It] is manifestly unfair and unjust, and . . . lays the predicate for, and practically invites, endless litigation. . . . It is the belief of the council that the view of no private citizen should be permitted to interfere or conflict with the larger interests of the people as a whole." Publicly exposed and forced into a corner, Pope conceded and the next day agreed to submit a more acceptable bill. The newspaper counted its blessings, "This action means that the fight as to what methods to pursue in going ahead with this project is now at an end" (Feb. 16, 1919), and hoped for a conflict-free month ahead. "Mayor Roy Miller and other members of the City Council apparently are to again be elected without opposition. The overwhelming demand upon the part of the citizenship, as expressed by the fact that five hundred three of the qualified electors of the city have petitioned him to again become a candidate . . . indicates a practical unanimity upon the part of citizens for his continuance in office" (*Corpus Christi Caller*, Feb. 27, 1919).

But it was the paper's parting shot that galvanized Pope: "True it is that we have a few men of nagging disposition who are never ready to line up with the majority and with the builders on any proposition, but we should be thankful that such men compose a very small minority." Within four days after Parr took his contested seat and three days after the revised Bayfront Improvement bill passed the senate, a small notice appeared in every newspaper in town: "I hereby announce myself as a candidate for the office of Mayor of Corpus Christi at the ensuing election." Signed by Gordon Boone, the names of three other men followed, each declaring for a post as city commissioner. At the eleventh hour, Pope had fielded an opposition ticket against Miller, headed by his own law partner.

For the first time in a decade, Roy Miller faced an opponent worthy of his respect; moreover, the incumbent was campaigning in a city that was virtually a testament to his own skills and leadership. In the fifteen years since the young Houstonian had arrived, Corpus Christi had at least doubled in population, and that was counting none but permanent residents.

Tourists had become a staple of the economy, and only partially because of the facilities moneymen had begun to provide: three major hotels—two downtown fronting Water Street and one farther up the little peninsula between Nueces Bay and Corpus Christi Bay, now known as North Beach—plus a myriad of smaller hotels, rooming houses, and summer cottages. The national health craze plus more practical designs in bathing costumes had made playing in the sea another opportunity for income. Soon bathhouses, elaborate cabanas "built out over the water where the people could emerge from the dressing areas and ease into the bay on slips of ladder," became part of the Corpus Christi vista. Extending along the beachfront between the wharves of the business district or jutting out into the bay from North Beach, they provided a perfect place for visitors as well as townsfolk to swim, wade, and simply get together with friends.[8]

Nor were bathhouses and bathing piers the only structures that had sprung up along the beach in the new century. One was Timon's magnificent building project, the county's new courthouse. Completed in 1914 and erected between Irishtown to the north and the business district to the south, it stood six stories high, its soft gray brick crowned by a red tile roof. A dignified main entrance, reached by a broad flight of steps, led into a massive interior from which courtrooms, offices, and hallways branched in three directions. With a sturdiness characteristic of the era, the top floors, overlooking Corpus Christi Bay, gave the best view in the region to incarcerated criminals, while lower floors housed jailers, their families, and other government officials. One of them was Walter Timon, who resoundingly won re-election to county judgeship a year after his voter abuse mistrial. Although appointed to the 28th District Criminal Court by

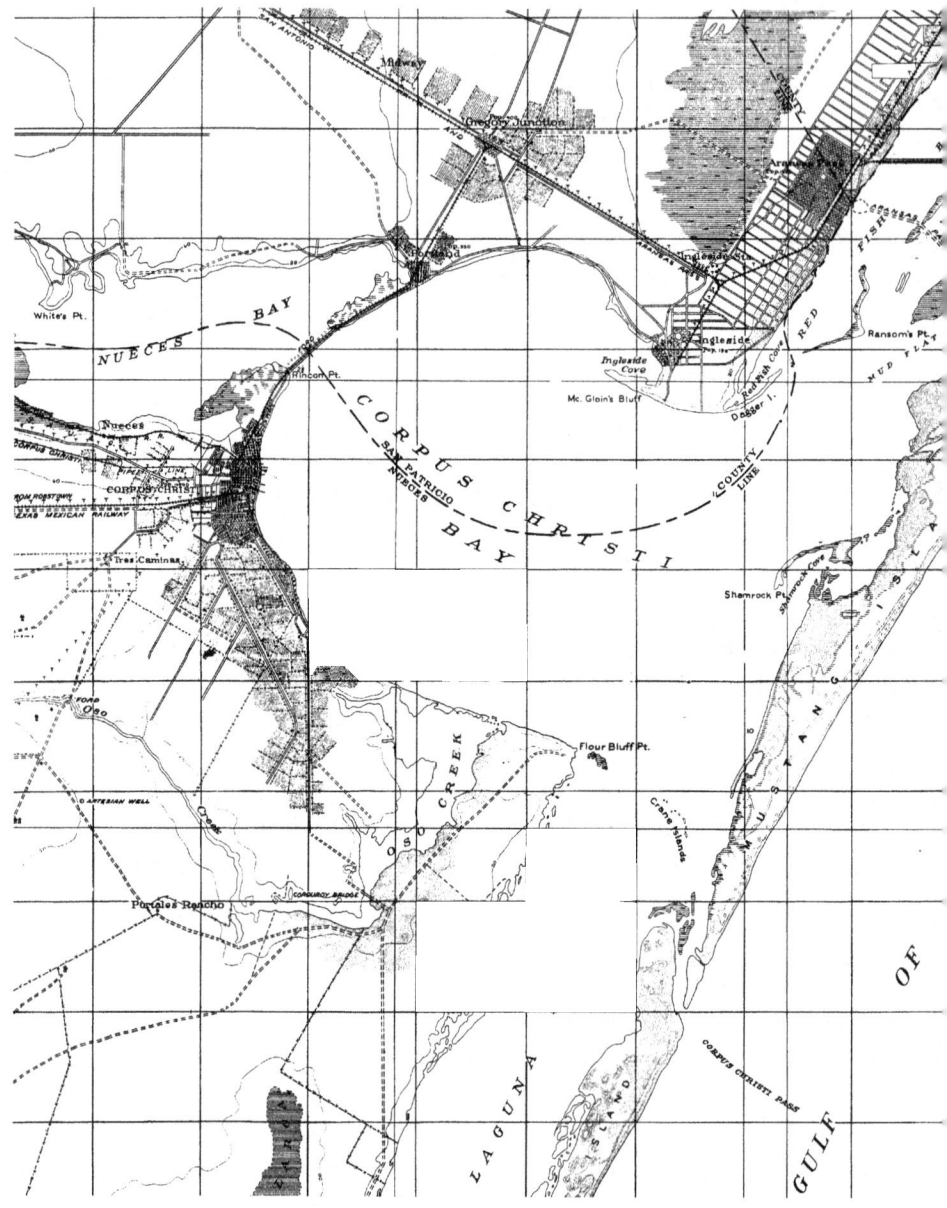

9. The city of Corpus Christi and its bays, as surveyed
in 1918. *Courtesy Corpus Christi Public Libraries.*

Ferguson just before the governor's impeachment, Timon continued to occupy rooms in the courthouse he had helped erect.[9]

Other structures of vastly different type had also begun to emerge on North Beach, where, eschewing the "old money" mansions on the bluff, young and successful businessmen had started to build. By 1915 their substantial year-round residences rivaled those on Broadway Street and included the concrete-bolted home of Judge H. D. MacDonald, the four-storied Mayfield house on Pearl Place, and the elegant two-story brick on Bushnick that Lester Gunst, now owner of his father's Stationery and Book Company, had designed for his bride May. Mayor Miller and his wife Maud, young physician A. E. Spohn, and cotton company executive Dave Locker also had homes along the bay's edge, as did merchants Wayne Greathouse, Joe Fuller, and Elliot Wright. Intermingled with the summerhouses and rent cottages that had long been there, over two hundred residences now perched on the peninsula between Corpus Christi and Nueces bays.[10]

But the queen of establishments along North Beach as the second decade started was neither a courthouse nor a home; it was a hospital. Desperate to provide more immediate medical care for his Corpus Christi patients than that offered by the nearest hospitals in San Antonio or Galveston, long-time physician Arthur Spohn contacted the nursing nuns of the Sisters of Charity of the Incarnate Word, and in the early 1900s they agreed to establish a sanitarium in the city.[11] But agreeing was easier than doing, and, although Alice Kleberg, wife of the King Ranch border boss and daughter of old Richard King himself, conducted the money-raising campaign, she ran into conflicts almost immediately. One was the reluctance of her propertied friends to contribute to the venture. Many had already invested their funds in a new hotel, designed to attract more railroads into the area, while others refused to help because the hospital was to be run by Catholic sisters. Another problem was location. The original site was to have been on "valuable grounds beautifully located on the Bluff" and donated by rancher John Kenedy, Doctor Spohn's brother-in-law. Then, abruptly and without official reason, Kenedy changed his mind. By the time the hospital was dedicated in 1905, it was wood, had only partially been paid for, and lay less than one hundred yards from the water on North Beach.[12] Moreover, it was less than well-received by the elite of Corpus Christi. "Although the sanitarium had been established in great part through the financial support of prominent Corpus Christi families, it was never considered an institution primarily for the rich. . . . In fact . . . in the early years, 'the wealthy people of Corpus Christi went to San Antonio when they needed surgery or special care. . . . Persons who could afford the trip and the service of . . . distinguished doctors never went to Spohn. Some went to Houston and Galveston, but most of them went to San Antonio.'"[13]

But the warmth and the effectiveness of the nuns soon charmed all of Corpus Christi. "Spohn was crowded with patients from the very beginning. Just one year after the opening it was necessary to add more rooms, and an annex was constructed adjoining the main building. By 1911, a separate chapel was built, and in 1912 a steam heating plant was added." By 1915, Spohn Sanitarium was a showplace, an extremely large, two-storied frame building facing the bay, with long veranda porch walkways on each floor and the wings. Basking in bayfront breezes, its door-sized windows, one in every room, opened onto the verandas, except for those of the centrally located furnace room. Sufficiently removed from the neighboring residences to secure quiet and privacy, the frame structure served as an occasional haven for San Antonio sisters recuperating from illness or stress. But most importantly, for the people of Corpus Christi, especially those "of very ordinary means [or] . . . who could not afford to pay for health care at all," it became hope personified.[14]

Bridges brought all these people—patients and businessmen, nuns and nurses, tourists and "townies"—together. A wooden causeway now straddled the bay connecting North Beach with the community of Portland, making northern entry or exit from Corpus Christi much more convenient. A smaller lumber bridge spanned Hall's Bayou, a low piece of ground near Irishtown, connecting North Beach with the city proper. Since this mud flat tended to flood every time the tide came in or rain fell particularly hard, the bridge, which could handle "cars, buggies, anything you wanted to go across," added considerably to residents' mobility. Texas-Mexican locomotives chugged onto and out from the bay on a new and larger city wharf, and the Southern Pacific/San Antonio Aransas Pass railroad was scheduling regular stops at the North Beach Breakers Hotel just for the tourists.[15]

New sets of trolley lines, seven operating within the city with about fourteen cars on duty, brought bathhouses and beaches within easy walking distance, and city streets, once so susceptible to mud that carriages would line up sideways so that ladies could step from buggy to buggy without getting dirty, were paved. City businesses in the downtown district had diversified, and specialty shops such as a bakery, a millinery shop, a coffee emporium, and a motion-picture house had taken up residence on Chaparral Street alongside veteran establishments like Corpus Christi National Bank and Morris Lichtenstein's department store. The Gunst Stationery and Book Company remained, but Lester Gunst had broadened his inventory to include office supplies, pianos, and the fabulously new Victor talking machine. Even the scraggly, weedy hillside of trash into which the bluff had degenerated looked new. Now "the joy of every citizen and the praise of every visitor," it had been landscaped, terraced, and graced with a balustrade and fountain that rivaled the neoclassicism of the courthouse.[16]

More than bathhouses, businesses, trolley lines, and paved roads attracted newcomers, however. Although the breezy climate was still uppermost in visitors' minds, the U.S. military was considering the city in a different way. Wilson's federalization of state militia into the National Guard and subsequent deployment of "five cavalry regiments, one infantry regiment, the major elements of two field artillery regiments, recently augmented by two new brigades . . . of cavalry and artillery" along the Texas-Mexico border in 1915 gave the Coastal Bend's location a strategic value. Gulf access (albeit limited) enhanced it. Soon commanding officers decided that Corpus Christi itself would make a good base, and Camp Scurry, located south of town along Chaparral, became a reality by 1916. Although Wilson's withdrawal of an armed expedition into Mexico finally bought a stalemate to border hostilities by 1917, the resulting pullout was a mixed blessing for Corpus Christi merchants who, like their forebears in 1846, had come to depend upon servicemen. So they loudly applauded the efforts of Representative Pope to establish a Naval Reserve school in the city, while Mayor Miller became a hero for personally persuading Gen. John Pershing to revive Camp Scurry as a junior military training camp. President Wilson's request to Congress, "to declare that a state of war exists with Germany," less than two weeks later further assured them that Corpus Christi would stay central to South Texas martial operations for a while longer.[17]

By the end of the Great War, for which the city had furnished 838 names for the first draft alone, over thirty young men from the area had died, with many more injured. It was for these injured, and others returning home in questionable physical and mental state, that the next military endeavor developed in Corpus Christi. Acting finally on an 1846 observation that the area "combines more advantages of position and salubrity [sic] . . . than any other point on the Gulf or Southern Atlantic coast," the surgeon general of the United States purchased Breakers Hotel on North Beach and began its immediate conversion into Army Hospital #15, a postwar convalescent center. Just a few weeks later, with the enthusiastic support of the city, he approved the additional establishment of a rest camp even closer to the shore. Tented at first until the 37th Infantry could build more permanent quarters, the enclave was to provide a brief spell of relief and relaxation for troopers who still patrolled "the hot sands and desert land" of the border. Between the two, city fathers estimated that from five hundred to one thousand more khaki-clad citizens would soon augment Corpus Christi's population.[18]

They arrived promptly, young enlistees like PFC Earl Carter, commanding officers like Captain B. M. Egeland, company mechanics like Noah Blanton—all came to Corpus Christi by train. The Texas-Mexican line coming east from Laredo was still dominant in the city, although the San Antonio and Aransas Pass, taken over by Southern Pacific in 1904, was running a close second with its direct route north across the bay. The St. Louis, Brownsville, & Mexico Railroad continued to carry farm families from the prairies to Kleberg town sites, while the newest line, the San Antonio, Uvalde and Gulf (S.A.U. & G.) ran directly west to Odem and Mathis, then northwest to John Nance Garner's Uvalde ranch. Catering to farmers and shippers along the way, it was known affectionately in Corpus Christi as the "sausage line." Nor did the rail lines stint on depots. Tex-Mex finally moved from its Berry Street terminal to share the brick-lined Union Depot with the St. Louis/Brownsville/Mexico in 1908. The S.P./S.A.A.P. built magnificent headquarters on North Broadway, and the "sausage line" raised a small unpretentious station along West Broadway. Each railroad had its own specialty, but together all depended upon the people of South Texas. They, in turn, were just as dependent upon the lines because, outside of the rapidly proliferating automobile, trains were still the only fast and efficient way to leave Corpus Christi.[19]

The port was neither, a situation that local and regional leaders had been well on their way to remedying—until the Parr imbroglio erupted. Determined to persuade the Rivers and Harbors Committee to commission a new survey after the abortive 1910 attempt, Roy Miller had been haunting the halls of Washington for years, buttonholing congressional aides, pressuring old poker partners, and lobbying lawmakers from as far away as Kansas. W. E. Pope had done his part in Austin as well, introducing a bill to allocate fifteen years of state ad valorem taxes to the city in order to finance a harbor-friendly Bayfront Improvement Plan. Flanking their moves were

Senator Parr on the legislative front, Robert Kleberg on the rural front, and Representatives Jim Slayden from San Antonio and John Nance Garner on the Washington front. Garner was particularly helpful now that he had become Democratic Party whip and leading minority member of the House Ways and Means Committee.[20]

In their struggle for government assistance, city leaders had even agreed in 1915 to build a seawall, a hurricane-protective barrier deemed unnecessary years earlier. But, desperate to get funding, and with an eye to future development, the council instructed its engineer to build the barrier "low"—and add a marina.[21]

Single-mindedly, Corpus Christi's drive for a deep water port continued in the midst of *Villista* raids along the border, growing casualty lists from the Great War, and city quarantines enjoined by the Spanish Influenza. Finally, just four days before Germany submitted her first conditional surrender, a Tennessee Trust Company offered to buy the $600,000 in seawall securities, and within six weeks after the signing of the Armistice, Mayor Miller's council had ratified the selection of a citizens' advisory committee and approved the seawall bond issue. Two months later, the senate approved the Waterfront Bill, the legislature acquiesced, and Governor Hobby signed it. "The last legislative obstacle to the improvement of the bayfront [has been cleared]," rejoiced the *Corpus Christi Caller*. "[W]ork is soon to begin."[22]

But, again, the *Caller* exulted too soon. Although the city had accepted seawall requirements and secured state funding for bayfront enhancements, Congress's Rivers and Harbors Committee had not yet decided to resurvey the coast, much less to designate Corpus Christi as a deep port site. Vital to federal funding was the continued exertion of the Parr/Pope/Kleberg/Miller coalition, but that alliance had shattered even before Governor Hobby signed the authorization law. The epithets, insults, and lies that had been hurled during the Parr investigation brought long-festering antagonisms to the surface; anger still rankled.[23]

Gamely the *Corpus Christi Caller* strove to heal the breach with an optimistic January 26, 1919 forecast. "The year ahead promises so much for Corpus Christi and Nueces County, that [it] is well worth the attention of those who have the interest of the city at heart . . . to help . . . put [its] projects 'over the top.' . . . It is not at all far-fetched to say that no city in the South begins the new year with greater prosperity." The paper even congratulated incumbent Mayor Miller for entering a fourth municipal campaign with no opposition, proving "a practical unanimity on the part of citizens for his continuance in government" (Feb. 27, 1919). "Now that the friction as to plans has been eliminated," it added a week later, "the Council will be prepared to make an immediate start . . . on improving the waterfront" (March 7, 1919).

But wounds had gone too deep. Fallout from the Progressive attack on Parr, and his surrogate Walter Pope, would soon spray everyone in the Miller administration with accusations of hypocrisy and greed, while a quiet, unassuming war vet strode to the forefront of the fight.

Actually Gordon Boone limped, an old injury from his past slowing his pace slightly as he walked the streets of Corpus Christi in the early months of 1919. So dignified that even in their personal correspondence, his closest partner called him "Judge," Gordon Boone was a rarity: a studied, deliberate moderate with ties in both Democratic camps.

Partnered with Pope since Madisonville days, he had shared victories with him, fielded instructions from him, and forwarded letters to him when the legislature was in session at Austin. At the same time, Boone joined the Hobby camp in August of 1918 and had publicly endorsed Miller for re-election just three years earlier. A retired brigadier general from the Spanish-American War and former chief magistrate of the 12th Judicial District, he did not commit himself lightly. For Boone to run for mayor, a post he later admitted he did not like and would never run for again, there had to have been a compelling reason.[24]

It came out five days after a *Caller* editorial enjoined the opponents to "Keep Cool." In a strident and explosive ad appearing in every city daily, Boone connected a series of recent rate hikes, passed without public input during the Miller administration, to a $325 monthly secret "salary" the mayor began getting at the same time. The implication of chicanery was obvious, and Boone pounded it home in every succeeding ad: "325 (Reasons)—Count Them!" and "Well, Look Who's Here—$325!"[25]

Included in his ads were pointed questions about the supplemental fund: "Is it paid by corporations or by Individuals?" "WHAT is it paid for?" "Is it legal?" One carried a total of Miller's official salary over the past eight years, $11,800, printed next to his sub rosa increment. Others hammered at the secrecy involved and asked repeatedly for the names of businessmen who had contributed. Another even questioned the council's pursuit of the port without public consent. The last ad, published on the day of the election, threw Miller's self-proclaimed piety back at him, "It is safer to vote

10. Gordon Boone, Spanish-American war veteran, former district judge, and candidate for mayor of Corpus Christi in 1919. *Copyright 1926, Courtesy* Corpus Christi Caller-Times.

for a man with a CONSCIENCE! And a man who only wants to DO RIGHT will consult that CONSICENCE before consulting his lawyer."[26]

For Miller had consulted his lawyer. One of several articles refuting Boone's allegation was written by city attorney H. A. Savage, but his argument, that Miller had indeed taken the money only as a form of "employment by businessmen of the city, to advance the commercial and military interests of Corpus Christi," fell flat, countered by Boone's austere, "the salary of $1800.00 provided by law for the Mayor of Corpus Christi is sufficient. I will ask no more." Miller's allegation that the Boone campaign was funded by "the Timon-Pope-Pease Combination" was offset by Boone's calm assertion of independence, "I am bound to no man," and his subtle reference to Robert Kleberg, "I am opposed to domination, dictation, or control by any man or set of men, resident or non-resident." The mayor's avowal that "war conditions" necessitated the silent hike of telephone rates was belied by a statement from the postmaster general of the United States, and his attack on Walter Pope for purchasing "second-hand homes . . . while drawing a salary from the city as attorney" simply made no sense.[27]

What did emerge from Miller was a deep hatred for his old antagonists and a genuine fear that his years-long struggle for bayfront development and the deep water port would result in "a wholesale donation of the waterfront to a few schemers."[28] "There is nothing in the law to require the City Council to proceed forthwith to carry out the bayfront plan. The law is silent in respect to the time when the work shall begin save that it must be begun within five years and be completed within ten years. Therefore, a City Council not favorable to the City plan . . . might very well postpone the work, until by some hook, crook, or politics, they might get the present law changed or amended [to benefit their own interests]," Miller wrote in the *Caller* on March 24, 1919. By the end of the campaign, Roy Miller had maintained his respect for Gordon Boone and even extended him "both sympathy and regret for the auspices that attend him" (*Caller*, March 24, 1919). But he was almost incoherent in his appeals to the public to support his re-election: "The future of Corpus Christi as a TRULY GREAT CITY is dependent upon ONE THING ALONE—DEEP WATER. AND IT IS ON THE WAY; IT IS ALMOST HERE. . . . Mr. Voter: Are you going to permit prejudice or politics to interfere with the carrying out of the program of progress?" (*Caller*, March 29, 1919).

The answer lay in voter turn out on April 1, and already Progressive inroads in the traditional vote were apparent. From a high of 1,820 poll fees paid in 1916, the year of a Prohibition referendum in Nueces County, city receipts had dropped 54 percent. But the real shock came in wards four and five, traditional centers of The Hill vote. By the January 31 deadline for registration, no more than 315 had signed up from those precincts, 60 percent less than those who had registered three years earlier.[29] The decrease was spectacular enough to warrant a *Caller* comment: "There is one condition in the elections of this year that is unusual and that is the fact that the vote among the Mexicans is comparatively light but 87 poll taxes having [been paid so far]. . . . In this connection it will be interesting to recall that the Dean Election Law is now in effect and it will be impossible to vote illiterates, as has been the custom in past elections" (March 31, 1919).

Whether it was the new law disenfranchising aliens and non-English speakers, or disinterest stemming from the last uncontested mayoral election, voters on The Hill did not flock to the polls that April as they had in years gone by. City residents who did go, however, went with a vengeance; turnout measured almost 90 percent of qualified voters, and they trounced Miller. Although the business section and the North Beach area, where he and so many other young businessmen made their homes, did support him by a narrow margin, the remaining precincts rejected him, some by as much as 60 percent. Boone and Pope's carefully selected commissioners were now in charge of Corpus Christi.[30]

A torpid dullness descended over the city, accompanied by a dreary rain the day election results were announced. Three days later, the new administration was sworn in, and Roy Miller's direst fears, that bay and seaport development would be held hostage to Walter Pope's ambitions, began to come true. Within a month after taking office, and against Boone's strong protest, the new city commissioners withdrew seawall funds from the Kleberg controlled bank and attempted to deposit them in the institution owned by Clark Pease. Only the intervention of a lawsuit, an injunction, and a denied appeal to the Fourth District Court stopped the process.[31] In the meantime, the council replaced the city engineer, hired a new attorney, and began to consider a plan to remove three feet of shoal along the bayfront floor. This would accommodate a barge docked alongside the municipal pier for the transfer of goods, a ruinously expensive project and poor substitute for a dredger-channeled harbor. But it was attractive in its normalcy. Corpus Christi's wharfs could function as they always had, and shoreline property owners like Pope could profit as they always had; nothing need disturb the insidious ennui settling over the city.[32]

Bayfront development itself and the concomitant seaport plan had not even appeared on the council's agenda, the *Caller* noted in late May, since the group first began meeting. By June, citizens were irate. "Deep water could be made possible if a united effort were made . . . but at the rate we have been going, we will never get it," several complained at a Rotary meeting. Others grumbled about the rights of businessmen and the responsibilities of public officials.[33]

But grumble as they might, no one responded, and slowly, inexorably, Corpus Christi slipped into a long, somnolent summer. Race riots raged in Chicago, cotton and grain prices plunged, and Texas ratified women's suffrage. But city readers' attention was on vice raids in local brothels and a move to register boarders in hotels. *Banditos* kidnapped army fliers, oil derricks rose overnight, and President Wilson presented the Versailles Peace Treaty to the Senate, but local interest centered upon a bathhouse pier collapse and an explosion that sent two workers to Spohn Sanitarium.[34] Finally, in mid-August, about the same time that Army Hospital #15 opened on North Beach, the state land commissioner set a valuation rate for property adjoining the proposed seawall, and the bayfront improvement project began to slog forward. But there was little fanfare. The weather was hot, air was heavy and humid, and city dwellers had settled into the inertia of a late Coastal Bend summer.[35]

Even a brief mention in the *Caller* of a tropical storm heading for Florida caused no concern. Was not the city impervious to hurricanes? Regardless of whether one took Reeder's assurances (he was after all a meterologist) seriously, the last two that hit South Texas seemed to confirm his words. The 1915 storm, although fatal to 116 people in the Galveston area, had no effect in Corpus Christi. The 1916 hurricane, which damaged Harbor Island and destroyed Riviera Beach with ninety-mile-per-hour winds, disturbed only flimsy wood structures along Water Street, leading the *Caller* to conclude, "The City is Practically Storm Proof." Its lead headline, "Corpus Christi Defies Tropical Hurricane," said it all.[36] So the city sweltered and slumbered in the heat, and out in the far eastern part of the Caribbean Sea, a tropical depression began to spiral toward the gulf.

10 Devastation and Death

The disturbance began as a mass of thundershowers and disturbed air off the Virgin Islands in the far eastern Caribbean some days earlier. Constantly veering west, aided by a wind shift unusual for the season, it began to coalesce into spiral formations circling a low-pressure center. It was not until it approached the Bermuda High, however, that it took direction. The high, a semipermanent high-pressure zone in the Atlantic so dense and cool that it can repel large air masses, was unusually broad in the late summer of 1919 and extended all the way down the Florida peninsula. Had it been less, it may have caught the disturbance along its outer edge and tossed it northward toward the East Coast, pushing it onto land too soon to become a danger. But that fall the Bermuda High was huge. It blocked the depression from an East Florida course and sent it westward into the gulf, "much as a spinning top follows the contours of a wall." There, the storm became a hurricane, that is, its nebulous low-pressure center spun itself into a well-defined column of fast-rising air, getting lighter, growing hotter, and leaching heat from the sea below. The faster the air rose near the center, the swifter the spiraling wind storms rushed into it, and the deeper the waters surged under it.[1]

When the *Caller* mentioned the storm, it was just invading the Florida Straits. At that point, air pressure at Key West had fallen far below normal to 28.81 mercury inches. By the time the hurricane passed, the pressure had hit 28.35, winds had passed eighty-four miles per hour, and the Key's anemometer (a device that measures wind speed) had blown away. As the system moved over the Dry Tortugas on the tenth, the pressure dropped to 27.51. A nearby ship reported a reading of 27.36, and gales began along the entire Gulf Coast. Ten vessels sank in the Florida Straits, among them a passenger liner with 488 people on board.[2]

The *Caller* dutifully reported the damage done, "Havana, 9/9: Cyclone winds are sweeping in from the gulf tonight, driving mountainous waves over the sea walls, which are flooding adjoining sections of the city at some places to a distance of six blocks," and the impact upon Key West, "South Florida Prostrate by Gale; Property Loss Appalling." But its last comment that week about the hurricane was the most ominous, "Storm Passes into Gulf. . . ."[3]

Then began an agony unique to meteorologists of that time; they lost the storm. "Once a hurricane reaches the area between the east Tradewinds and prevailing westerlies, usually around 25°-30° N, it often finds only weak air flows to guide it and may pause or wander aimlessly for days. This is a dangerous time because stationary hurricanes over water can strengthen quickly, and their next move is never certain."[4] In those days, the only way to track a hurricane before it made landfall was from ships at sea, and any left in the area of this storm were too crippled to report their observations. Moreover, barometric readings along the gulf shore never gave definite indications of the storm's intensity and direction. There was no lack of effort on the part of Isaac Cline, now chief of the regional weather center in New Orleans, and his staff to send out what information they had.[5] "Sept. 10, 1919 Following message sent from N.O. at 715 am. . . . Tropical disturbance . . . will enter the Gulf of Mexico Tuesday night and continue its northwestward movement. . . . Tropical storm probably over extreme southeastern Gulf of Mexico this morning and moving northwest. No reports thus far today from immediate vicinity. . . . Tropical storm probably about latitude 26 longitude 85 moving northwest. Dangerous winds Thursday over southeast Gulf."[6]

But "probablys" and "likelys" far outnumbered "certainlys." "Sept 11, 1919 Following message sent from N.O. at 320 pm received at 437 P.M. Tropical storm . . . still moving northwest probably near 25 and longitude 87; will likely reach middle gulf coast tonight. . . . Repeated hurricane warning order Louisiana Coast to Carabelle Fla. [Later on that night:] storm warnings ordered nine pm Port Arther [sic] to Velasco, Texas [area near Freeport]."[7] By Thursday of that week, uncertainty and frustration had reached fever pitch. Coastal warnings were given, then changed, and finally the district head promised to keep his office open after hours. "Sept. 12, 1919 sent 920 am. . . . Hoist northwest storm warning nine am Texas coast of West of Velasco to Corpus Christi Change to Northeast warning Pt. Arthur to Velasco Tropical disturbance in Gulf will cause increasing northerly winds next 24 hours probably reaching gale force Precautions should be continued. . . . [A positive] response to . . . request[s] for office to remain open."[8] By Saturday morning a Gulf ship finally reported in with a barometer reading of 27.50. Because the vessel was three hundred miles south of New Orleans, hope began to grow that the hurricane's landfall would be in Louisiana, "From N.O. at 907 am . . . Louisiana coast tropical storm moving northward into Louisiana west of mouth of Mississippi River . . . high tides. Every precaution should be exercised in southern Louisiana." San Antonio papers reported that the storm had already landed in that area, and even though a heavy shower hit the Coastal Bend late Friday, local officials ordered the storm warning flags along the beach and wharves in Corpus Christi to be lowered the next day.[9]

Some citizens had worried, but most paid little heed. Drained by a sultry summer, they welcomed the hint of change in the air. Winds were blowing from the north without heavy humidity, the temperature had cooled, and fish were biting from the back bay all the way down to Baffin Bay near Kingsville. For the first time in months, people felt energized. It was a good time to be outdoors and enjoy one last weekend before fall, or at least go to the shoreline and watch the waves.[10]

The waves *were* unusual for a September: huge wide breaking swells, coming slowly and magnificently, alternating with the normal, frothy white caps so usual in the bay.[11] It became almost a game, looking out over the water and trying to see how far one of those big swells stretched along the horizon before it finally broke.

But by late Saturday the northerly wind had picked up in speed, and it had started to rain again. The tide came in higher than usual. Then an engineer at Port Aransas called a friend at the Corpus Christi Weather Bureau with an ominous message, "The storm must be near the coast." Water was coming into his office, which was perched on piling fifteen feet above mean low tide.[12]

His words were a warning, the northerly wind on a September afternoon had been a warning, the huge numbers of fish near the surface, feeding in anticipation of coming turbulence—all had been a warning. Direst of all had been those strange waves, long, big, and slow breaking. They were *swell*, "low lines of . . . waves [that] move about three times faster than the storm itself," and the precursor of *surge*. They were still breaking upon the business district and North Beach on Saturday night, but the time between them was growing longer, one more marker indicating the intensity of the coming storm for those who would take heed.[13]

Few did, however, and plans for the following day went on much as usual. At the Nueces Hotel, vacationing teacher Lucy Caldwell left a late wake-up call with the desk before going to sleep. She had not gone bathing in the bay that day as usual; a "peculiar restlessness of the water" had stopped her. But she wanted to get in a swim before noon the next day. In his Camp Rest tent near Military Hospital #15, PFC Earl Carter also caught some quick shuteye. Company I's struggle to keep rain from washing out stakes and light poles climaxed a hectic week, and showers were still coming down. Up on the back part of the bluff overlooking Nueces Bay, Thomas Hickey's granddaughter, Marian Dodson, prepared her children for bed and planned Sunday dinner at the same time. Aunt Nelly was coming by on the morrow, and Marian's housemaid Lucretia would be in early to help.[14]

Annie Mays was not planning a normal Sunday, however. The continuing rains precluded evening Mass at Holy Cross the next day, so she took daughters Alclair and Anita to stay with her mother Saturday night. Sally's house had windows that, if necessary, could be boarded. Besides, the girls would have a good time giggling on quilts with their cousin. Down on North Beach, Teddy Fuller and his big brother were also pondering the weather. Never had they seen so many fish in the bay, and the murky sky carried its own tension, "There was something exciting [in] the wind." Farther south on the beach, the surf pounded even harder on Water Street. Still living next door to the ice plant, Lorenza and Manuel Sánchez watched while the children, Roy, María, and baby Ramón slept. Their brick-and-frame structure had easily weathered the 1915 and 1916 storms, but the sea sounded different this time.[15]

At midnight the phone rang at the Corpus Christi Weather Bureau. It was Houston with a message from New Orleans; the disturbance was in the central gulf, apparently south of Galveston. However, its center could not be located, and what came next was more of a plea than an order, "Watch barometer carefully during night and take all possible precautions against rising winds and higher tides especially if barometer begins to fall steadily." The last message transmitted while lines were still up arrived later on Sunday; the center was now definitely near the south coast of Texas. Hurricane warning flags went back up.[16]

The storm came hard that early Sunday morning; wind blew from the north-northwest and by eight o'clock had reached over forty miles per hour. Along the beachfront of Corpus Christi, rain was so thick "you could hardly see across the street,'" Lucy Caldwell noted, gusts throwing the water of the bay "exactly as you would dash a bucket of water on to a fire." Still, veterans of previous hurricanes shrugged off the weather. Sister Mary George, formidable mother superior of Spohn Sanitarium, had no qualms about seawater lapping the steps of her hospital; the tides had been that high "many times before," she assured her nurses. Corpus Christi native Lester Gunst was also unconcerned as he headed downtown to pick up an edition of the *Caller.* Papers were never delivered on Sundays, and this would be a good chance to get together with friends for coffee. In his own house down the street from the Gunsts, Teddy Fuller wakened to dark skies and frothy waters. He felt no alarm, however; everything "appeared to be south of us . . . the barometer was steady."[17]

Up on the bluff, a persistent hammering nudged young Alclair out of sleep. The adults were boarding up the windows of her grandmother's home and talking in hushed tones. Farther west on Palm Street, Sam Dodson moved his livestock to the lee side of the house. Although the rainfall did not seem terribly threatening, he still wanted the animals out of harm's way.[18]

By 10:00 A.M. the winds had shifted again to the north, and even though the local weather bureau was advising that the approaching storm would be small, some beach residents were beginning to feel concern. One was former mayor Roy Miller, who hastened his wife and little boys to the Nueces Hotel as waters began to swell in their street. Gunst was another. His casual jaunt downtown had become a hurried trip home to bring his family back to the hotel for the squall's duration. Reluctant to leave her beloved house, May took only one change of clothes for little Marian and insisted her husband hire a cab; she didn't want their new car to get wet. Rushing next door, Gunst added one more person to the group, Dave Locker, who had planned to ride things out until Lester persuaded him to accompany them.[19]

Other beach residents who moved to safer shelters through the driving rain included Evalena Wright's family, who hurried to the Bidwell Hotel facing Mesquite Street, her cousin Gertrude Wright, whose father brought her to the Nueces Courthouse, and Matt Pellegrino, who led his mother and sisters from a downtown funeral parlor up the bluff to a schoolhouse. Also moving higher were Laura and Manuel Sánchez. Reluctant to abandon Water Street but convinced now of the severity of the storm, the young couple grabbed their children, bundled the baby in blankets, then scrambled up the bluff to their Carrizo Street house.[20]

Heading to shelter in the opposite direction were Claude Greathouse and his wife and daughters who fled their beach house so abruptly that little Lemmawayne left barefooted. "My daddy carried . . . my baby sister Mayfair in the rubber sheet from her bed. . . . My mother held my older sister and me by the hand. I got a sticklebur in my foot, but she wouldn't let me stop to get it out. I cried all the way to the hospital."[21]

The hospital to which Lemmawayne's parents took her was Army Hospital #15, the North Beach hotel that had become the military convalescent center just a month earlier. Brick-walled, three-storied, and imposing, it evoked the same sense of security as the Nueces County courthouse, which also began to fill with anxious families. But not all residents were that concerned. Camp Rest commander B. M. Egeland, stationed in Corpus Christi for the past two months, had fallen in love with the sea and refused to believe it could bring danger. Firmly ensconced in his North Beach home, he and his wife encouraged several of his staffers to join them and ride out the excitement their little bay promised.[22]

Others on the beach also taking the storm in stride were Robbie Simpson and his family, anticipating homemade doughnuts and fried chicken for dinner, the Fullers, preparing to take Teddy's Aunt Doshie to the train station, and SAAP railroad conductor Terrell Brooks and his wife. They, assured of complete safety within a home that had weathered the 1916 hurricane, had elected to stay there with their two babies. Others were also complacent, many just sitting down to their noontime meal. "Oh no, I can't leave home," W. P. Helscher replied to an anxious caller. "We're having coconut pie for dinner." The Reddicks on Furman Street were also hungry. "We had cooked this fine chicken dinner," Mrs. Reddick remembered, "so we decided we should eat it before we left."[23]

By this time, food was farthest from anyone's mind at the weather station. Gales, blowing from the northeast now and approaching seventy miles per hour, had smashed the sunshine recorder and broken the instrument shelter. Phone lines were whipping in the wind, lights were flashing off and on, and rain was streaking through closed windows. Even more threatening was the barometric reading. Obeying the directive to "watch barometer carefully," Corpus Christi meteorologist Charles Heckathorn checked the instrument in between attempts to re-establish contact with his headquarters. Then, at 10:30 A.M., he noted the pressure indicator dip below 29.5 inches. At that point, he issued the first, and only, official warning of the day: "Direct people in exposed places to seek places of safety."[24] "This was given to the police department and to a large number of persons who had [gathered to render] assistance in case of danger. Immediately the police sent messengers in automobiles to the north of town and began distributing the warning from house to house. The men who had collected in the office gave the warning . . . in the vicinity of the business district and telephoned to as many as could be reached in that manner so that few were missed and many warned several times."[25]

But not all. Growing concern had led the sisters at Spohn Sanitarium to call the weather bureau several times during the morning, only to be assured that if a real storm did come they would be warned. But no one called nor came, and within an hour after Heckathorn issued his warning, their telephone lines were down, their electricity gone, and Corpus Christi Bay was sweeping across the peninsula, cutting off any escape to the bluff or higher portions of the city. By noon the two bays were surging into one, the smaller buildings near the hospital were beginning to rip apart in the waves, and the bathhouse was collapsing. With the staff and a few citizens who had come the night before, Mother Mary George and her assistant, Sister Thaís, started carrying patients onto the second floor of the south wing, hoping they would be less exposed to the swelling tides. But not all could be lifted, and several, including one paralyzed and another seriously burned, had to be left behind. Straightening blankets, mopping foreheads, comforting in voices muted by the assault of the storm, nuns and lay nurses rotated in shifts from the upstairs patients to the small room in the north annex. Immobile but terrified, the two patients on the first floor lay help-less, Milton Plum, limbs paralyzed and still, and José Hernández, scald wounds still suppurating from the power plant explosion. Assured by the soothing words of Sister Thaís and aide Theresa Reece, they stared at the creaking ceiling, while a wind-whipped stairwell away, the rest of the patients clustered to pray and listen to the storm.[26]

Within another hour, the barometer had dropped again, this time to 28.65. In meteorological terms, that registered to 927 millibars, the lowest barometric pressure recorded up to that time in the United States.[27] This storm was heading straight for Corpus Christi.

But what began to convince the townspeople—the holdouts, the die-hards, the long-term residents who still considered Corpus Christi im-pervious to hurricanes—was the ever-rising tide. By 9:45 A.M. water was almost up to the gutter on the street closest to the bay. By noon it was still rising. At 1:00 P.M. the water was running eighteen inches in Chaparral Street; forty-five minutes later it was five feet deep. The storm surge had started coming in, and that, coupled with the normal tides and the long, hurricane swell waves, was thundering over North Beach and the busi-ness district.[28]

People panicked. The Fuller family fled their house on Water Street, determined to reach the railroad track, the highest point of land on North Beach. In the dark and confusion only Mr. Fuller and Brother made it. Pushed beyond even their mother's reach by the water's rapid rise, Teddy and his older sister Esther took refuge in an abandoned house, watched it collapse around them, and then climbed onto the remains of the roof. Blackened with storm clouds, flashing with lightning, throbbing with noise, their world narrowed down to that fragile roof-raft dipping and tilting in the waves. Even then, it was not just the wind and the water and the rain. Those barrier isles, Mustang and San José, that were to have protected the city, had been scoured by the hurricane on its way inland. Bombarding the seas holding Teddy's float were huge barrels of oil swept from Port Aransas docks, telephone poles ripped from the dunes, and bulls, heifers, and near-grown calves already drowned in fourteen-foot high waves that had enveloped the islands. Additional loose lumber, rail ties and beams torn from the Southern Pacific trestle made the sea a shrapnel-laced explosive. Boards, poles, planks, and furniture hit their faces, pounded their bodies; nails stabbed and lacerated them.[29]

Others didn't even survive that long. Captain Egeland finally fled with his wife from his North Beach home as tides began to rock its foundations. Blocked from the railroad tracks by a drifting building, they used it as refuge until it too cratered into the surge. Springing from the collapsing roof, Egeland snatched a rail from the thrashing debris, pulled his wife and himself onto it, then secured their one life preserver between them. When last seen alive, they were clasped tightly together, careening out into the waves.[30]

Terrell Brooks's shelter had also proven too fragile for this storm. The tides, the winds, the surge, the constant slamming tore the two-story structure apart, and by 6:00 that evening, he and his wife were clinging to boards and pieces of lumber, desperately struggling to hold their two little ones above water. Then a swirling tangle of window casement and tree limbs swept the youngest from her arms, and Mrs. Brooks, tied to her baby for safety, went under. A thunderclap later, the older child disappeared. Mr. Brooks, exhausted, disheartened, too spent to hold onto the boards, let go. He drowned.[31]

As did others. Huddled inside the hospital's most secure ward, fingering rosaries silently as Monsignor Jaillet recited *Ave Marias* and *Paternosters*,

Spohn patients stared sightlessly forward, absorbed by the quaking of their building and the thudding of debris against the windows. Suddenly, in a startling moment of silence, they heard Hernández's voice from the north wing, "Sister Thaís!" The nun sprang from her knees, thrust open the door, and started down the stairwell. "Just as she did . . . there was a terrible crash. The north wing . . . split open, the roof fell in, and the annex blew away." Sister Paula, "sensing the danger for all, used . . . her strength to close the door," but Sister Thaís, Theresa Reece, and the two men in the downstairs room were gone.[32]

The waters were deadly. "Three great waves struck the town at the storm's height, with the greatest wave arriving at about 5:00.[33] [They] boom[ed] against the bluff facing the water. They sucked houses and debris with them out toward the gulf, to meet other big tidal waves coming in. As the waves came together they crushed buildings and wooden timbers like eggshells."[34]

They were channeled. "The water [surged] through the business district . . . to the north where the bluff disappears. . . . [Funnel-like] the bluffs on both sides of Corpus Christi Bay . . . compressed and concentrated the tide and its massive force over North Beach and across the mouth of Nueces Bay to the bluffs of Portland. . . . The tide reached 16 feet at White Point on the north shore of Nueces Bay."[35]

They scoured. "Along the southern portion of Corpus Christi Bay, the high clay bluff was worn away by the heavy seas to a depth of forty feet in many places. Along the waterfront in the business district, the seas tore away . . . nearly whole lots."[36]

By 3:00 P.M., the time the eye landed twenty-five miles south, waves were crashing over fourteen feet high, North Beach had disappeared, and Nueces and Corpus Christi bays had merged into a single raging maelstrom. Fifteen more hours of horror later, the storm subsided, leaving a shattered city behind.[37]

As Monday's dawn broke, bluff residents like the Dodsons and Popes and Mays checked their home's interiors and mopped up wind-blown rain, relieved the damage had been so slight. Then they went outside—and into shock. "We just stood upon the bluff," Alclair Mays remembered later, "and looked down and saw all of this water . . . and . . . dead bodies . . . and buildings and parts of buildings floating in the water."[38]

Over nine hundred structures were destroyed below the bluff, and water

11. Downtown Corpus Christi after flood waters receded, 1919.
Courtesy Corpus Christi Public Libraries.

stood eight to nine feet deep in those that remained. The beach was solid wreckage with houses, cars, boats, streetcars, and railroad tracks intertwined with bloated livestock and sea-drenched clothing.

Most of the business district from Chaparral Street to the water line was gone, and all of North Beach had been swept clean, except for the top stories of the military hospital, one remaining wing of Spohn Sanitarium, and the Henry Macdonald House, which was leaning so far over after the storm that one could step off the upstairs porch onto the ground.[39]

F. J. Mulligan, business agent for John Kenedy, described the desolation in a report to his boss.

> Everything on the beach, from the Tex-Mex railway to the Sap [San Antonio and Aransas Pass railroad], is destroyed. . . . West of Water Street, back to Mesquite Street, from one end of the town to the other, is wrecked. The water rose ten feet and ruined everything that the wind did not destroy. . . . The streets are impassible. . . . The debris is covered with crude oil, and that makes it very difficult. . . . The sand is piled up on the beach from two [to] ten feet. The [former] Mayor's front is a sand bank. Hundreds of people took refuge in the courthouse, the City Hall, and the post-office. These people lost all that they had. . . . Many are missing, and it is not known just how many are lost. Up to the present time, a number of bodies have been recovered. The bluff did not suffer much. It was on the beach that the damage was done.[40]

Nor was it simply the beach area that had suffered. That great wall of water rushing from the gulf had poured Corpus Christi Bay into the Nueces, inundated its river, then swept onto the surrounding plains. Floodwaters reached inland almost as far as Odem, twenty miles northwest of the city, and washed out tracks to the SAU & G railroad. A ten-foot swell along the Matagorda peninsula deluged the region. "Summer homes in Victoria were leveled, and the cotton crop was destroyed. An eight-foot storm surge overwashed Sabine Pass. At Port Aransas, the steamship *Media* was lifted onto the docks." The little town of Aransas Pass was nearly destroyed, and Mustang Island was almost completely flooded. At Rockport "the tides were higher than ever before and every store was damaged. The town's only ice plant and Heldenfels Shipyard was wrecked. Water lapped at the third story of the local hotel and other buildings."[41]

The worst, however, were the dead. Bodies were everywhere, imprisoned in the wreckage, buried under sand, floating onto shore with the

12. The Lone Star Ice Company on Water Street, another casualty of the hurricane. *Photo by Doc McGregor, Courtesy Corpus Christi Public Libraries.*

tides, many stripped bare by the elements and all covered with oil from the wrecked storage tanks. "And, oh, the condition they were in," wrote Lucy Caldwell. "Arms and legs off, heads almost severed, all the hair gone, swollen beyond conception, and black from the oil . . . hair entangled with seaweed and the bodies so mutilated that identification was impossible."[42]

But at that point, immediately after the storm, one was geared for death. It was later, when one had briefly forgotten the horror and was thinking of something else—that was the worst, admitted young fifteen-year-old Chris Rachel, who lived across Nueces Bay at White's Point where so many victims had floated ashore. "Days and weeks and months after the storm, we were still finding bodies."[43]

There were many. Although some who had died from the storm had been visitors to the city, like late-summer tourists and rest camp soldiers, at least 90 percent of the dead were residents. Of these, most had lived in the newer sections of town, either on the beach just south of Hall's Bayou or on North Beach itself, both areas less than four feet above sea level. Bluff residents, including most of the city's minorities, had survived relatively unscathed except for workers like young Dr. Spohn's cook, who died trying to escape her employer's flooded home.[44]

But the winds and sea had played no favorites. George Demotsis lost his whole family; Teddy Fuller lost his mother, his aunt, and a best friend; Juan Martinez lost his wife and six children; H. K. Graham lost his son.[45] Remorseless in its details, the *Corpus Christi Caller* listed whole households that had perished.

Mason—child (1)
Mason—child (2)
Mason, Christopher Columbus
Mason, Miss Amanda
Mason, Mrs.
Nichols, Dorothy, age 10 (daughter of W. E. Nichols)
Nichols, Elvin, age 7 (little daughter of W. E. Nichols)
Nichols, W. E.[46]

It listed those that died alone.

Almanza, Pablita
Van Cleave, Robert

Conley, baby of Mrs. D. D. Conley

Wright, D.N. Confederate soldier[47]

It listed those that had no names.

> Unidentified male, white, about 55, 5 feet, 10 inches . . . 75
> pounds . . .
> Unidentified female, Mexican, about 12 or 13, wore gray coat, light
> dress, button shoes . . .
> Unidentified white female child, 7 years, light hair bobbed
> Unidentified female, white, about 9 years old, red bath suit with black
> trimmings. . . .[48]

To the best of their abilities, like disaster survivors the world over, citizens of Corpus Christi tried to control the horror. Monday's early light found residents like Samuel Dodson resolutely pulling on rubber boots, then taking wagons to pick up bodies or commandeering boats to cross floodwaters still raging between North Beach and the bluff.

A soggy red signal blanket, hoisted by the Spohn nuns from the only room left in the hospital, got immediate attention, and soon a small fleet of rescuers launched themselves across the truculent bays to the rooftop of the sanitarium's boiler room. There, as the men carefully placed a few patients and a sister in each boat, they heard the tragic story, broken by tears and shudders. The last to be rowed across was Mother Mary George.[49]

But the tidal surge was still strong, and it was late afternoon before the final boat ground against upper courthouse steps and delivered the mother superior into the arms of volunteers. There she, her nuns, the staff and the patients were warmed, clothed, and fed; and there, in time, the congregation was made whole again when Sister Mary Thaís's body was brought in, still in her black habit with her beads entwined about her waist.[50]

The Nueces County courthouse, its walls resolutely withstanding the worst of the waves, had become the region's initial command center. It was to its doors that rescuers first brought the living and carried the dead. It was in its basement that volunteers cleansed oil from the corpses so they could be identified. It was on its main floor, as the water receded, that Marian Dodson and her aunt Nelly helped distribute clothing to the three thousand left homeless after the storm.[51]

Nor did the outburst of generosity stop at courthouse steps. Up on the

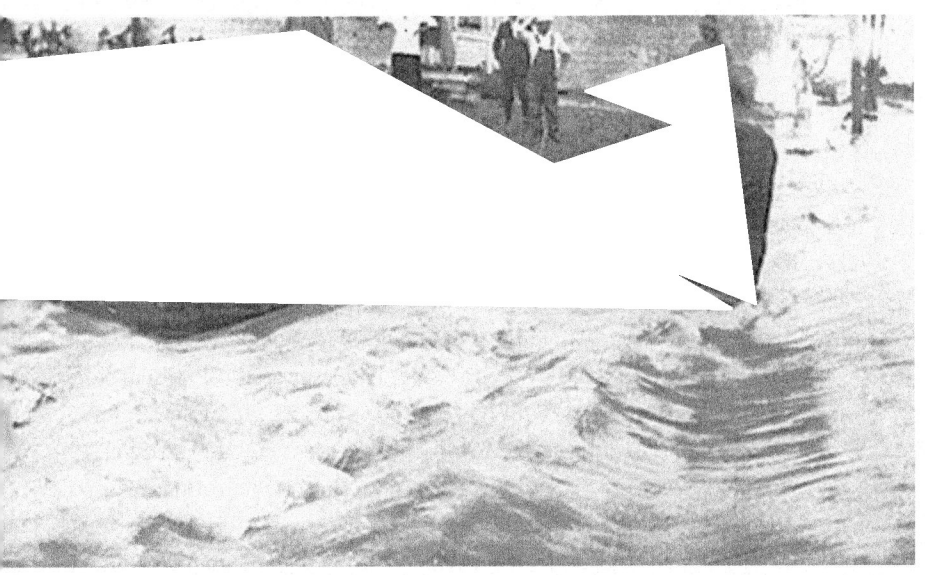

13. Boater in the storm tide, 1919. Courtesy Jim Moloney.

bluff, neighbors rushed hot meals to harried physicians like Dr. Heaney, shored up broken buildings like those of Holy Cross convent, and opened their homes to bereft families like the Greathouses. Farther north, before even the first bridge had been repaired, a young reporter swam across a swollen river to let Corpus Christi know of survivors washed up on the lower Nueces shores. It was on the first train to leave the city three days later, then, that Joe Fuller came to Sinton, and there, on the steps of the station he stood until a car drove up, its doors opened wide, and Teddy and his sister Esther rushed into their father's arms.[52]

But it was in city hall that the next significant actions occurred. Acutely aware that initial altruism would soon wane, Mayor Boone first contacted the governor to secure martial law, then called upon the U.S. Army and the Red Cross for aid. By the time waters in the business section had receded to an oil-slick wallow, new faces were entering the devastated town.[53]

The Red Cross was one of the first, actually activated on Sunday when local chapter members telephoned volunteers during the night and urged them to report for duty on the morrow. By the next day the entire southwestern division of the organization was in action. Relief trains accompanied by workers from Laredo and San Antonio were on their way to Corpus Christi, while a ship loaded with food, clothing, and medicine headed for Rockport. Within a week a staff of thirty-five emergency specialists were at work in the devastated areas, including a bacteriologist, social workers, and a nursing corps. Canteens and clinics were set up, clothing was dispersed, and vouchers, useable "only for the specific articles called for," were being distributed at designated stations across town. By June of the following year, when the organization tallied its books and prepared to leave Corpus Christi in the hands of its local workers, the organization had expended "over $250,000 [in] appropriations . . . [to] Corpus Christi families and the farmers nearby."[54]

What lingered most, however, were the memories of those who had been helped. Little Marian Gunst was one, describing the very early aftermath when Red Cross planes flew overhead, dropping bundles of food and clothing and milk. Evalena Wright, whose family returned to a shambled house empty of everything but sand, was another. "They had a mess hall in one of the big tents to eat. I remember going in there at breakfast time and there were scrambled eggs and after being hungry for so long . . . that was really good looking food."[55] Lucy Caldwell was a third. "They worked night and day. Under the leadership of Major McCann . . . the local Red Cross collected every bit of available food and clothing in Corpus Christi and distributed to the suffering. I saw Major McCann at the railway station with a handbag of money, distributing funds to refugees—taking no receipts and asking no questions."[56]

Less numerous on that first relief train, but just as needed, were the Reverend Mother Mary John O'Shaughnessy from Incarnate Word headquarters in San Antonio and a small contingent of nurses. Determined to succor her sisters, Mother O'Shaugnnessy had made elaborate plans to set up a makeshift hospital, sort out the remaining Spohn patients, and send the surviving staff away to recuperate from their loss, plans that received an immediate set-back once the Corpus Christi nuns heard them. United in suffering with the city, the sisters insisted upon remaining; after all, there was the temporary hospital to be equipped, patients to tend, assistance to be acknowledged.[57]

Within a week of the disaster, Mother Mary George had placed a "Card of Thanks" in the *Caller*, expressing her appreciation to the townspeople and commemorating Sister Thaís's death in the only way she could. "Grateful thanks is tendered for the expressions of sympathy from all sides for the loss of Sister M. Thaís, who gave her life for a Mexican patient. Hers was a martyr's death and the sisters feel her supreme sacrifice obtained God's special providence for the remaining inmates of the sanitarium, as their preservation from drowning was truly miraculous."[58]

Not long afterwards, a relic of the destroyed hospital, a small statue of the child Jesus, was salvaged from the wreckage and returned, almost unscarred, to the nuns. Three weeks later, Mother Mary John was back in San Antonio with her original corps of nurses. Time would come for the Spohn sisters to be replaced, one by one, and allowed to rest. Now, it was far more important that they heal with the people with whom they had suffered.[59]

The U.S. Army was the third relief institution responding to Mayor Boone's September 15 request. On his way as soon as he received Brig. Gen. F. C. Marshall's order, Lt. R. M. Eichelsdoerfer led the first in a series of troops who brought food and medicine, organized tent cities, dug latrines, and patrolled the streets in a city still in shock. Coming up from Brownsville on a designated express, he arrived in Corpus Christi early Tuesday morning with six thousand rations, one thousand beds, five hundred loaves of bread, and soldiers to police the storm area. By that evening,

Col. John A. Porter, the same commander who supervised rescue work after Galveston's devastating storm, had enforced martial law, set up district relief headquarters in city hall, and created a working military presence. In an area ringed with shell-shocked survivors, rotting animals, wet lumber, and bursting oil tanks, Porter's men were an oasis of calm. Stopping an incipient riot, running a refugee camp, monitoring a smallpox scare, and keeping track of $81,927.41 worth of supplies, they took on every job.[60]

They also took care of their own, and here is where the devastation had to have hit Porter hard. One officer and sixteen enlisted men of the 37th Infantry, stationed to staff the rest camp, had died in the hurricane, many heroically. Two had helped Esther and Teddy Fuller escape their collapsing shelter, keeping the "compressing walls apart with . . . outstretched hands" until the youngsters were atop the roof. Another had saved young Myrtle Ball from drowning, only to die himself in the havoc. Others had physically pulled panic victims from shattering buildings, or caught them from being submerged by debris, or carried them through strong undertows to safety. Many like H. E. Johnston, Mike Swatt, and Herbert Montgomery survived to commendations and esteem. But it was the dead who were nameless in their heroism, and it was up to Porter to identify them as best he could, "Private First Class Earl Carter . . . Dan Madiarini . . . Richard Hopps . . . Eukle Shonk," bury their pitifully decomposing bodies as quickly as possible, then ask his commander to notify the families. So the adjutant general did, sending telegram after telegram to Illinois and Wisconsin and Chicago homes, telling unsuspecting fathers or mothers or wives that their loved one had been lost in a storm in a place no one had heard of, along a seashore everyone considered safe.[61]

It was the final action Gordon Boone took that Monday morning, however, that became the most significant; he created a general rescue committee, composed of the most bitter political factions in the city, to coordinate relief, then put his old opponent in charge. Within days of the storm's landing, Roy Miller had launched seventeen active subcommittees, each headed by a major civic leader operating in his own specialty. Clark Pease was in charge of the Finance Committee, Hugh Sutherland in charge of rebuilding, and Judge Timon in charge of employment. Walter Pope coordinated salvage operations, and a carefully neutral city police chief provided flashlights and lantern wicks for nightly guard patrols. Mayor Boone himself issued emergency proclamations, directed citywide registration, authorized day passes, estimated property damages, escorted government officials, set up shore patrols, and soothed ruffled egos, all on a collapsing card table in a makeshift office, having bequeathed his official quarters to the military.[62]

Committee chairman Miller, in between authorizing sewage repairs and mediating contribution disputes, may have had the hardest job, however: piecing together descriptions of recovered bodies to publish for possible identification. Day after day he and his *Caller* staff sifted through each pencil-scrawled message, some from retrievers across the bays at Portland and White Point, several from Colonel Porter, others from local undertaker Maxwell P. Dunne. Interspersed between the stoic reports on the remains were personal, almost painful details that did not see print: "fishing tackle in pockets . . . beard about three days old," "diaper pinned with extra large safety pin," "high black button shoes, common sense heels." Some told of silent struggles to survive: "Female child, unknown . . . deep cut under left knee bandaged with torn rags and hemstitched pocket handkerchiefs, bandaged very tight to stop flow of blood." Others told of triple tragedies: "Add to your list Mrs. Marguerite Pruden, wife of Major Pruden. . . . One child born at Spohn after Major Pruden's death, lost in the flood and so far we are unable to get any trace of it." Implicit in every account were the survivors who made their way to the courthouse basement to identify their kin: Donnie Mullen's mother, Mildred Slagt's parents, and Zaharian Pitsota's comrades in arms.[63]

Every scrap of death making its way to Miller's Central Committee office emerged later as neatly typed lists on bond onionskin paper, eventually part of the disaster documentation demanded by bureaucracies and assistance agencies. But it was the centrality of effort and the spirit of cooperation, especially among erstwhile enemies, that most impressed relief operatives in Corpus Christi, and it was this "most hearty and cordial co-operation [of] all city officials" that Colonel Porter saluted when he turned the stricken area over to the National Guard five days after the hurricane hit. From that point on, with state militia in the Corpus Christi district "bringing conditions . . . back to normal," the city was essentially back in the hands of its people.[64] What would they do? Abandon it, as had the citizens of Indianola, and flee to safer inland boroughs? Or remain, as had the people of Galveston, only to wither in Houston's backwash?

Recovery and Resurgence

The answer was simple. Not far removed from the risk-takers of Henry Kinney's generation, the people of 1919 Corpus Christi elected to stay. That they never considered leaving was obvious Monday after the hurricane when a rumor that the city would be abandoned caused a near-riot of resistance downtown. But just as patently obvious was the need to clean the place up. The day after the hit, "there was so much wreckage you couldn't tell which . . . planks had gone [where]; the city [had to use] bulldozers to shift the piles from blocking the roadways." But within seven days, laborers had opened up the streets, cleared off the ruined lots, and stacked the lumber.[1]

The boards were put to immediate use. An outsider's bald assessment, that Corpus Christi businesses were permanently paralyzed, rang too true for many, and by the end of the year, 45 percent of those affected by the hurricane had indeed ceased to exist. But the rest remained, chose to rebuild, and used rescued lumber and new stock loaned at cost to reopen.[2] By November, the *Caller* was able to report even less bankruptcies in the city than had occurred the year before, bank dignitaries were exulting over "more money now than we have had in any previous year," and new congressman Carlos Bee[3] and the San Antonio Chamber of Commerce had already petitioned the federal government to allocate low-credit loans to Corpus Christi storeowners. Farmers were shipping over $500,000 worth of grain on the reconstructed railroads, and the downtown section of the city was ringing with the blows of carpenters and mechanics by the hundreds. Although the city's population had taken a hit, schools were reopening, a new fishing wharf was in the offing, and a unit of at least one hundred small cottages with roofs and sides thatched with palmettos was poised to rise on North Beach.[4]

The final step was almost inevitable. Boone's inspired appointment of Roy Miller to lead the Central Rescue and Relief Committee had been a stroke of organizational genius. The ex-mayor's unabated energy, even in the midst of devastation, had blended with the new mayor's quiet dignity. Now that Corpus Christi was recovering, what more could the two leaders achieve? The answer came at a special meeting with Congressman Bee in early October. There, in a crowded city hall, Boone announced the plan he and Miller had devised.[5] "'We want to build a seawall,' [he] said . . . [Boone] then spread out a map of the city and the two bays, showing how it would be possible from a geographical standpoint to construct the seawall around the city and through Hall's Bayou into Nueces bay . . . thus providing a *fully protected, land-backed harbor which could handle shipping of all classes.*"[6]

Rising from the oil-laden wreckage of their city, the two had led their people to stability; now they challenged them with a greater cause, the same method others had used in the midst of devastation. For San Francisco after the 1906 earthquake, the cause had been financial expansion; for Chicago after the Great Fire, it was expanded land use; for Galveston, it was a better way of government; for Corpus Christi, it would be a seawall. To Boone, the idea symbolized his rejuvenated city; for Miller, it fulfilled his dreams. Not only would the need for such a barrier never again be questioned; hooking its construction to that of a land-backed, international maritime harbor removed deep water from politics and made it a practical necessity—plus a lot easier to sell. With the influx of nationwide attention brought by the disaster, the heady boomtown atmosphere generated by rebuilding, and the poststorm spirit of cooperation still resolutely alive, the city needed only its congressman to secure a new survey by the Army Corps of Engineers.[7]

Reluctant to commit before consulting with coastal rivals Aransas Pass and Rockport, Bee did promise to take the plan to Washington. A month later both he and Texas Senator Morris Sheppard introduced bills supporting federal funds for a seawall, under the auspices of relief for the storm-stricken region. The port then got a prod when Bee's proposal to the Rivers and Harbors Committee, that it resurvey possible "harbor facilities on the Texas coast contiguous to Rockport, Aransas Pass, Corpus Christi, and Port Aransas," was accepted.[8]

Corpus Christi's next step was to convince the Committee's chief engineer, Major L. M. Adams, that not only was the city the logical place geographically and economically for a port, but that the entire region supported it. Here Miller's editorial expertise came to the fore with the 1921 publication of a magnificent brochure, *The Corpus Christi Port Project*.

Emblazoned with a bird's-eye view of the city, the bay, and a proposed twenty-five foot channel opening into the gulf, the frontispiece graphically captured the city's location behind three barrier islands, while sturdily

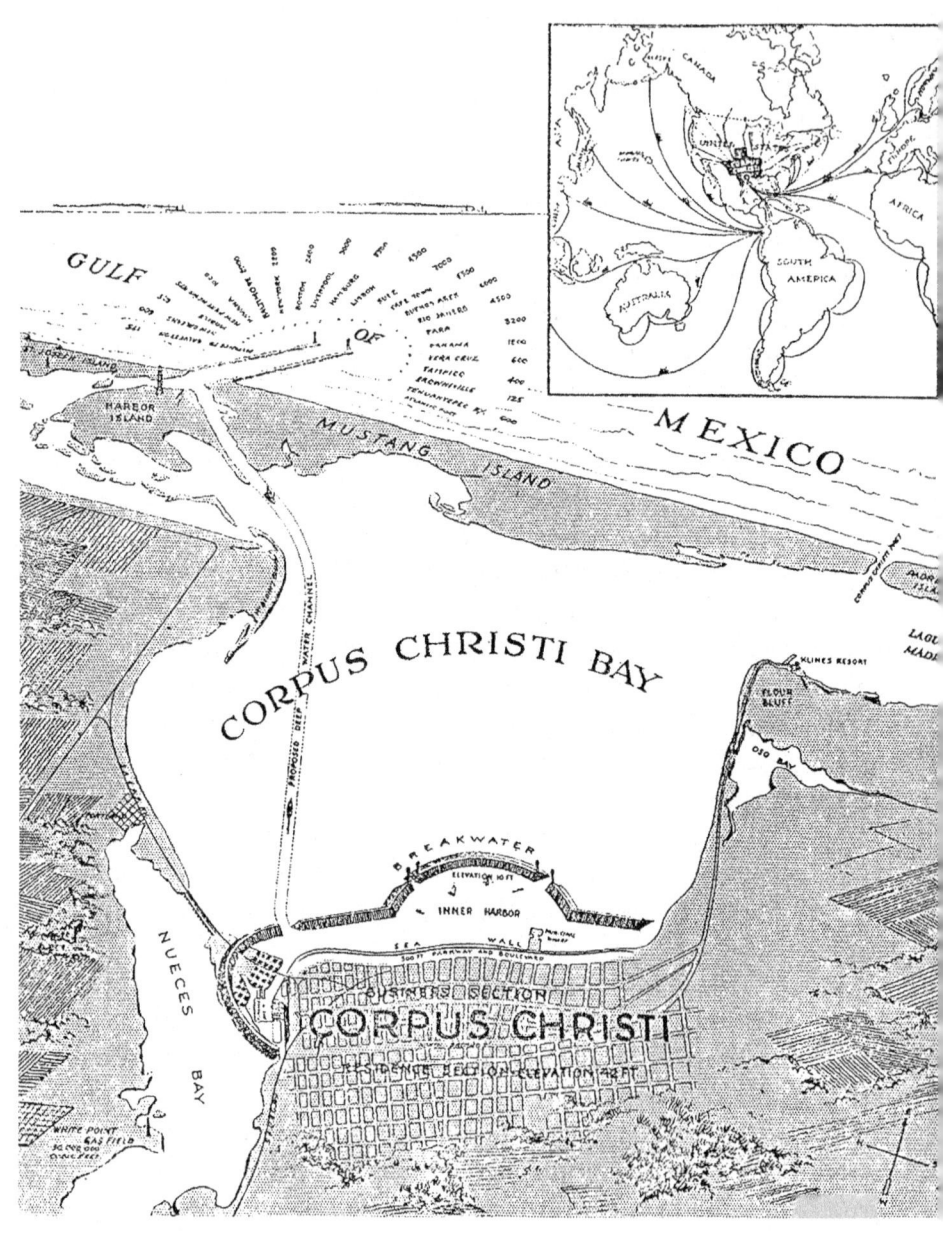

14. Frontispiece of *The Port of Corpus Christi Project*, showing the projected impact of a deep water port in Corpus Christi. *Courtesy Port of Corpus Christi Authority.*

drawn breakwaters and seawalls demonstrated the advantages of its forth-coming man-made protection. At the mouth of the channel where it flowed into the gulf, the names of twenty-two ports, ranging from Rio de Janeiro to Havana, were drawn radiating outwards, each with their exact distance from Corpus Christi listed in mileage. A small insert map of the world, showing the city as large as Texas with sea routes leading to it from every continent on earth, completed the imagery of a port located at the cross-roads of the world.[9]

The brochure then described the economic advantages deep water would bring to the area. Building upon the extraordinary expansion of South Texas agriculture in the early century, Miller stressed the elevenfold increase of Nueces County cotton from 1910 to 1920, the recent harvest of ninety-one thousand bales a surprising jump from estimates a few months earlier.[10] He then added the 400 percent growth in general cultivation over the same period and area, where annual shipments of cabbages, cucum-bers, onions, and even strawberries demanded much quicker and more reliable transport than that provided by Galveston or Houston.[11]

Freight rates also figured in tallying potential benefits. Regardless of final destination, every shipper had to deal with the controversial fees de-manded by the two ports, and it was not only farmers who suffered. Retail-ers who imported goods entrained from Galveston paid over 15 percent more than they would if products came locally, estimated the traffic man-ager of the Texas-Mexican Railway. His input added another dimension to Miller's case; rather than fighting a new southern port, the major railroads of Texas were supporting it.[12]

"We have been endeavoring for some time to figure a plan under which we might . . . assist the irrigation companies in the Rio Grande Valley to get fuel oil at a reduced cost," the freight agent for Gulf Coast Lines wrote Miller. "A port at Corpus Christi would immediately solve that difficulty and we could and would establish a rate which would save them in the neighborhood of 45 or 50 cents per barrel per year . . . a net saving . . . to be passed on to the farmers and shippers of the Rio Grande Valley, of ap-proximately $225,000.00 per year."[13]

Moreover, railways opened up regions. The growth Miller had activated as agent for Kleberg when, by 1911, twenty-two towns with populations of more than fourteen thousand nestled "along the track . . . between Browns-ville and Corpus Christi, where there had been only five ranch houses seven years [earlier],"[14] had to have figured prominently in his next argument.

"The future of a large section of Texas . . . now meagerly developed, waits upon the provision of large and cheaper transportation facilities to enable it to grow. . . . A seaport, properly located and equipped, adequately served by connecting railroad lines, will exert an influence of tremendous force in stimulating and hastening the settlement and development of an area larger than many States of the American Union, an area—productive though it is today—yet barely more than ten per cent developed."[15]

Finally, Miller had to convince Major Adams that Corpus Christi was the place to build such a "properly equipped seaport," and here he used every gambit at his command:

history: "[S]ince the admission of Texas . . . Corpus Christi has been . . . the oldest city . . . [and] the trading center of this section . . . of the State;"[16]

placement: "A portion of the business district . . . the Beach section . . . has an elevation of from 5 to 10 feet. The remainder of the city . . . more than ¾ of its corporate area, is located on a high bluff . . . [with] an elevation of from 35 to 50 feet;"[17]

monetary worth: "The City's . . . taxable values amount to $10,005, 990.00 while the actual value of its property exceeds $20,000,000.00;"[18]

infrastructure: "The city has about 13 miles of street paving, complete systems of storm and sanitary sewers, modern lighting and power plants, and a street railway system. It has three banks, with combined resources of about $6,000,000.00 . . . hotels and public buildings;"[19]

civic responsibility: "When railroads were built . . . they were built out of Corpus Christi largely financed by Corpus Christi business men. The construction of the San Antonio and Aransas Pass Railroad, the Texas Mexican Railroad, and the St. Louis, Brownville and Mexican Railroad, now a part of the Gulf Coast lines, was originated and started by citizens of Corpus Christi."[20]

At the same time, he took every opportunity to disparage upcoast rivals. "The townsite of Aransas Pass . . . has been sold and re-sold by lottery schemes and mail order methods to countless hundreds all over the country who are ever ready to embrace any get-rich-quick device."[21]

He emphasized their isolation. "Attached hereto are letters from the traffic officials of the Gulf Coast Lines, the San Antonio, Uvalde & Gulf

Railroad, and the Texas Mexican Railroad. . . . The letters state clearly that those lines are opposed . . . to the establishment of the port at Aransas Pass and that they will not make extensions to that point if the port is located there."[22]

He stressed his city's centrality. "Corpus Christi is approximately 21 miles west of Port Aransas and 22 miles by rail from the town of Aransas Pass, and it is by just that distance closer to the territory which the port should serve."[23]

Finally, Miller had to assure Adams and the Corps of Engineers that not only would deepwater facilities in Corpus Christi be safe, they would also be financed. Here he elaborated upon the legislature's donation of twenty-five years of ad valorem taxes to the city. "In order that the Federal Government might know of the vital interest of the people of Texas in securing the establishment of a seaport at Corpus Christi . . . the appropriation in this law is conditioned; it provides, first that the plans for the construction of such seawalls and breakwaters 'for port purposes' at the City of Corpus Christi shall be approved by the Government Engineers, and second, that the appropriation shall not be available in any event unless and until Corpus Christi is designated by the Federal government as a deepwater port."[24]

That the state would help build breakwaters and seawalls for the city, therefore, was certain only if it officially became deepwater headquarters. In order to attain that, Miller and his cohorts made one more commitment: if the federal government dredged the channel, the people of South Texas would finance the necessary terminal and harbor facilities themselves.[25]

The means to do this developed years earlier when supporters of the Buffalo Bayou waterway, determined to make channel-dredging as attractive as possible to the Corps of Engineers, persuaded the state to create quasi-governmental navigation districts. Such institutions would, upon approval of voters involved, "have the power to . . . issue bonds to pay for improvements to . . . rivers, bays, creeks, streams and canals" (emphasis added). Washington officials loved the "Houston Plan," and it became a cornerstone of subsequent federal projects.[26]

"Prior to Houston's offer," wrote one backer, "no substantial contribution had ever been made by local interests to secure the adoption of their projects, and no project has since been adopted by the national government without promise of local contributions and assurances that the waterfront would not be privately controlled."[27]

Now, Miller was making those assurances on the part of his city. "The requirement of adequacy simply means adequate terminal facilities. The citizens of Corpus Christi and Nueces county . . . have submitted a proposal to the Federal Government agreeing without limitation or reservation to provide such publicly owned and operated wharfage, warehouse and terminal facilities as the Federal Government may deem necessary to meet the requirements of commerce which will move through the port of Corpus Christi. In order to provide funds for this purpose, it is proposed and guaranteed to create, under State law, a Navigation District . . . to vote bonds in such amount as may be necessary to provide the facilities which . . . will insure the adequacy of the harbor."[28] Such adequacy would be guaranteed by an already-hired "expert terminal engineer," who, even as *The Corpus Christi Port Project* went to press, had begun plans for docks, warehouses, and piers should the channel be approved. All that was lacking was the government's acceptance.[29]

No terminal construction would ever be undertaken, however, without voter endorsement of the navigation district, and getting that was something that Miller and Boone had been working on since Congressman Bee's visit eleven days after the hurricane. Like other leaders who had transformed devastation into growth, the two were relying on already established political entities—congressmen, representatives, commissions, councils—to push through required legislation. But funding for this deepwater port was going to require grassroots support, something never attempted in Corpus Christi before.[30]

First, though, they had to win the region. Unexpected commercial opposition from strongly mounted Aransas Bay interests had undercut the city port project of 1909; this time area support had to be unanimous. Thanks in no small part to Robert Kleberg, it was. Calling in markers from railroad line representatives, shipping executives, bankers, businessmen, ranchers, farmers, and mayors from all over South Texas, he ordered them to a booster meeting in Kingsville in March 1921. There, despite his declining health, he organized the Corpus Christi Deep Water Association with himself as chairman, Roy Miller as secretary, treasurer, and chief lobbyist, and, in a feat of political pragmatism, old antagonist Walter Pope as head of the executive committee. Such work bore quick rewards; not long after the gathering, letters of support from groups as varied as the Southwestern Cattle Raisers Association and the Beaumont Chamber of Commerce began flooding the desks of congressional committee members. A single-space listing of nearly three hundred county and commercial endorsements for the Corpus Christi site filled two full pages of the *Port Project* brochure.[31]

But indifference from the north soon dampened enthusiasm in the south. San Antonio's obvious disinterest in a Corpus Christi port led to rumors that chief officers of the city's chamber of commerce "had taken an option on Harbor Island and were using their best efforts to direct the location of the port at Aransas Pass." Fearful of the past repeating itself, a delegation of over fifty city residents, led by Pope and Miller, stormed a chamber meeting in April 1921 and watched gleefully as their leaders battered down every objection to a Corpus Christi port. By the time the dust had settled, San Antonio chambermen had voted to override their president, endorse a port which "would save the business interests of that city $917,000.00 a year through the medium of reduced freight charges," and join Corpus Christi's lobbying effort.[32]

The move to convince local citizens came next. To coordinate the chamber's work with those of the Deep Water Association and the Commercial Association, a reinvigorated civic resource for the port, Boone set up a Citizens' Central Committee. Chaired by himself, featuring Miller and Pope as government pointmen, and headed by businessmen expert in banking, trade, and public relations, Boone led the committee into harbor acquisition with rancorless zeal. Even Walter Pope's old crony Clark Pease served enthusiastically on the finance board.[33]

But old wounds continued to fester, and, during plans for a D.C. lobbying junket a year after the hurricane, Pope's antipathy to Miller suddenly erupted. It took all Boone's tact and common sense to put his partner back on course for the port. "With reference to Miller—In one sense [I] did make him representative of the city—but I knew perfectly well that he was going to see those people while he was in Washington and I thought the best thing to do was to make him feel that he had to report something. You can find out just how much and what he did. And since he is bound to butt in always, the only thing to do is to use him when we can or have to."[34]

Placated, Pope went ahead with the trip, established his own contacts with army and federal officials, then returned to Austin to push the breakwater bill though the legislature. A month later he thrust personal antipathy aside yet again to join Miller in confronting the San Antonio Chamber of Commerce. Succeeding years would see more of the same, the two even journeying together to Washington in a last-minute sweep of Congress during Port Designation week. Although nowhere near rapprochement with his old antagonist, Pope could afford to swallow his pride in the fight for the port.[35]

But giving up his land along the waterfront, real estate now so valuable that its potential commercial worth far outdistanced even Pope's wildest estimates—that would be a hard sell. And it was. A carefully worded letter from Russell Savage, the city attorney, writing at Mayor Boone's behest, reviewed the city's need for the "riparian and littoral rights along the shore": "Since the funds which the city has available for these improvements—a sea wall at about 600 ft. from the shore . . . and a break-water at about 4000 ft from the shore—are very limited, the city will not be in a position to pay for any of these claims, because every dollar spent in this way would be that taken from the amount needed for the proper protection of the city and its people."[36] Then in the mildest manner possible, Savage requested Pope "do your part in this great and necessary work by donating your riparian rights to this property"—property which included three city lots, a full neighborhood block, and four acres along Hall's Bayou, virtually the entire stretch of bayfront access property.[37]

Pope balked, so much so that Savage pulled off the gloves in his next letter. "Dear sir: I received your letter in which you state your indisposition with reference to the grant of riparian rights desired by the city. . . . I am surprised at you, you are so liberal. . . . A man who has been permitted to house rotten hay and the *Evening Times* in the same building without interference by the sanitary officers. A man who has been permitted to feed his cows on waste paper and his goats on corrugated iron without interference from the Humane Society. A man who has denied his employees in his building the privileges of answering a call of nature and left them upon the cold charity of their neighbors. . . . A man who has been permitted to claim squatter rights on every water hole and dumping ground in the city . . . ought not to act that way."[38]

Savage's parting shot, "Your public spirit sounds like that which usually emanates from Kingsville," was doubly vicious in that it conjured up the old Kleberg/King Ranch connection so abhorrent to Pope. In time, the representative conceded, an act so important that Miller included the letter, "offering and guaranteeing to convey, without cost to the United States government whatever lands owned by [Pope] that may be required in connection with the establishment of the proposed harbor at Corpus Christi," in Major Adams's packet touting the city's strengths in 1921. But the concession was reluctant on the part of the man rumored to "own one third of the town . . . at least one half of the county . . . and half of the bay!"[39] And his evident discontent had to have added to Mayor Boone's burdens.

His burdens grew even heavier when plans for a seawall were dumped. Boone's enthusiasm for the protective structure highlighted the meeting that introduced the harbor proposal to Congressman Bee on October 1, and his support intensified as the city council authorized their engineer to develop detailed specifications. "There is nothing that will indicate to the rest of the nation," said Mr. Boone, "that Corpus Christi is not only determined to 'come back' but is actually doing it, than for the city to set to work on the building of the seawall."[40] Within a few months, comprehensive blueprints for a "twelve-foot wall of mass concrete [that would] rest on piling . . . driven down to impervious clay . . . [extending] two feet above the highest water on record at Corpus Christi" had been submitted to city fathers.[41]

Two and a half weeks later, the seawall was dead. At a clamorous meeting held in city council chambers on February 26, 1920, Clark Pease and Walter Timon announced to a breathless public that "it is in the best interests of Corpus Christi that elaborate plans for the building of a seawall be changed and that instead a breakwater be built in front of the city." As part of a three-man tour of Great Lakes and gulf cities, the duo had become convinced that forty-foot surges could be "tamed by a breakwater, as at Buffalo, Cleveland, and other points that we visited." Even the city's structural designer agreed. "Eminent engineers," he asserted, "were of the opinion that such protection would break the force of a storm . . . and that water that would come into the city would not do any appreciable harm." Moreover, a breakwater built in thousand-foot sections with five-hundred-foot gaps would have the advantage of still providing the enclosed harbor necessary for a deepwater port, but at cheaper cost. People left city hall happily that night, convinced of the efficacy of the smaller barrier. Little was said of Gordon Boone, the only member of the three-man tour boycotting the meeting.[42]

Despite understandable misgivings, however, when the city council officially approved the breakwater-only plan, Mayor Boone acquiesced.[43] Vague hopes of building a seawall later would have to suffice for now. In the meantime, maintaining the enthusiasm demonstrated at the February meeting was imperative, a job Roy Miller had already begun.

Commitment and Construction

Already practiced at selling the city as a port to outsiders, Miller now faced his greatest challenge: selling the port to his own city. Less than a month after the disaster, he initiated the first move, a series of front-page *Caller* editorials alerting his readers of their golden opportunity "to make Corpus Christi a real city":[1] "Our representatives in congress . . . sincerely profess their eagerness to help us *now*. Let them, then, see to it that Corpus Christi's just claims for harbor development receive immediate attention. We also assure them, as well as ourselves, that every red-blooded upstanding forward looking Corpus Christian (and that's one hundred percent of our population which hasn't been shrunk by a single quitter since the storm) is on the job and will stay on the job until Corpus Christi gets Deep Water."[2]

Succeeding editorials stressed a port's advantages: "The people . . . will get all the benefits . . . absolute safety, lower rates, and all of the facilities for the convenient, efficient and expeditious transaction of business." They touted the city's worthiness:

"For years [Corpus Christi] has accepted graciously and contentedly the decision of the Engineers. . . . She is within her right [to demand] her just station." And most importantly, they stressed its resilience: "Corpus Christi Still Lives."[3]

If Corpus Christi still lived, surely not so many had died. Now that the city was promoting itself as the safest spot to harbor an inland port enclosed by natural and man-made barriers, it became imperative to downplay the impact of the September 14 hurricane. Although a statement by the Relief Committee, eight days after rescue efforts began, said that "the known dead . . . now stands in excess of 400 . . . [with] more than 100 . . . missing," press reports in March of the next year lowered the official toll to 277, all victims from the surrounding area. It mattered little that earlier substantiated fatalities included two visitors from Waco, a couple from Laredo, and soldiers from Wisconsin, Illinois, and Georgia, nor that other sources estimated up to one thousand dead, many crushed by debris into the glutinous bottom of Nueces Bay.[4] Like Chicago after its 1871 fire,

San Francisco after its 1906 earthquake, and Galveston after its 1900 storm surge, Miller needed to decrease Corpus Christi's risk identification, and the *Caller's* revised mortality list helped do this.[5]

At the same time, the city had to appear ready for a port, and here Miller's special Thanksgiving Day edition set the tone. Congratulatory ads from the governor, announcing proudly that, "Corpus Christi has 'come back,'" ranged alongside more informative messages like that of the Guaranty Title Company: "Yes, We Suffered a Heavy Loss in the STORM. However, our most important and valuable records were protected by our vault." Pithier spots included those of Sam's Candy Kitchen, "Coming Back? Sure!" and Southwestern Tractor and Implement Company, "Come Back? No! Continue? Yes!" Even Nick Mora's employer, the Lone Star Ice Factory, virtually eradicated by the hurricane, bought a spot to announce its rebuilding on the bluff "near the Tex-Mex depot."[6]

In addition to the affirmative articles and congratulatory ads, however, Miller exalted the city's own concept of itself. Employing two of the nation's most evocative images of that time, helpless virgins and noble statesmen, he featured a three-column drawing on the front page of the business section showing a beautiful young maiden kneeling on a cross-strewn shore, her arms upraised, her robes bearing the name "Corpus Christi."

Gazing upon her from a radiant sky, a martyred President Lincoln, his Gettysburg words appropriately edited, beamed down a blessing: "That this city, under god, shall have a new birth and this city of the people, by the people, and for the people shall not perish from the earth." The message was evident: just like other cities stricken by nature, Corpus Christi would achieve its own unique sanctification.[7]

Sanctification, in this case, meant a deepwater port, and by the time Timon, Pease, and Boone returned from their Great Lakes tour, citizens across the area were ready to take a hand in getting one. Wise enough to include the public in the decision for a breakwater, area leaders now canvassed them for financial commitment as well, promising that successful federal government designation was "as sure to come as the money is to be raised." Not quite receiving the anticipated $30,000 desired, the Central Committee still had enough funds to present their case to Major Adams and his cohorts at a special fact-finding conference in Galveston on October 14, 1921. Along with a thick packet that included *The Corpus Christi Port Project*, the Corps of Engineer's chief officer also accepted a formal request

15. The City of Corpus Christi and Abraham Lincoln, symbolically
illustrated in the *Corpus Christi Caller*'s Thanksgiving Edition.
© 1919, *Courtesy* Corpus Christi Caller-Times.

for the entire board "to make a personal rout of investigation of the territory in and around the . . . area under consideration" in March of the next year.[8]

Not listed officially but vastly more important to the success of a local port was Miller's final ploy—an opportunity for Adams to roam Robert Kleberg's domain, the largest, most secretive private rangeland in the country.[9]

> Roy came to me and asked if I could arrange a hunt at the King Ranch. I called Bob Kleberg and the hunt was arranged. The three of us drove to the ranch. It was an extremely hot day in December. Major Adams, the perfect Army officer at all times, came in uniform. We drove around most of the day but it was extremely hot and no bucks were sighted. Later in the afternoon, the ranch hand . . . driving the car told me, in Spanish, that because it was so hot all the animals were up in the brush and that the only way to get a deer was to walk into the brush. I related this information to Major Adams who without hesitancy and even though in uniform . . . went with the ranch hand into the brush. After a substantial period of time, we heard a shot. After another waiting period, out of the brush came Major Adams and the ranch hand dragging a nice buck. Major Adams' neat uniform was askew. He had a slight torn tear in his jacket but was grinning from ear to ear.[10]

> Roy . . . asked if I could arrange for a bottle of whiskey. . . . [He] took it with him into Major Adams's room. Two or three drinks later Roy came out of the room, came to my room, knocked on the door, opened it and said, "We've got it."[11]

But pledges secured by hard liquor have a tendency to evaporate, and it was with anxious hearts that the members of the Citizens Central Committee awaited the formal inspection of the U.S. Army Corps of Engineers on March 1, 1922. Arriving Wednesday morning in a private car on a rail line owned by Kleberg interests, the engineers, led by Adams, enjoyed a large breakfast at the Nueces Hotel before paying obligatory visits to port competitors Rockport and Aransas Pass. After a Thursday morning session in Corpus Christi, they took a slow train to Kingsville, ate a sumptuous lunch hosted by Robert Kleberg and his wife Alice, toured the small town named after her father, then geared up for another night at the ranch—the second for Major Adams, his earlier stay discreetly unnoted.[12]

Leaving the next morning, the delegation visited Uvalde, stopped at other designated trade territories on the way back to San Antonio, returned to Washington, then sat in silence for two months. Confident assertions began to ring hollow as the Army Corps deferred action week after week. In the midst of controversy over Prohibition and a revived Ku Klux Klan, a distinct air of discouragement began to permeate city hall. Then, on May 25, in the midst of last-ditch lobbying by Pope and Miller, word spread through the halls of Congress that the decision had come down. A short time later, a triumphant telegram arrived at the *Caller*: "We win." In his report to the secretary of war, Major Adams had gone against his own commander to recommended Corpus Christi as the only site offering the "development of a safe and adequate port" for the West Gulf Coast. The board unanimously seconded Adams, and the Rivers and Harbors Committee acceded.[13] The port project now an established fact, Corpus Christi had indeed won.

Now all that was needed was the creation of the government entity "to build, finish, and maintain [the] terminal railways, wharves, warehouses, and bulkheads" so vital to a successful port. Even before Adams's designation, a group of thirty-five citizens had already petitioned Nueces County commissioners to establish a navigation district, and by November 1921, a date had been set to hold an election "to determine whether or not such navigation district shall be created and whether or not tax shall be levied . . . to redeem [its] bonds at maturity."[14]

By the time the polling actually commenced, the election date had been changed twice, finally falling on Halloween the following year. In the meantime, district boundaries were set, election judges assigned, and the bond value set at $1 million, already partially defrayed by private gifts and a city donation. An additional $2 million for the breakwater would come from state remits, and the $1.8 million expense of actually digging the channel, plus its annual maintenance, was on the federal government's ticket.[15] Corpus Christi was getting a good deal, and once again old boosters reunited to convince the people. Fighting off increasing frailty, Robert Kleberg set up two groups, the Corpus Christi Waterways Committee and the Port Development Association; headed once again by Miller and Pope, they coordinated a no-holds-barred campaign to secure the district.[16]

Dreary, rainy weather and a stubborn recalcitrance by Robstown residents were not enough to offset local enthusiasm for the port. At three o'clock on October 31, 1922, the city vote was already 2,279 in support— two malcontents in the third ward keeping the count from total unanimity.

By the time commissioners canvassed county-wide polls, the total favoring a navigation district had climbed to an overwhelming 3,754. Not only did Corpus Christi now have its port, it now had an ardent public eager to provision it.[17]

Three months later county officials elected the first Commissioners of County Navigation District No. 1, and the trio, Walter F. Timon in the lead, accepted salaries of a dollar each. Also receiving a dollar was Walter Pope, whose final and formal cession of bayshore land earned him no more than "the customary [federal fee] in such cases," but garnered reams of favorable publicity. Within months, the district's bonds had been purchased, "the money . . . placed in local banks . . . for harbor improvement,"[18] and the building of the port began.

For youngsters like Alclair Mays who liked to "drive visitors around" showing off her city, the changes of the next few years must have seemed almost magical. First to emerge in the water were long, cement-based jetties, flat on the top and encrusted on their sides with one hundred thousand tons of rocks, offloaded from a special train track built specifically into the bay for that purpose. Designed with separation gaps between each thousand-foot section, the jetties first encompassed the business area, then, as port plans expanded, snaked northward. By the time the harbor was dedicated, the breakwater stretched six miles long and was already "forming a bulwark against which waves . . . threaten in vain." Never built to block but only to check sea surges, the breakwater was the first tangible sign of bayfront improvement.[19]

But its impact was dwarfed by the arrival in January 1925 of the Matagorda, a dredger tiny in comparison to standard vessels but sufficient to make yet another alternation in the bayfront: the transformation of Hall's Bayou. One of the notorious low spots in Corpus Christi and ever subject to the ebbing and flowing of tides, the bayou had served mainly to separate residents of North Beach from the city proper. Now, widened and deepened by the Matagorda and successive dredgers, it became the port's turning basin. Within months it acquired new accouterments: transfer sheds, some more than four city blocks long; wharfs, buttressed for rough moorings; and rail tracks, networked in between warehouses and storage bins.

In addition, scooped-out bottom mud had been restructured into a stout levee, protecting its north side from Nueces Bay overflows.[20]

More was yet to come. Soon following in Matagorda's wake was the John Jacobson, a huge dredger, majestic and deliberate in its lumbering

16. Transfer sheds, rail tracks, and wharves along the turning basin, formerly Hall's Bayou. *Courtesy Murphy Givens.*

progress from the gulf. As its powerful cutters chewed deep into loosened bayfloor, suction tubes drew the soil upwards, then spewed it out into strategic spoil islands—brand-new perching havens for pelicans and cormorants curious about the flurry of activity. By the time the old year had ended, the *Jacobson* had nearly completed its job, and within a month into 1926, a twenty-five-foot-deep channel extended from the North Jetty at Port Aransas through the Laguna Madre and all the way across Corpus Christi Bay.[21]

The culminating change, however, the one that every day reminded everyone of their new harbor, had nothing to do with water and everything to do with land. It was the brand-new bascule bridge, erected to span the shores of the new turning basin. Where once a plank bridge had crossed Hall's Bayou to connect the city with its northern tip, now engineers had designed an elaborate steel contraption fitted with electric motors and weighted counterbalances. Construction began in May 1925, and by March of the next year the central span was in place. Within nine months after the *Jacobson* left the bay, the last part of Corpus Christi's dream had become reality: a ninety-foot-long automobile and railroad bridge that raised its full length as often as thirty times a day, allowing ships and freighters to enter a reassuringly deepwater port.[22]

The dream was complete, though far from perfect. Along with expected construction growth, new industries were impacting the area. Natural gas wells sunk off White's Point had been feeding city outlets for three years; now a contract with Houston would necessitate heavier equipment. Wildcatters were flooding in with derricks and rigs, hoping to create additional Spindletops in West Nueces. Chemical engineers were checking alkali deposits in the locality with an eye for future chemical plants. In the meantime, coastal cotton was dominating all other crops, leading the state in production and already monopolizing the district's four cargo docks. It was painfully clear that the freshly-cut channel would not be near deep enough for burgeoning sea trade, and already plans were being made to petition the government for additional dredging. But the port itself had been realized; now it was time to celebrate. In setting the date for the celebration, Corpus Christi demonstrated once again that danger-daring bravado so characteristic of its early founders; port dedication festivities would start on September 14, 1926, exactly seven years after the 1919 hurricane hit.[1]

The day dawned bright, shining with unique clarity on the people hastening through flag-bedecked streets toward The Hill. The first official event of the two-day program, the "Combined Military, Naval, and Civic Parade," was scheduled to start there at ten in the morning, and participants were scrambling to their assigned spots. Placement was everything, especially for elected officials crammed into automobiles, and as the multiband, thousand-person spectacle began high-stepping its way down the bluff, each politico waved as if he were the only person on display. For most constituents cheering from the curbs, the officeholders were nameless but necessary irritants, doing little more than separating the marching bands from the beauty pageant contestants. But the men in the cars shared one thing in common with the people on the sidewalks; each had weathered their own storms in the years since the hurricane.[2]

One was Roy Miller. Vice-chairman of the Port Celebration Committee and master of ceremonies of the dedication itself, he was all over Cargo Dock #1 when the parade ended, greeting friends, glad-handing buddies, and herding honored guests toward the speakers' platform. His day had started well, and comments made by dignitaries would soon emphasize

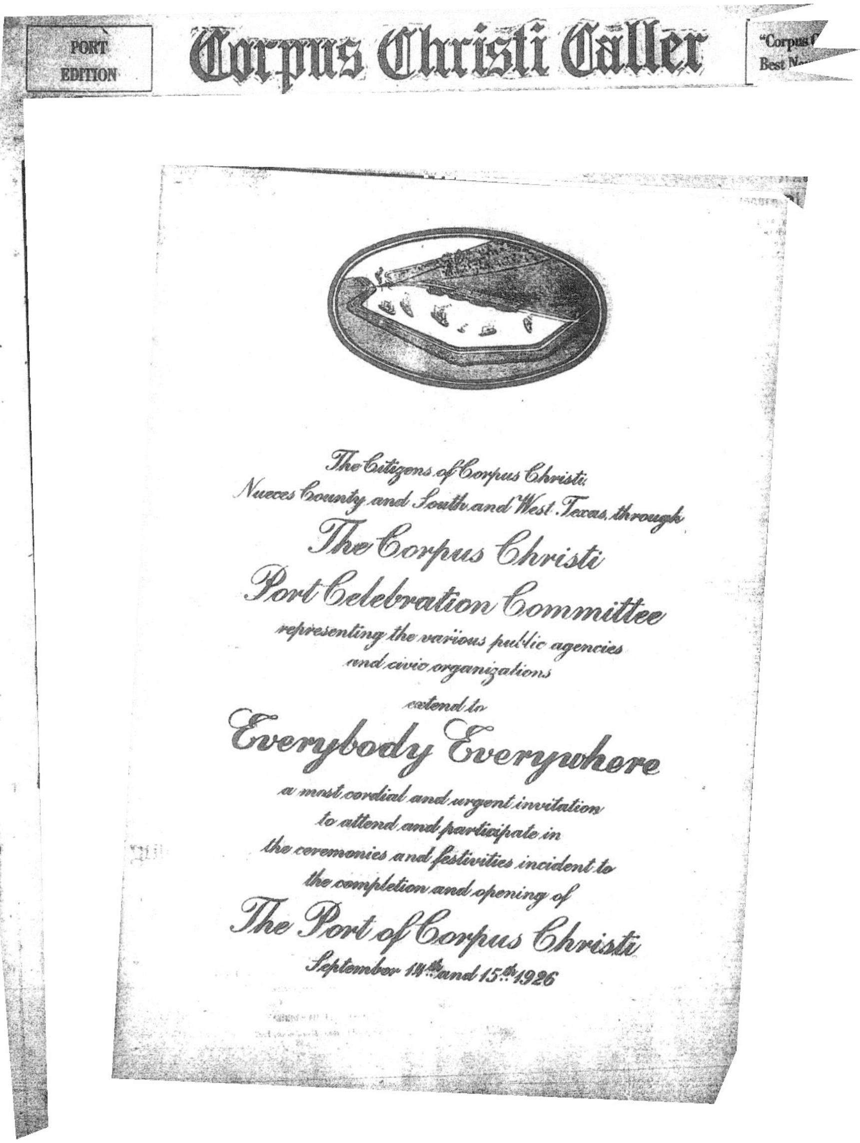

Corpus Christi Caller

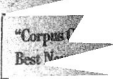

The Citizens of Corpus Christi,
Nueces County and South and West Texas, through

The Corpus Christi
Port Celebration Committee

representing the various public agencies
and civic organizations

extend to

Everybody Everywhere

a most cordial and urgent invitation
to attend and participate in
the ceremonies and festivities incident to
the completion and opening of

The Port of Corpus Christi

September 14th and 15th 1926

17. Corpus Christi's invitation for all to attend port dedication
ceremonies. *Courtesy* Corpus Christi Caller-Times.

18. Celebrants along the turning basin and on Cargo Dock #1 as the bascule bridge opened the Port of Corpus Christi to deep water trade. *Courtesy Murphy Givens.*

his effectiveness as a lobbyist. "I hope the completion of this waterway will not deprive us of the pleasure of having Roy Miller in Washington," one congressman was to remark. "We think a lot of him there."[3]

But the sprightliness in Miller's step had diminished. His brilliance bringing people together for the port secured his primacy in the celebration, and his political savvy made him invaluable to officeholders and private developers alike. The secret salary, however, remained like a sore tooth, souring his image with many of the public. That, and the loss of his baby son and namesake less than two years after the storm, had blunted the vaunted enthusiasm of the "Boy Mayor of Corpus Christi." He and Maud would commute between the Coastal Bend and Washington to raise their remaining three boys, but his role would now be behind the scenes, pushing Corpus Christi's interests—and his own—in other ways.[4]

Just as benighted was his old antagonist, Walter Pope. Emerging triumphant from the scandal that tainted Miller, Pope saw his land donations and port legislation enhance his status statewide, leading him to dream of the gubernatorial chair, a position of power far greater than that of mere representative. So in 1924, Pope left his seat in Austin, entered the Democratic race for governor—and failed to even make the run-off. But possibly the greatest blow came from Archie Parr. After overtly encouraging the younger man to run for governor for years, his lack of support in the actual campaign was obvious, even to Pope's friends.[5] "We should suggest to you that you write to your old friend Archie Parr, who you have assisted so often and so much, as while we were in Duval County the other day, we saw pictures of Lynch Davidson [Pope's main opponent] posted everywhere and were given to understand that that County would be for Lynch Davidson. We do not believe you should lose Duval County."[6]

Parr's letter after the loss casually waved away his betrayal, "When I saw how things were going I gave my vote to Lynch. . . . Sorry you were not elected," then turned back to his favorite subject, his own vote count. "I think I will beat Berniski between 4500 and 5000 votes." The message was clear: Pope was as valuable as Parr would allow him to be. Introduced by Miller that dedication day only as the public's "Former State Representative," it would be another year before Pope ran for his old seat again, but he would.[7]

One who would never run again, or ride, was Robert J. Kleberg. Chosen as honorary chairman of the celebration committee because of his "long fight for the designation of Corpus Christi as a deepwater port site, his leadership in the development of South Texas, and his untiring work in behalf of the local port," Miller's old friend was not on the platform with the others. Just months earlier Kleberg had suffered a stroke that, combined with the palsy, left him crippled and at home. His mind had not gone, however, and his promise, "to take an active interest . . . in the development of the port," was as real as his determination to build it had been. It was just his body that had given out.[8]

The same could not be said of Archie Parr. Among the "Distinguished Guests" milling about on the platform waiting to be introduced that bright September day, Parr seemed to have aged the least. Exultant in his triumph over the Progressives in 1919 and so necessary as lawmaker to the survival of the port that even the *Corpus Christi Caller* had recently lauded him, "one of the outstanding members of the state senate," Parr continued to wield power bluntly and openly. As concerned with the welfare of his workers as Kleberg or Wells had ever been, he was also quick to quell upstarts, as he did when Pope overstepped his boundaries. But his aim remained fixed upon county domination, and it was not without reason that lobbyists and lawmakers termed his rule a "reign," his family a "dynasty," and he himself the "Duke of Duval."[9]

But if not in Duval, things were different in neighboring areas of South Texas. The border disruptions before World War I had dislocated many Hispanics forever, and although others had moved into the region after the war, a large number made their living as migrant pickers or as "patch" croppers. Forced to live in dirt-floored shacks and hire their children out at the age of three, these workers felt none of the gratitude toward their managers so characteristic of the old patrón system; consequently, valley voting patterns were changing.[10]

As were those in the city. A significant number watching the politicians parade along Leopard Street that early September morning were the very citizens those men had disfranchised. Just three years earlier the once-optional "white primary" had become mandatory, and although groups across the state had already challenged the law, blacks in Corpus Christi were finding increased discrimination difficult to deal with. One of those was Annie Mays. Because no place in the city provided schooling beyond eighth grade for African Americans, she had been forced to board Alclair at Prairie View for three years. Now she had to send Anita away, and even with education, nothing ensured her daughters good jobs. Officially graduated and holding a teaching certificate, Alclair could not get hired by the school district. As her oldest daughter cleaned houses and as her youngest made ready to leave, Annie began a quiet activism of her own, hosting visiting NAACP advocates who hoped to "work the politicians to get [voting] rights."[11]

Also working the politicians was Annie's old neighbor, Ben Garza. From his vantage point at the Metropolitan Café, Garza had become convinced that equal justice would come only if people used their own judgment when balloting. In the future, Garza would form a group where one's personally paid poll tax receipt would act as entry; in the present, all he could do was urge friends, even if it was too late for themselves, to educate their children.[12]

This was something Lorenza Sanchéz, Nick Mora's daughter, was determined to do. The hurried move she and Manuel had made up the bluff during the hurricane had become permanent; now Caldwell Street was the family home, and, once classes started, Cheston Heath, their children's new school. Not as close as George Evans Elementary, Heath was designated for "Mexicans" and center of the English-only curriculum the state now required. Learning the national tongue was important for Roy, María, and Ramón Sanchéz, and not just so that they could vote when they got older. The regimen was difficult, however, and it was a happy threesome that greeted the holidays granted by Superintendent Carroll the day of the dedication.[13]

So did Eleanor and Anne, Marian Dodson's daughters. Even though they attended parochial school, they would be performing in the grand pageant that night. Moreover, despite mounting attacks upon Catholicism recently, Miller had asked Bishop Ledvina to give the benediction closing the ceremonies. His participation and the inclusion of Laredo's Saint Augustine Band in the musical program reassured Corpus Christi Catholics of their continued value to the city. But threats existed. The power of the Ku Klux Klan had intensified since its regeneration a few years earlier, and the election of two Klansmen to Nueces County offices had shaken Irishtown as well as The Hill. With daily newspaper accounts of hooded parades and cross-burning initiations, it was not for nothing that Sam Dodson gave a pistol to his wife for protection when he was away.[14]

Voices quieted and tuning trills softened to intermittent squeaks from the orchestra as Miller made his way to the front of the platform. Having checked one more time that all invited "Members of Congress, Government Officials, and Distinguished Guests" had been seated, he turned to the crowd.[15] Only seventeen years had passed since he received that triumphant telegram from Garner in 1909 announcing a deepwater survey, but a multitude of changes had occurred: reputations tarnished, careers destroyed, enmities solidified, whole segments of the population disenfranchised in the name of progress; wars fought overseas and in the next county, natives and aliens alike displaced, beaten and killed; and such an upsurge in the seas as to wipe away a full city beach. Time had not been gentle to this community, but, basking in the brilliance of its bay, it still stood.

Invocation ended, he turned to the man who had soothed the city in its time of troubles, enabling it to rebuild and then create the port. Haltingly but firmly, Gordon Boone took the stand.[16]

Notes

PROLOGUE

1. Texas wrested independence from Mexico in 1836 and endured a precarious existence as a republic for the next ten years. *Corpus Christi 100 Years* (Corpus Christi, Tex.: The Corpus Christi Caller-Times, 1951), 31–32; Walraven, *Corpus Christi*, 37.

2. "Corpus Christi 1900," *Corpus Christi Caller* Centennial Edition, 1983, CF-16, file 65, George Coalson Files, South Texas Archives, Texas A&M University–Kingsville (hereafter cited as STA).

3. Lea, *King Ranch*, vol. 2, 493, 539.

4. Garner's telegram was quoted in "Survey of 25 Foot Channel is Assured," *Corpus Christi Daily Caller*, January 27, 1909.

5. Ibid.

CHAPTER ONE

1. Brown and Brewton, *Environmental Geologic Atlas*, 12, 23–24.

2. R. A. Morton, "Regional Geology of the N. W. Gulf Coastal Plain," *Sedimentary Processes and Environments*, ed. Nummedal, 54; Dag Nummedal, "South Jetty, Aransas Pass," in *Sedimentary Processes and Environments*, 49–50; "A Trip to Padre Island," *Corpus Christi Caller*, April 9, 1887, 4.

3. Brown and Brewton, *Environmental Geologic Atlas*, 12.

4. "City and Country," *Corpus Christi Caller*, June 2, 1888.

5. "A Trip to Padre Island," *Corpus Christi Caller*, April 9, 1887.

6. Crimmins, "Notes and Documents," 352.

7. "City and Country," *Corpus Christi Caller*, June 2, 1888.

8. McClintock, "Journal of a Trip," 157.

9. Wynn, "Lewis Harvie Blair," 267.

10. Ibid., 267.

11. Price, "Reduction of Maintenance," 248; Crimmins, "Notes and Documents," 353.

12. "City and Country," *Corpus Christi Caller*, June 2, 1888.

13. *New Orleans Weekly Picayune*, September 8, 1845, quoted in Payne, "Camp Life," 328.

14. Price, "Reduction of Maintenance," 248; Payne, "Camp Life," 329.

CHAPTER TWO

1. Corbin, "Archeological Materials," 61.

2. Newcombe, "Indian Tribes of Texas," 1.

3. Chipman, "In Search of Cabeza de Vaca's Route," 136, 147; Campbell, *Gone to Texas*, 28–30.

4. Chipman, *Spanish Texas*, 33–34, 36.

5. For more information on smuggling activities, see the 1847 *Harper's* article by Captain W. S. Henry, "Campaign Sketches of the War with Mexico," included in the Paul Schuster Taylor Papers, "Mexican Labor in the United States, 1919–1934," 10.7, Bancroft Library, BANC MSS 84/38c, University of California at Berkeley (hereafter cited as Bancroft MSS), 732. For information on Corpus Christi's culpability, see Graf, "Colonizing Projects in South Texas," 436.

6. The dispute that allowed the haven to thrive resulted from Mexico's denial of Texas' claim to the Rio Grande. Adams, "British Correspondence Concerning Texas," 326; Payne, "Camp Life," 340.

7. For information on Kinney's duplicity, see Walraven, *Corpus Christi*, 37. Walraven also covers Kinney's promotion efforts, as does the *Corpus Christi Caller* article "Immigrant Irishmen," Dan Kilgore Collection #7312, Special Collections Room, Texas A&M University–Corpus Christi (hereafter cited as SCM).

8. For statistics, see Payne, "Camp Life," 327–34; for the quotation, see Wallace, "General William Jenkins Worth," 161.

9. For information about Maria and Felix von Blücher's characters and backgrounds, see von Blücher, *Maria von Blücher's Corpus Christi*, 3–9, 28. Facts on early Corpus Christi are in Walraven, *Corpus Christi*, 44–45; facts on Kinney are in Amelia W. Williams, "Kinney, Henry Lawrence," in Webb and Carroll, *Handbook of Texas*, vol. 1, 962.

10. Williams, "Kinney, Henry Lawrence," 962; Anna Moore Schwein, interview by Paul Schuster Taylor, Corpus Christi, Tex., August 1929, 10.7, Taylor Papers, Bancroft MSS, 111; Nueces County Historical Society, *History of Nueces County*, 63, 65–68; "A Letter from Corpus Christi," *Corpus Christi Caller*, May 16, 1886.

11. Authorities agree upon the number of slaves in 1860 Nueces County, 216; the total in prewar Corpus Christi differs according to the areas considered city proper. Taylor listed 38, this writer counted 55, and Schwein gave two sets of figures: 56 and 75. Schwein interview, 107, 109; Campbell, *Grass-Roots Reconstruction in Texas*, 193; Taylor, *American-Mexican Frontier*, 92; U.S. Department of Commerce, U.S. Census Bureau, *1860 Population Schedule Texas–Slave Schedules*; Murphy Givens, "Early roots of black life in Corpus Christi," *Corpus Christi Caller-Times*, May 29, 2002.

12. Alclair Mays Pleasant, interview by Rue Wood, Corpus Christi, Tex., February 25, 1998, tape recording in possession of South Texas Archives, Texas A&M University–Kingsville, Kingsville, Tex. (hereafter cited as STA); Pleasant, inter-

views by the author, Corpus Christi, Tex., May 4, 2002, and November 11, 2003; *Thirteenth Census of the United States: 1910*.

13. Schwein interview, 109; Anne Dodson, James Rowe, and Bill Walraven, "The Heritage of the Black Man: Why Was I Born, Why Am I Living?" *Corpus Christi Caller-Times*, Sept. 15, 1968.

14. Vera, "Cisneros Genealogy," 16; Vera, "Juan José de la Garza Montemayor," 8; Crimm, *De León*, 82; Walraven and Walraven, *Gift of the Wind*, 17.

15. Alonzo, *Tejano Legacy*, 179; Montejano, *Anglos and Mexicans*, 114.

16. Haines, "Early Transportation History," 7, 10; Coffee, "Logs Reveal Texas," 231.

17. Bruce Cheeseman, *Handbook of Texas Online*, s.v. "King, Richard," http://www.tsha.utexas,edu/handbook/online/articles/KK/fki19.html (accessed November 21, 2005); John Ashton, *Handbook of Texas Online*, s.v. "Kenedy, Mifflin," http://www.tsha.utexas.edu/handbook/online/articles/KK/fke23.html (accessed November 21, 2005).

18. Murphy Givens, "The History of Corpus Christi," *Corpus Christi Caller-Times*, July 18, 1999; Lea, *King Ranch*, vol. 1, 115, 153–56.

19. Haines, "Early Transportation History," 7–8; Lea, *King Ranch*, vol. 1, 297–98, 334–36, 339–40; Jordan, "Black Tracks to Texas," 13.

20. Nueces County Historical Society, *History of Nueces County*, 56–58, 62.

21. Haines, "Early Transportation History," 11–22; "The First Excursion," *Corpus Christi Caller*, November 14, 1886.

CHAPTER THREE

1. Murphy Givens, "Storms opened way for city's port," *Corpus Christi Caller-Times Online*, http://www.caller.com/mgivens/single22.html (accessed March 15, 2001; site now discontinued).

2. Alperin, *Custodians of the Coast*, 4; Crimmins, "Notes and Documents," 353.

3. *U.S. Coast and Geodetic Chart*, 1875, *U.S. Coast and Geodetic Chart*, 1884, *U.S. Coast and Geodetic Chart*, 1887, Bulletin board display (n.p., n.d.), University of Texas Institute of Marine Biology, Port Aransas, Texas.

4. Nueces County Historical Society, *History of Nueces County*, 163.

5. Schwein interview, 111.

6. Lea, *King Ranch*, vol. 1, 335; Walraven, *History of a Texas Seaport*, 64, 73; Nueces County Historical Society, *History of Nueces County*, 164–65; Almonte, 177.

7. "Council Proceedings," *Corpus Christi Caller*, September 19, 1886; "From Corpus Christi: A Texas Town That Will Soon Have A Boom," *Corpus Christi Caller*, May 2, 1886.

8. Alperin, *Custodians of the Coast*, 41, 119, 127–30; "What Texas Gets," *Corpus Christi*

Caller, August 19, 1886; "At Aransas Pass," *Corpus Christi Caller*, November 24, 1899.

9. Alperin, *Custodians of the Coast*, 52, 128–29; Bixel and Turner, *Galveston and the 1900 Storm*, 3–4.

10. "Rejoicing in Corpus Christi," *Galveston Daily News*, May 5, 1900.

11. "The Texas Appropriations," *Corpus Christi Caller*, April 18, 1886.

12. "Indianola and Galveston," *Corpus Christi Caller*, August 29, 1886.

13. "Is the *Galveston News* Mad?" *Corpus Christi Caller*, October 13, 1886.

14. "Plans for the Harbor," *Galveston Daily News*, April 25, 1900; "The Coast Inlets," *Corpus Christi Caller*, Aug. 27, 1887.

15. Fuller, *When the Century and I*, 9. For more information on Corpus Christi's civic improvement, see the following articles from the *Corpus Christi Caller:* "Council Proceedings," October 10 and October 24, 1886; "Street Improvements," October 10, 1886; "It Cops the Climax" and "Council Proceedings," November 14, 1886; "City and Country" and "The City by the Sea," July 9, 1887; and "Corpus Christi: the Seaside Attractions of a Lovely Bay City," August 27, 1887.

16. Taylor, *American-Mexican Frontier*, 92, 96, 159.

17. Alonzo, *Tejano Legacy*, 207, 256.

18. Doughty, "Sea Turtles in Texas," 44, 59.

19. Doughty, "Sea Turtles in Texas," 63; Taylor, *American-Mexican Frontier*, 92.

20. Ramon Sanchez, interview by Thomas Krenek, September 17, 1991, tape recording in possession of SCR; *Montgomery's City Directory of Corpus Christi, Texas: 1907–1908* (San Antonio, Tex.: Montgomery Publications, 1907), 85; Ruiz, *Triumphs and Tragedy*, 305–307; "Felix A. Blucher." Available from "Old Bayview Cemetery," http://168.53.172.250/oldbayview/blucherbiographicalinfo.http (accessed November 17, 2002; site now discontinued); Von Blücher, *Maria von Blücher's Corpus Christi*, 245–46; *Thirteenth Census of the United States: 1910; Corpus Christi City Directory: 1913–1914* (Asheville, N.C.: Piedmont Directory Company, 1913), 182.

21. Eleanor Dodson, interview by Mary Jo O'Rear, Corpus Christi, Tex., July 6, 2001; "Important Changes in Officials of Corpus Christi National Bank Made at Annual Meeting Tuesday," *Corpus Christi Caller*, January 15, 1919, 5; *Best's City Directory of Corpus Christi, 1919* (Corpus Christi, Tex.: D. H. Best, 1919), n.p.

22. Marian Gunst Browne Crutchfield, interview by Mary Jo O'Rear, Corpus Christi Tex., July 11, 2001; *Thirteenth Census of the United States; Best's City Directory of Corpus Christi, 1919.*

23. "Corpus Christi: 1900," *Corpus Christi Caller*, Centennial Edition, 1983, CF-16, file 65, George Coalson Files, STA; Procheska, "Czechs in Nueces County," 39–40.

24. Caterino Lerma, interview by Paul Schuster Taylor, Harlingen, Tex., September

21, 1929, Taylor Papers, 10.7, Bancroft MSS; *The Javelin*, September 2, 1911, 12:23, Bancroft MSS; Montejano, *Anglos and Mexicans*, 114, 115; Neil Foley, *White Scourge*, 8, 10, 11.

25. Texas Mexican, interview by Paul Schuster Taylor, Nueces County, September 9, 1929, 12:23, Taylor Papers, Bancroft MSS; Henry Allsmeyer, interview by Paul Schuster Taylor, San Benito, Tex., December 1928, Taylor Papers, Bancroft MSS; Coalson, *Migrating Farm Labor System*, 14; Neil Foley, *White Scourge*, 42.

26. Eisenhauer and Starnes, *Corpus Christi*, 36, 37, 38, 72; "Street Improvements," *Corpus Christi Caller*, October 10, 1886; Sullivan, *Our Times*, vol. 1, *The Turn of the Century*, 14, 285, 580, 600.

27. Fuller, *When the Century and I*, 6, 239; Burr, *Billboard Guide to Tejano*, 74.

CHAPTER FOUR

1. Williams, *Weather Book*, 141; "Anatomy of a Storm," *Corpus Christi Caller-Times*, May 31, 1998.

2. Williams, *Weather Book*, 146.

3. Ibid.

4. "More Particulars of the Blow," *Corpus Christ Caller*, August 26, 1886.

5. Roth, "Texas Hurricane History," 4, 18.

6. Patricia Bellis Bixel, "It Must Be Made Safe," in *American Disasters*, ed. Biel, 233.

7. I. M. Cline, "West Indian Hurricanes," *Galveston Daily News*, July 16, 1891.

8. "Is the *Galveston News* Mad?" *Corpus Christi Caller*, October 13, 1886.

9. "Story of the Hurricane Which Swept Galveston," *Galveston Daily News*, September 12, 1900.

10. Isaac Cline, "Special Report on the Galveston Hurricane of September 8, 1900," *National Weather Service Stories and Tales*, www.history.noaa.gov/stories/cline2.html (accessed December 3, 2003; site now discontinued).

11. "Galveston's Calamity," *Corpus Christi Caller*, September 14, 1900.

12. "Storm Notes," *Corpus Christi Caller*, September 14, 1900.

13. "Had an Enjoyable Time," *Corpus Christi Caller*, September 14, 1900.

14. "Editorial," *Corpus Christi Caller*, September 14, 1900.

15. Ibid.

16. San Antonio visitor quoted in "A Field for Enterprise," *Corpus Christi Caller*, November 14, 1886; Fort Worth Gazette quoted in "Deep Water for Texas," July 2, 1887, and "Corpus Christi: the Seaside Attractions of a Lovely Bay City," August 27, 1887, *Corpus Christi Caller*; the Texas-Mexican Railroad brochure quoted in "The City by the Sea," *Corpus Christi Caller*, July 6, 1887; Galveston tourist quoted in "A Visit to Corpus Christi," *Corpus Christi Caller*, April 2, 1887.

17. "The Texas Storms," *Corpus Christi Caller*, October 20, 1886.

18. Ibid.

19. George Reeder, "Corpus Christi's Advantages," *Corpus Christi Caller*, December 20, 1901.

20. Ibid.

21. "Corpus Christi as a Safe Harbor and Deep Water Port," *Corpus Christi Caller*, July 30, 1909.

22. Taylor, *American-Mexican Frontier*, 92, 96.

23. Jenny Strasburg, "Forgotten Neighborhood: History of Northside's Isolation Has Been Unwritten," *Corpus Christi Caller-Times*, February 8, 1998.

24. Alclair Mays Pleasant, interview by author, November 11, 2003.

25. The first African American schoolhouse was erected on land donated by Richard King in 1873. See Jordan, "Black Tracks to Texas," 12–14.

26. Strasburg, "Forgotten Neighborhood," 28 (cited in note 23).

27. Since national census figures did not include Mexican Americans as a separate ethnic group in the early twentieth century, most authorities estimated their numbers in Corpus Christi to be 30 to 35 percent of the Anglo population. See Fernández, *Mexican-Americans in Corpus Christi*, 1, 5–6; "Corpus Christi: 1900," *Corpus Christi Caller-Times*, Centennial Edition, 1983, Coalson Files #65, STA.

28. Fernández, *Mexican-Americans in Corpus Christi*, 1.

29. Sánchez interview.

30. Jordan, "Black Tracks to Texas," 14.

31. "Corpus Christi: 1900," Coalson Files #65, STA; "John Mircovich dies, Resident 68 Years," *Corpus Christi Caller*, n.d., n.p., Kilgore Collection, #73212, SCR.

32. Bette Hunter Ash, August 15, 2001, conversation with author, Robstown, Texas; Painter, *Standing at Armageddon*, xxix–xxxiv; Eleanor Dodson, interview with author, July 6, 2001, Corpus Christi, Tex.; "Assessor's Abstracts of City Lots: 1917–1920," LHR; *Best's City Directory of Corpus Christi: 1919*; Flanney, *Irish Texans*, 107–116; "Immigrant Irishmen," Kilgore Collection #7312, SCM.

33. Flanney, *Irish Texans*, 107–108; Johnson, *History of the American People*, 305.

34. Taylor, *American-Mexican Frontier*, 92; Blodgett, *Texas Home Rule Charters*, 2–3; Eisenhauer and Starnes, *Corpus Christi: A Picture Postcard History*, 84–89; Reeder, "Corpus Christi's Advantages."

CHAPTER FIVE

1. Garner's nickname derived from his support of the cactus bloom as the official Texas state flower. His choice lost, but the moniker stuck. See Fisher, *Cactus Jack*, 17.

2. "Meets with Mr. Garner," *Corpus Christi Caller*, January 30, 1903.

3. Fisher, *Cactus Jack*, 37.

4. Fisher, *Cactus Jack*, 23, 33, 36–37.

5. Alonzo, *Tejano Legacy*, 235–39; Crimm, *DeLeón*, 240; Barnes, *Farmers in Rebellion*, 111, 196; Senate Commission on Industrial Relations, *Final Report*, 64th Cong., 1st sess, 1916, S. Doc. 415, 8951, 8953, 8957.

6. Alonzo, *Tejano Legacy*, 110–12; del Castillo, *La Familia*, 11; Mr. Johnson, interview by Taylor, El Paso, Tex., November 17, 1928, BANC FILM: 2649:1, Taylor Papers, Bancroft MSS, 107a; Jovita González, "Social Life in Cameron, Starr, and Zapata Counties" (Master's thesis, University of Texas, 1930), 52.

7. Ruiz, *Triumphs and Tragedy*, 102–105.

8. Ibid, 104.

9. Alonzo, *Tejano Legacy*, 45.

10. González, "Social Life in Cameron," 50–51.

11. Catarino Lerma, interview by Taylor, Harlingen, Tex., September 21, 1929, 10.7, Taylor Papers, Bancroft MSS; "Property and History Notes," 12:31, Taylor papers, Bancroft MSS; Montejano, *Anglos and Mexicans*, 80–81.

12. Montejano, *Anglos and Mexicans*, 80.

13. Juan Estrada, interview by Taylor, Aqua Dulce, Tex., August 14, 1929, BANC FILM: 2649:1, Taylor Papers, Bancroft MSS, 694; González, "Social Life in Cameron," 84.

14. Richard King, interview by Schuster Taylor, Corpus Christi, Tex., August 14, 1929, BANC FILM: 2649:1, Taylor Papers, Bancroft MSS, 691.

15. Bedford (foreman of King Ranch), interview by Taylor, Agua Dulce, Tex., August 14, 1929, BANC FILM: 2649:1, Taylor Papers, Bancroft MSS, 694.

16. Starting in 1859 and for the next sixteen years, Juan Nepomuceno Cortina led a series of uprisings against Anglo Americans along the lower Rio Grande valley. See Thompson, *Cortina*, 1–9, 200–202, 222–23; Rosenbaum, *Mexicano Resistance in the Southwest*, 42–45. Triplett and Hauslein, *Civics: Texas and Federal*, 96; Texas Legislature, *D. W. Glasscock, contestant, vs. A. Parr, contestee, Supplement to the Senate Journal: Regular Session of the 36th Congress, 1919* (Austin, Texas: Texas State Senate, 1919), 862, Texas State Archives (hereafter cited as TSA); *Corpus Christi Weekly Caller*, July 24, 1918, 12:33, Taylor Papers, Bancroft MSS; Anders, *Boss Rule in South Texas*, 16; Lerma interview; Anders, "Boss Rule and Constituent Interests," 279–80.

17. Taylor, *American-Mexican Frontier*, 230; Anders, *Boss Rule in South Texas*, 6–7.

18. Baulch, "James B. Wells," 61, 87, 92; Anders, "Boss Rule and Constituent Interests," 279–83.

19. Anders, *Boss Rule in South Texas*, 15.
20. Anders, "Boss Rule and Constituent Interests," 285–86.
21. D. W. Glasscock, *vs. A. Parr*, 862, TSA.
22. Anders, *Boss Rule in South Texas*, 13; Baulch, "James B. Wells," 54; Venesssa Santos-Garza, "Vaqueros of the Kenedy Ranch," *Corpus Christi Caller-Times*, August 3, 2003; Isabel Scarborough, "The King Ranch Schools," in *Kleberg County, Texas: A Collections of Historical Sketches and Family Histories* (Austin, Texas: The Kleberg county Historical Commission, 1979), 81–85; Pleasant, interview by Wood.
23. González, "Social Life in Cameron," 88–89.
24. Ibid.
25. González, "Social Life in Cameron," 87; Anders, *Boss Rule in South Texas*, 13, 14.

CHAPTER SIX

1. Lea, *King Ranch*, vol. 2, 483, 489, 498, 513, 540–44; Frank Goodwyn, *Life on the King Ranch*, 25; Kate Bluntzer, "Robert Justus Kleberg," *Corpus Christi Caller*, 10, November 6, 1932, Vertical Files—Biography: Kleberg, LHR.
2. Lea, *King Ranch*, vol. 2, 506, 539, 545–46; William E. Curtis, "Ranchmen Give a Wealthy Empire," *Weekly Corpus Christi Caller*, April 21, 1911; *The Javelin*, June 19, 1909, 12:27, Taylor Papers, Bancroft MSS; Anders, *Boss Rule in South Texas*, 139–40.
3. Lea, *King Ranch*, vol. 2, 550, 556; Curtis, "Ranchmen Give a Wealthy Empire"; *History of Nueces County*, 94.
4. "Corpus Christi: 1900," Coalson Files, STA; Montejano, *Anglos and Mexicans*, 110, 114–15, 168; Quadrilla, interview by Taylor, El Paso, Tex., November 13, 1928, BANC FILM: 2649:1, Taylor Papers, Bancroft MSS, 89; Mexicans near W.T. Young Ranch, interview by Taylor, Acala, Tex., November 15, 1928, BANC FILM: 2649:1, Taylor Papers, Bancroft MSS, 95; quotation from Bedford interview.
5. González, "Social Life in Cameron," 64.
6. "A Glimpse of Missionary Conditions in Texas by a Passionist Missionary," *Extension Magazine: the Catholic National Monthly*, X (October 1915): 9.
7. González, "Social Life in Cameron," 65.
8. "Vattman, Texas," in *Kleberg County, Texas*, 347; Anders, *Boss Rule in South Texas*, 75; Johnson, *History of the American People*, 304–305; "How I Spent My Vacation by a Southern Missionary," *Extension Magazine*, 20; Fialka, *Sisters*, 5–6, 50–51; Slattery, *Promises to Keep*, vol. 1, 123–24; quotation from John F. Quinn, review of *Catholicism and American Freedom*, by John T. McGreevy, *Catholic Southwest* 16 (2005): 88–89.

9. "A Glimpse of Missionary Conditions in Texas by a Passionist Missionary," *Extension Magazine*, 10; Mrs. Allsmeyer, interview by Taylor, December 1928, BANC FILM: 2649:1, Taylor Papers, Bancroft MSS, 26.

10. "A Glimpse of Missionary Conditions," 10.

11. Thaddeus Stevens, quoted in Foley, *White Scourge*, 54.

12. Terms used are in the context of the time. "Whites," "Anglos," and "Americans" were commonly accepted designations of the ruling Caucasian leaders of segregated, Texas society. See Foley, *White Scourge*, 5–7. "Mexican" referred to all native-born Americans of Mexican descent. See Taylor, *American-Mexican Frontier*, xi, 241–42. *Mestizos* were the people of Mexico, descendents generally of the *Indios* and the conquistadores, "the progeny of Spaniard and Indian." See Ruiz, *Triumphs and Tragedy*, 12, 37. Alan Taylor, *American Colonies*, xiii, 140, 157, 212, 436, 443; Zinn, *People's History of the United States*, 204–209.

13. W. D. Hatter, interview by Taylor, Banquete, Tex., 1919, 10.7, Taylor Papers, Bancroft MSS, 167.

14. Mr. Bloodworth, interview by Taylor, Kingsville, Tex., October 1928, 12:10, Taylor Papers, Bancroft MSS.

15. Henry Baldwin, interview by Taylor, Corpus Christi, Tex., August 31, 1929, BANC FILM: 2649:1, Taylor Papers, Bancroft MSS, 710.

16. H. R. Sutherland, interview by Taylor, Corpus Christi, Tex., August 19, 1929, 10.7, Taylor Papers, Bancroft MSS, 92.

17. Andrés de Luna, interview by Taylor, September 1929, 10:7, Taylor Papers, Bancroft MSS, 195–196; Ben Garza, interview by Taylor, Corpus Christi, Tex., August 29, 1929, 10:7, Taylor Papers, Bancroft MSS, 123; V. Carl Allsup, *Handbook of Texas Online*, s.v. "Hernandez v State of Texas," http://www.tsha.utexas.edu/handbook/online/articles/HH/jrh1.html (accessed March 14, 2006); González, "Social Life in Cameron," 111; "Quotations from Deed Records of Nueces County, Texas, Benovsky Addition, Bishop, Texas," January 28, 1913, 10:7, Taylor Papers, Bancroft MSS; Genevieve Cox, interview by author, Corpus Christi, Tex., January 22, 2004.

18. N. D. Collier, interview by Taylor, El Paso, Tex., November 13, 1928, BANC FILM: 2649:1, Taylor Papers, Bancroft MSS, 69.

19. González, "Social Life in Cameron," 106–108.

20. Ibid.

21. Montejano, *Anglos and Mexicans*, 116, 125–27, 133.

22. Laurie Jasinski, "Memories of Early Sarita, 1905–1910," (paper presented at South Texas Historical Association, Kingsville, Texas, November 1, 2003); Laurie Jasinski, "Sarita, Texas," *The Handbook of Texas Online*, http://www.tsha.utexas

.edu/handbook/online/articles/view/CC/eec12.html (accessed June 4, 2004); Lea, *King Ranch*, vol. 2, 558–59; Montejano, *Anglos and Mexicans*, 111–12, 130.

23. Garraty and Carnes, *American Nation*, 600–601, 606–607, 609–611; Foley, *White Scourge*, 6, 204; Schneider and Schneider, *American Women in the Progressive Era*, 67–69, 94, 124–25, 166–67; Sullivan, *Our Times*, vol. 5, *Over Here: 1914–1918*, 162–63.

24. Chudacoff and Smith, *Evolution of American Urban Society*, 184–87; Link, and McCormick, *Progressivism*, 6, 21–25; Sally Satel, "A Better Breed of American," review of *Better for All the World*, by Harry Bruinius, *The New York Times Book Review*, February 26, 2006, 6; Grantham, *Southern Progressivism*, xvii–xviii; Garraty and Carnes, *American Nation*, 605–615.

25. Grantham, 107, 122, 156–57, 173, 253, 289, 402.

26. Violence was an ever-present threat to African Americans in Dixie. Between 1882 and 1951, an estimated thirty-four hundred Blacks were lynched nationwide, 90 percent in the South. See Robert A. Gibson, "The Negro Holocaust: Lynching and Race Riots in the United States, 1880–1950," *Yale-New Haven Teachers Institute*, http://www.yale.edu/ynhti/curriculum/units/1979/2/79.02.04.x .html (accessed March 21, 2006). Grantham, *Southern Progressivism*, 112, 115–116, 125, 231–233; Doyle, *New Men, New Cities*, 261, 266.

27. Gould, *Progressives and Prohibitionists*, 4, 6–7, 42–44; Calvert and De León, *History of Texas*, 227, 278, 283–85.

28. Stoney, "Suffrage in the South, Part I: the Poll Tax;" Campbell, *Gone to Texas*, 337; Anders, *Boss Rule in South Texas*, 47–48, 90–91.

29. *The Javelin*, August 5, 1911, 12:27, Taylor Papers, Bancroft MSS (emphasis in original).

30. *The Javelin*, July 26, 1913, 12:27, Taylor Papers, Bancroft MSS.

31. Moseley, "Citizens White Primary," 526.

32. Moseley, "Citizens White Primary," 531.

33. *The Javelin*, May 29, 1914, 12:27, Taylor Papers, Bancroft MSS.

34. Moseley, "The Citizens White Primary of Marion County," 531.

35. "Vote for Amendment,'" *Corpus Christi Caller*, October 24, 1902.

36. "Terrell on Poll Tax Amendment," *Corpus Christi Caller*, September 12, 1902.

37. Grantham, *Southern Progressivism*, 112–15, 118–19; Gould, *Progressives and Prohibitionists*, 6; Moseley, "Citizens White Primary," 524; "Grandfather Clause is Held Unconstitutional," *Corpus Christi Caller and Daily Herald*, June 22, 1915; Stoney, "Suffrage in the South, Part I: the Poll Tax," 2; Stoney, "Suffrage in the South, Part II: The One Party System," 9.

38. Democrat primary winners were virtually guaranteed victory in the general election. See Janice C. May, *Handbook of Texas Online*, s.v. "Government," http://tsha .utexas.edu/handbook/online/articles/GG/mzgfq.html (accessed July 9, 2004). *The Javelin*, July 10, 1914, 12:27, Taylor Papers, Bancroft MSS; "Statement to Women Voters," *Corpus Christi Caller*, July 23, 1918; Moseley, "The Citizens White Primary of Marion County," 527.

39. Moseley, "Citizens White Primary," 525.

40. *The Javelin*, July 7, 1916, 12:27, Taylor Papers, Bancroft MSS.

41. Chandler Davidson, "African Americans and Politics," *The Handbook of Texas Online*, http://www.tsha.utexas.edu/handbook/online/articles/view/AA/wmafr .html (access July 9, 2004).

42. Stoney, "Suffrage in the South, Part II: The One Party System," 9.

43. *The Javelin*, June 12, 1914, 12:27, Taylor Papers, Bancroft MSS.

44. George Scott, interview by Paul Schuster Taylor, Big Wells, Tex., April 7, 1929, BANC FILM: 2649:1, Taylor Papers, Bancroft MSS, 303.

45. Grantham, *Southern Progressivism*, 113–14; Schwein interview; Roy Miller, interview by Paul Schuster Taylor, Corpus Christi, Tex., August 31, 1929, 10:7, Taylor Papers, Bancroft MSS, 118–119; Senate Committee on Industrial Relations, *Final Report*, 8951, 8953.

46. Nueces County Tax Rolls 1846–1910, yr. 1898, LHR; Victoria County Tax Rolls 1846–1910, yr. 1898, LHR; O. Douglas Weeks, "Election Laws," *The Handbook of Texas*, Vol.1, 551; "Terrell, Alexander Watkins," *The Handbook of Texas*, Vol.2, 725.

47. All Terrell's quotes come from "Terrell on Poll Tax Amendment," *Corpus Christi Caller*, September 12, 1902.

48. Anders, *Boss Rule in South Texas*, 90–91

49. These figures are based upon annual wage estimates for agricultural workers of $212.97 and for city workers of $1200.00 in Taylor's *American-Mexican Frontier*, 123, 158. The poll tax's regressive impact in modern times would be approximate to a college instructor paying about $76.00 a year to vote. See Bureau of Labor Statistics, U.S. Department of Labor, *Occupational Outlook Handbook*, 2006–07 Edition, Teachers—Postsecondary, on the Internet at http://www.bls .gov/oco/ocos066.htm (accessed April 22, 2006). "Poll Tax Payments Nueces County Now Amount to 2648," *Corpus Christ Caller*, January 31, 1917; Davidson, *Race and Class in Texas Politics*, 23.

50. "Vote of 1,400 or More is Expected in Today's Election," *Corpus Christi Caller and Daily Herald*, April 6, 1915; Stoney, "Suffrage in the South, Part I: the Poll Tax," 5.

51. Anders, *Boss Rule in South Texas*, 92–93; Triplett and Hauslein, *Civics: Texas and Federal*, 95–96; Davidson, *Race and Class in Texas Politics*, 22–24, 51; Calvert and De León, *History of Texas*, 292–93.

CHAPTER SEVEN

1. J. Baughman, "The Evolution of Rail-Water Systems of Transportation in the Gulf Southwest, 1836–1890," *Journal of Southern History* 34 (August 1968): 371, 374, 378–379, 381; "Railroad Commission," *Handbook of Texas*, 429–430; "Joseph Hirsch to the Bankers at Corsicana; Need of Another Port," *Weekly Corpus Christi Caller*, February 28, 1908; Marilyn McAdams Sibley, *The Port of Houston: A History* (Austin, Tex.: University of Texas Press, 1968), 135–136.

2. "Marcellus E. Kleberg," "Robert Justus Kleberg," "Rudolf Kleberg," *Handbook of Texas*, 2:968–69; Lea, *King Ranch*, 2:492; Graham, *Kings of Texas*, 199. Since all communities between the Rio Grande and the Nueces River numbered less than ten thousand inhabitants, wealthy patróns like Kleberg could still influence votes. See Anders, *Boss Rule in South Texas*, 91–92.

3. Anders, *Boss Rule in South Texas*, 122–23.

4. For an overview of Miller's early career, see the following articles: "Roy Miller, Former *Caller* Editor," *Corpus Christi Caller*, November 26, 1933, and "Roy Miller Dies in Baltimore Hospital," *Corpus Christi Caller*, Vertical Files—Biography: Roy Miller, LHR.

5. Quotation by Richard King, interview by Taylor, Corpus Christi, Tex., August 14, 1929, BANC FILM: 2649:1, Taylor Papers, Bancroft MSS, 691.

6. Kinney quoted in Taylor, *American-Mexican Frontier*, 233–34.

7. Ibid.

8. Sutherland interview. For more information on Irish American and Mexican American advancement, see Flanney, *Irish Texans*, 109, and Taylor, *American-Mexican Frontier*, 94, 159, 177, 235.

9. Ben Garza, interview by Taylor, Corpus Christi, Tex., August 29, 1929, 12:23, Taylor Papers, Bancroft MSS, 125.

10. *Corpus Christi Weekly Caller*, quoting from *El Echo del Gulf*, May 8, 1914, 12:33, Taylor Papers, Bancroft MSS.

11. For more information on African Americans in Corpus Christi, see the following: Campbell, *Grass-Roots Reconstruction in Texas*, 219; Taylor, *American-Mexican Frontier*, 239–240; Fernández, *The Hill*, 6, 9, 11.

12. Nueces County Tax Rolls 1846–1910, yrs: 1898, 1899, 1901–1910, LHR.

13. Nueces County Tax Rolls 1846–1910, yrs: 1898, 1901, 1904, 1905, 1906, 1910, LHR.

14. Press Foreman of *Corpus Christi Caller*, interview by Taylor, 1929, BANC FILM: 2649:1, Taylor Papers, Bancroft MSS, 625.
15. Sutherland interview.
16. Taylor, *American-Mexican Frontier*, 92; "Official Returns from Nueces County," *Corpus Christi Caller*, November 13, 1900; Nueces County Tax Rolls 1846–1910, yr. 1900.
17. *Polkitas* are little polkas, and *corridos* are narrative ballads sung to a polka beat; see Burr, *Tejano and Regional Mexican Music*, 19.
18. Montejano, *Anglos and Mexicans*, 133–35; Douglas Foley et al., *From Peones to Politicos*, 19–21.
19. "Miller Rally at Leonard Hall Attracted Big Crowd," *Corpus Christi Caller and Daily Herald*, April 1, 1915.

CHAPTER EIGHT

1. Assessor's Abstracts of City Lots, [Corpus Christi]: 1917–1920, LHR. For more information about Pope, see Thomas Kreneck, "W. E. Pope Papers—A Biography Brief," Introduction to W. E. Pope Papers, http://rattler.tamucc.edu/dept/special/pope.html (acccessed May 26, 2003); Political Autobiography by W. E. Pope, n.d., Pope Papers, file 81.1, SCR.
2. Roy Miller, *Statements Regarding A Safe and Adequate Harbor at Corpus Christi, Texas*, file F-1067, Port of Corpus Christi Archives (hereafter cited as PofCCal.), 1; "Deep Water for Corpus Christi," *Corpus Christi Caller*, January 10, 1908; Mary C. Riley, "The History of the Development of the Port of Corpus Christi" (Master's thesis, University of Texas, 1951), 103.
3. Anders, *Boss Rule in South Texas*, 185.
4. Ibid., 185.
5. Baulch, "James B. Wells," 299.
6. Hays Dix Deposition, September 7, 1912, file 34.7, W. E. Pope papers, SCR; "To Investigate Duval," *Corpus Christi Caller and Daily Herald*, September 4, 1915.
7. John E. Green Jr. to T. W. Gregory, October 7, 1915, Department of Justice papers, file 176178, RG 60, National Archives [hereafter cited as NA]; W. Wallace Jr., "Memorandum on the Duval Count, Texas, Election Fraud Cases," October 22, 1915, Justice papers, NA; Gould, *Progressives and Prohibitionists*, 157–59; Anders, *Boss Rule in South Texas*, 188–89.
8. Green to T. W. Gregory, May 14, 1915, Justice papers, NA.
9. "Federal Grand Jury Will Probe General November Election."
10. T. D. Wilson to J. E. Green, "Indictment Filed in the District Court of the United

States of America, for the Southern District of Texas, in the Fifth Circuit," April 24, 1915, Justice papers, NA.

11. Texas Rangers and Tejanos had long endured a hostile relationship. See *Handbook of Texas Online*, "Texas Rangers," http://www.tsha.utexas.edu/handbook/online/articles/TT/met4.html (accessed December 2, 2007).

12. "Synopsis of Evidence in Corpus Christi Election Case," March 15, 1916, Justice papers, NA.

13. Nor did they. In 1917, the Fifth Circuit Court of Appeals reversed the entire verdict on a technicality. See *Tom Dunn et al, Plaintiffs in Error, vs. The United States of America*.

14. Green to Gregory, January 24, 1917, Justice papers, NA.

15. Charles Johnson, "The Corpus Christi Outrage," *State Topics: A Journal of the People*, 6 (September 25, 1915): 2, TSA.

16. The nickname epitomized Ferguson's deliberate appeal to his rural constituents. See Anders, *Boss Rule in South Texas*, 241–42.

17. Cumberland, "Border Raids," 302.

18. Anders, *Boss Rule in South Texas*, 232–33, 244.

19. Calvert and De León, *History of Texas*, 287–89.

20. Moore, "Valuable Work in State House Is Pope Record," and Hardeman, "Representative W. E. Pope, One of Few Legislators Born in Log Cabin," LHR.

21. Anders, *Boss Rule in South Texas*, 234, 248–49.

22. The following are all in the W. E. Pope Papers, SCR: Roy Miller to W. E. Pope, February 17, 1917, file 56.4; Roy Miller to Senator Archer Parr, February 17, 1917, file 56.4; W. E. Pope to Roy Miller, February 19, 1917, file 56.5; The Citizens' Bay Front Advisory Committee to state legislature, February 21, 1917, file 58.16; W. E. Pope to City Engineer H. A. Stevens, April 23, 1918, file 59.6.

CHAPTER NINE

1. Enacted in a special session early in 1918, these laws allowed women to vote in primary elections, forbade judges from assisting voters except in cases of physical disability or age, and outlawed anyone but full-fledged U.S. citizens from voting. The use of written ballots whereon the names of unwanted candidates had to be scratched out, leaving only the desired candidate's name clear, supposedly certified the literacy of the voter.

2. *D. W. Glasscock vs. A. Parr*, 1033–34, TSA.

3. *Glasscock vs. Parr*, 864–65; Anders, *Boss Rule in South Texas*, 258–60.

4. *Glasscock vs. Parr*, 864, 1033; Anders, *Boss Rule in South Texas*, 260.

5. Anders, *Boss Rule in South Texas*, 261.

6. "Glasscock-Parr Probe to be Deep," *Corpus Christi Caller*, January 19, 1919; "To Investigate Primary Also," *Corpus Christi Caller*, February 5, 1919; "Story of Primary in Duval County Told Legislature," *Corpus Christi Caller*, February 7, 1919; "Night Session May be Held in Senate Contest," *Corpus Christi Caller*, February 11, 1919; "Glasscock Rests Election Case, Parr Starts," *Corpus Christi Caller*, February 18, 1919; "Forty-Two Residents Nueces County Indicted Saturday; "*Glasscock vs. Parr*, 1034–1035, 1038, 1050, 1052; Anders, *Boss Rule in South Texas*, 263–265.

7. "Parr Seated as Senator from 23rd District," *Corpus Christi Caller*, March 14, 1919; *Glasscock vs. Parr*, 1053–1054; Anders, *Boss Rule in South Texas*, 265.

8. "Hotel Arrivals," *Corpus Christi Caller*, May 31, 1919; "Beach Hotel Roof Garden Was Opened for Summer Season," *Corpus Christi Caller*, June 25, 1915; J. R. Bluntzer, interview by J. L. Campbell, Corpus Christi, Tex., March 25, 1972, STA; Eisenhauer and Starnes, *Corpus Christi, Texas: A Picture Postcard History*, 30; Fuller, *When the Century and I*, 12; Alex Cox, interview by author, Corpus Christi, Tex., July 7, 2001.

9. "History of the 1914 Nueces County Courthouse," http://www.1914courthouse .org/history.htm (accessed July 20, 2002); Eisenhauer and Starnes, *Corpus Christi, Texas: A Picture Postcard History*, 59; "Nueces Democracy Triumphs over Independents," *Corpus Christi Caller and Daily Herald*, November 8, 1916; Wagner, *Handbook of Texas Online*, "Walter Francis Timon;" Dodson interview, July 9, 2001.

10. Crutchfield interview; Fuller, *When the Century and I*, 248, 259; Eisenhauer and Starnes, *Corpus Christi, Texas: A Picture Postcard History*, 149, 152; Murphy Givens, "The streets of the city," *Corpus Christi Caller-Times*, April 17, 1998, http://www .caller.com/mgivens/170498.htm (accessed March 15, 2001); Darren Barbee, "Service brings families together after deadly hurricane severed ties," *Corpus Christi Caller-Times*, September 13, 1919, http://www.caller.com/1999/september/ 13/today/local_ne/718.html (accessed March 15, 2001).

11. Copy of unsigned letter, May 24, 1903 (San Antonio, Texas: Archives of the Motherhouse of the Sisters of Charity of the Incarnate Word. Not to be reproduced without proper authorization of the archives. Hereafter cited as AMSCIW). Although no author or recipient were listed in the transcript of this letter, Sister Margaret Patrice Slattery, historian of the Sister of Charity of the Incarnate Word, San Antonio, Texas, considered it to be written by Bishop Verdiger and sent to Dr. Spohn, based upon its context and its origin in Laredo, Texas. See Slattery, *Promises to Keep*, 2:386.

12. Slattery, *Promises to Keep*, 2:159–65.

13. Ibid.

14. Ibid.; unsigned document, "History of Spohn Hospital," n.d., AMSCIW, 1;

Golden Jubilee Souvenir of the Congregation of the Sisters of Charity of the Incarnate Word,
1869–1919 (San Antonio, Tex.: 1919), AMSCIW, 35.

15. Cox interview; Bluntzer interview; *Corpus Christi: One Hundred Years,* 110–112.

16. "Bumpy, Slow, and Awkward—But Fun," *Corpus Christi Caller-Times,* Nov. 10,
1963, sec. B; Crutchfield interview; Greenwood, "Oyster shell Helped City
Improve Early Day Streets;" Eisenhauer and Starnes, *Corpus Christi, Texas: A Picture
Postcard History,* 36, 37, 38, 97, 98, 99; "Mr. Voter: These are Facts!" *Corpus Christi
Caller,* March 21, 1919; Lessof, "Public Sculpture in Corpus Christi," 195.

17. Cumberland, "Border Raids in the Lower Rio Grande Valley," 287, 308–309;
Fuller, *When the Century and I,* 110–11; P. T. Mason to Pope, February 5, 1917, File
56.5, W. E. Pope Papers, SCR; Pope to Commander of Cadets, February 6, 1917,
File 55.7, W. E. Pope Papers, SCR; "Pershing Selects Corpus Christi for Junior
Military Camp," *Corpus Christi Caller,* March 25, 1917, 1; "Joint Resolution Asks
for War," *Corpus Christi Caller,* April 3, 1917. During the Great War, Camp Scurry
served as a training center for the Fifth Engineers and the Fourth Field Artillery
of the Army. Givens, *Old Corpus Christi,* 47.

18. "Nueces County Furnishes Nearly 1500 for Selective Service War Draft," *Corpus
Christi Caller,* June 8, 1917; Walraven, *Corpus Christi,* 185; Crimmins, "Notes and
Documents: W. G. Freeman's Report on the Eighth Military Department," 353;
"Surgeon General Directs the Institution Be Held in Readiness for Immediate
Occupancy," *Corpus Christi Caller,* March 5, 1919; "Corpus Christi Hospital Is
Ordered Turned Over to Public Health Service," *Corpus Christi Caller,* May 10, 1919;
"Washington May Stamp Official Recognition of Idea of Rest Point in the City,"
Corpus Christi Caller, June 24, 1919; "'This Is the Life' Say Men at Rest Camp," *Corpus Christi Caller,* July 20, 1919; "Long Fight for Institution Is Finally Ended," *Corpus
Christi Caller,* March 4, 1919.

19. Major General Dickman to Adjutant General of the Army, Washington, D.C.,
Sept. 18, Sept. 20, 1919, General Correspondence, A.G.O., 1917–1925, Corpus
Christi, Box 1269, 370/79/23/06, RG407, NA; Bluntzer interview; Eisenhauer
and Starnes, *Corpus Christi, Texas: A Picture Postcard History,* 87, 88, 89; "Corpus
Christi, Texas: August, 1919," *Sanford Map Company* (Broadway, New York: Sanford Map Company, 1919); Sullivan, *Our Times,* vol. 2, *Pre-War America,* 339–40,
432–33.

20. "Survey of Twenty-Five Foot channel Is Assured;" "Roy Miller Dies in Balti-
more Hospital;" "A Resolution," Vertical Files—Biography: Roy Miller, LHR;
"Citizens Committee Is Appointed to Assist in Waterfront Improvement,"
Corpus Christi Caller, December 28, 1918; Richard Laune, *Battle for Prominence: The
Port of Corpus Christi* (Master's thesis, Texas A&M University–Kingsville, 2002),

58; Fisher, *Cactus Jack*, 53. The following are in the W. E. Pope Papers, SCR: Roy Miller to Archie Parr, February 17, 1917, file 56.4; W. E. Pope to Roy Miller, February 19, 1917, file 56.6; Clark Pease and T. King to W. E. Pope, February 28, 1917, file 56.1; W. Helscher to W. E. Pope, April 27, 1917, file 55.17.

21. "Waterfront Bill Now Before the Legislature," *Corpus Christi Caller*, May 21, 1915; "The Election At Early Date Certain," *Corpus Christi Caller*, October 6, 1917; "Construction work on Seawall Expected To Start Here Within Next Three Months," *Corpus Christi Caller*, January 11, 1920.

22. "Villa Holds Up Express Train from Chihuahua," March 24, 1916; "Former General Under Villa in Kingsville Jail," May 12, 1916; Casualty Lists," *Corpus Christi Caller*, November 9, 1918; "Measures Taken to Protect the Public Welfare," *Corpus Christi Caller*, August 7, 1918; "Council Receives Offer for Purchase of Sea Wall Bonds," *Corpus Christi Caller*, August 2, 1918; "Waterfront Fight Ends," *Corpus Christi Caller*, February 16, 1919; "Corpus Christi Waterfront Bill Is Unanimously Indorsed in Report of Senate Committee on Public Land," *Corpus Christi Caller*, March 7, 1919; "Governor Affixes Signature to City Bayfront Measure," *Corpus Christi Caller*, March 18, 1919; "Bayfront Bill Passes Senate," "Corpus Christi Bayfront Bill Passes Legislature," *Corpus Christi Caller*, March 15, 1919.

23. "Hobby Forces Control County Convention," *Corpus Christi Caller*, August 4, 1918; "Greater Corpus Christi, #3" "To the Democrats of the 23rd Senatorial District," *Corpus Christi Weekly Caller*, November 3, 1918; "Otto Wahrmund and Archer Parr;" J. F. Clarkson to W. E. Pope, May 1, 1919, file 57.2, W. E. Pope Papers, SCR.

24. Dodson interview, July 9, 2001. The following are in W. E. Pope Papers, SCR: W. E. Pope to Gordon Boone, January 25, 1917, file 55.3; Gordon Boone to W. E. Pope, June 26, 1908, file 53.2; W. E. Pope to Gordon Boone, January 20, 1917, file 55.3; W. E. Pope to D. W. Brown, August 10, 1917, file 55.4. "Citizens Give Reasons for Supporting Miller," *Corpus Christi Caller*, April 6, 1915; "Hobby Forces Control County Convention;" "Recruit Rally in Park Tonight," *Corpus Christi Caller*, August 12, 1918; "Judge Gordon Boone, Who He Is," *Corpus Christi Caller*, March 24, 1919; "Mayor Boone Tells of Steps for Making City Moral," *Corpus Christi Caller*, January 21, 1921.

25. "Keep Cool," *Corpus Christi Caller*, March 19, 1919; "Judge Gordon Boone, Who He Is;" "There's a Reason," *Corpus Christi Caller*, March 26, 1919; "Well, Look Who's Here—$325!" *Corpus Christi Caller*, March 30, 1919.

26. "Judge Gordon Boone, Who He Is;" "Politics Vs. Progress," *Corpus Christi Caller*, March 28, 1919; "A Word Before You Vote," *Corpus Christi Caller*, April 1, 1919; "This For an Example!" *Corpus Christi Caller*, March 30, 1919.

27. "City Attorney Explodes Attempts of Opponent to Besmirch Roy Miller," *Corpus Christi Caller*, March 29, 1919; "Judge Gordon Boone, Who He Is;" "Another One Nailed," *Corpus Christi Caller*, March 26, 1919; "To the Voters of Corpus Christi," *Corpus Christi Caller*, March 23, 1919; "Real Issue of City Campaign Set Forth by Mayor Roy Miller," *Corpus Christi Caller*, March 25, 1919; "The Net Closes," *Corpus Christi Caller*, March 27, 1919.

28. "Real Issue of City Campaign Set Forth by Mayor Roy Miller."

29. "Investigators Find Poll Tax Books Straight," *Corpus Christi Caller*, February 2, 1916; "Nueces County Prohibition to Become Effective on April 21," *Corpus Christi Caller and Daily Herald*, March 24, 1916; "Poll Tax Payments and Exemptions for Nueces County Totals 2195," *Corpus Christi Caller and Daily Herald*, February 4, 1919.

30. "Poll Payments in Nueces Fall to Below 3,000," *Corpus Christi Caller and Daily Herald*, February 1, 1917; "Campaign Continues Chief Topic on Street and in Stores and Offices," *Corpus Christi Caller*, March 31, 1919; "Entire Ticket Headed by Judge Gordon Boone Swept Into Office in City," *Corpus Christi Caller*, April 2, 1919.

31. "City News in Brief," *Corpus Christi Caller*, April 3, 1919; "Newly elected City Officers Are Installed," *Corpus Christi Caller*, April 5, 1919; "City National Bank Named as Treasurer," *Corpus Christi Caller*, May 2, 1919; "Investigation Is Ordered by City Council," *Corpus Christi Caller*, May 3, 1919; "Judge Hopkins Continues Temporary Injunction in Transfer of City Funds," *Corpus Christi Caller*, May 25, 1919; "Judge Hopkins' Decision in City Depository Case Sustained by Court," *Corpus Christi Caller*, June 19, 1919, 1.

32. "Commissioners at Head of Water and Police to Shift," *Corpus Christi Caller*, July 27, 1919. The following are in W. E. Pope Papers, SCR: J. Anderson to W. E. Pope, September 4, 1919, file 57.3; O. O. Woodman to Carlos Bee, August 29, 1919, file 57.3; Seaboard Transportation to W. E. Pope, September 5, 1919, file 57.3. "City May Be Port if Plans Are Approved," *Corpus Christi Caller*, June 24, 1919; "U. S. will Help Dredge Bay at Corpus Christi," *Corpus Christi Caller*, September 11, 1919; Rosen, *Limits of Power*, 20, 41.

33. "Deep Water is Vital for Corpus Christi Prosperity," *Corpus Christi Caller*, June 6, 1919.

34. "Negro Killed and Score of Whites Injured when Blacks Riot in Chicago," *Corpus Christi Caller*, July 28, 1919; "Cotton Values Descend with Violent Crash," "Grain Values Take Headlong Plunge Down," *Corpus Christi Caller*, August 5, 1919; "Suffrage Is Ratified by Texas House," *Corpus Christi Caller*, June 25, 1919; "Army and City Join Hands to Drive Vice from Corpus Christi," *Corpus Christi Caller*,

August 10, 1919; "Mexican Bandits Hold U.S. Army Officers," *Corpus Christi Caller*, August 18, 1919; "Oil Company Formed Here, Oil Fever Spreading to Bishop," *Corpus Christi Caller*, April 9, 1919; "Oil Activity in This Area at Fever Heat," *Corpus Christi Caller*, June 9, 1919; "Peace Treaty Is Formally Presented to Senate With Long List of Amendments," *Corpus Christi Caller*, September 11, 1919; "Excursionists Take Plunge in Bay Waters," *Corpus Christi Caller*, August 18, 1919; "Two Men Burned When Steam Pipe Nipple Blows Out," *Corpus Christi Caller*, September 14, 1919.

35. "Corpus Christi Public Health Service Is Now Great Asset to the City," *Corpus Christi Caller*, August 3, 1919; "Property on Bay Front is Valued at $2.00," *Corpus Christi Caller*, August 16, 1919.

36. "Tropical Storm Is Heading for Florida Coast," *Corpus Christi Caller*, Sept. 9, 1919; "Known Deaths at Galveston and Other Coasts Ports Total 116," *Daily Corpus Christi Caller*, Aug. 19, 1915; "Wind Velocity Monday Running 38 MPH," *Daily Corpus Christi Caller*, August 17, 1915; Richard A. Laune, "Life of a Texas Shortline, the Riviera Beach & Western Railway, 1912–1917," *The Journal of South Texas* 13 (Spring 2000): 88–89; "In Spite of Losses Citizens Feel Happy," "Corpus Christi Defies Tropical Hurricane," *Daily Corpus Christi Caller*, Aug. 19, 1916.

CHAPTER TEN

1. Russell Mozeney, untitled manuscript, Box 1.5, Russell Mozeney Papers, SCR, 2; David Roth, "Texas Hurricane History," http://www.srh.noaa.gov/lch/txhur .htm (accessed December 18, 2000; site now discontinued); Ellis, *Hurricane Almanac*, 44; Williams, *Weather Book*, 141–43.

2. Roth, manuscript, "Texas Hurricane History," 35.

3. "Havana Swept by Heavy Gale From the Gulf," *Corpus Christi Caller*, Sept. 10, 1919; "South Florida Prostrate by Gale; Property Loss Appalling," *Corpus Christi Caller*, Sept. 11, 1919.

4. Ellis, *Hurricane Almanac*, 45.

5. Mozeney, 1–2; Ellis, *Hurricane Almanac*, 72; Dan Kilgore, "The 1919 Storm," *Nueces County Historical Commission Bulletin* 2 (1989): 52; "Dr. Isaac M. Cline: A Man of Storm and Floods, Part 3: New Orleans," *Weather People and History*, http://www.islandnet.com/~see/weather/history/icline3.htm (accessed July 16, 2003; site now discontinued).

6. Larry Mooney, "Advisories for 1919 Storm," ed. J. McAuliff, (U.S. Department of Commerce: Weather Bureau, April 12, 1978), STA.

7. Ibid.

8. Ibid.

9. Ibid.; Roth, manuscript, *Texas Hurricane History*, 35; "Tropical Storm Gains Speed, Hits Louisiana on Mississippi River," "Heavy Squall Reported at Corpus Christi," *San Antonio Express*, September 13, 1919; Ellis, *Hurricane Almanac*, 72.

10. "The Great Hurricane," *Corpus Christi Caller-Times*, Sept. 7, 1969; Fuller, *When the Century and I*, 244; Ellis, *Hurricane Almanac*, 72; Mozeney, 2.

11. Ellis, *Hurricane Almanac*, 43.

12. "The Great Hurricane."

13. Ellis, *Hurricane Almanac*, 45; Fuller, *When the Century and I*, 244.

14. Murphy Givens, "Letter describe city's worst disaster," *Corpus Christi Caller-Times*, September 8, 1999, sec. A, 10; John A. Porter to Adjutant General of the Army, Washington, D.C., Sept. 21, 1919, NA; "Border Men Here to Forget Camp Life in Pleasure," *Corpus Christi Caller*, September 14, 1919; Dodson interview, July 9, 2001.

15. Pleasant interview, November 11, 2003; Fuller, *When the Century and I*, 247–48; Sánchez interview; "Corpus Christi, Texas: July 1914," *Sanborn Map Company*; *14th Census of the United States: 1920*; *Digital Sanborn Maps Key*, http://sanb orn.umi.com/HelpFiles/key.html (accessed June 14, 2006).

16. Mooney, "Advisories;" Mozeney, 10; Ellis, *Hurricane Almanac*, 72.

17. Kilgore, "The 1919 Storm," 51; Givens, "Letter describes city's worst disaster;" Georgia Nelson, "Hurricane of 1919 a Vivid Memory to Nun at Spohn," *Corpus Christi Caller-Times*, Sept. 11, 1960; Crutchfield interview; Fuller, *When the Century and I*, 248.

18. Pleasant interview, November 11, 2003; Dodson interview, July 9, 2001.

19. Kilgore, "The 1919 Storm," 52; Ellis, *Hurricane Almanac*, 72; "Mrs. Roy Miller, 82, Dies Here," LHR; Crutchfield interview.

20. Darren Barbee, "Service brings families together after deadly hurricane severed ties," *Corpus Christi Caller-Times*, Sept. 13, 1999, http://www.caller.com/1999/september/11/today/local_ne/640.html (accessed March 15, 2001; site now discontinued); Darren Barbee, "Finding those lost in 1919 a hard task," *Corpus Christi Caller-Times*, Sept. 11, 1999, http://www.caller.com/1999/september/11/today/local_ne/640.html (accessed March 15, 2001; site now discontinued); "Residents Who Weathered Storm Hold Vivid Memories," *Corpus Christi Caller-Times*, Sept. 7, 1969, sec. B, 2; Sánchez interview.

21. Givens, "The Streets of the City."

22. Murphy Givens, "Old courthouse stories," *Corpus Christi Caller-Times*, April 4, 2001; "Captain and Mrs. Egeland Perish on Raft Together," *Corpus Christi Caller*, Sept. 25, 1919.

23. Williams, *Weather Book*, 145; Fuller, *When the Century and I*, 248; "Woman Literally

Tarred and Feathered by Storm," *Corpus Christi Caller*, Sept. 29, 1919; "Early Resident Recalls Little Incidents about 1919 Hurricane," *Corpus Christi Caller-Times*, Nov. 9, 1955.

24. Mooney, "Advisories;" Charles Heckathorn, "Station Report of the Hurricane of 1919," National Weather Service, http://www.srh.noaa.gov/crp/docs/tropics/hisory/1919st.html (accessed March 15, 2001; site now discontinued).

25. Heckathorn, "Station Report of the Hurricane of 1919."

26. Nelson, "Hurricane of 1919 a Vivid Memory to Nun at Spohn;" Florence Patton, "Visiting Nun Recalls Storm in Old Spohn," *Corpus Christi Caller-Times*, Oct. 18, 1955, n.p.; Mary Helen Finck, *The Congregation of the Sisters of Charity of the Incarnate Word, San Antonio, Texas, a Brief Account of its Origin and its Work* (Washington, D.C.: The Catholic University of America, 1925), 198–99; "History of Spohn Hospital," n.d., AMCIW, 1; "Officially Revised List of the Dead and Missing Shows Only 357 Names," *Corpus Christi Caller*, n.d., file 34, Kilgore Papers, SCR; "Destruction of Spohn Sanitarium," *The Southern Messenger*, September 25, 1919, (Courtesy of the Catholic Archives at San Antonio. Not to be reproduced without the proper authorization of the Archives, hereafter cited as Cal.of SA).

27. Mooney, "Advisories for 1919 Storm;" Mozeney, 10; "Allen rivals the worst of Atlantic hurricanes," *Corpus Christi Caller-Times*, Aug. 8, 1980.

28. Heckathorn, "Station Report;" Ellis, *Hurricane Almanac*, 72.

29. Fuller, *When the Century and I*, 248–59; Heckathorn, "Station Report."

30. "Captain and Mrs. Egeland."

31. "Woman Literally Tarred and Feathered by Storm."

32. Nelson, "Hurricane of 1919 a Vivid Memory to Nun at Spohn"; "Visiting Nun Recalls Storm in Old Spohn"; Finck, *The Congregation of the Sisters of Charity*, 198–99; "Geraldine McGloin to Sister Francesca Eiken," January 29, 1999 (copy in possession of author); "Profiles in Faith" bulletin board display, (Corpus Christi, Tex.: Corpus Christi Cathedral Historical Committee, June 1999).

33. Kilgore, "The 1919 Storm," 52.

34. Crofford, *Pioneers on the Nueces*, 135.

35. Kilgore, "The 1919 Storm," 53.

36. Heckathorn, "Station Report."

37. Kilgore, "The 1919 Storm," 52–55; Ellis, *Hurricane Almanac*, 72.

38. Pleasant interview, November 11, 2003; Dodson interview, July 9, 2001.

39. Ellis, *Hurricane Almanac*, 72; Givens, "Letter describes city's worst disaster"; "Early Resident Recalls Little Incidents about 1919 Hurricane"; Bluntzer interview.

40. J. Mulligan to John G. Kenedy, Sept. 16, 1919, SCR.

41. Bill Walraven, "The next surge hurricane," *Corpus Christi Caller-Times*, May 19, 1988, SCR; Roth, "Texas Hurricane History," manuscript, 36; Ellis, *Hurricane Almanac*, 74, 76.

42. Walraven, *History of a Texas Seaport*, 80–81.

43. "Residents Who Weathered Storm Hold Vivid Memories," *Corpus Christi Caller-Times*, September, 1969; "Another Storm Victim Found," *Corpus Christi Caller*, March 13, 1920.

44. A rough count of the "Officially Revised List of the Dead and Missing Shows Only 357 Names" indicates 333 dead, thirty-two of whom were not residents of Corpus Christi. Six (2 percent) were listed as African American (colored), twenty-four (7 percent) appeared to be Mexican American, and the remaining 266 (80 percent) were Anglo American. See "Officially Revised List of the Dead and Missing Shows Only 357 Names," *Corpus Christi Caller*. "19,000 Registered Here First Week After Storm to Provide List of the Living," *Corpus Christi Caller*, March 14, 1920; "List of the Dead," *Corpus Christi Caller*, September 17, 1919; Fuller, *When the Century and I*, 248–49, 252–57.

45. "List of the Dead," *Corpus Christi Caller*, Sept. 17, 1919; "List of the Dead," *Corpus Christi Caller*, September 19, 1919; "Two Left Out of Sixteen," *Corpus Christi Caller*, n.d. 1919; Fuller, *When the Century and I*, 248, 258–60; "Officially Revised list of the Dead and Missing Shows Only 357 Names."

46. "Officially Revised list of the Dead and Missing Shows Only 357 Names."

47. Ibid.

48. "Description of Bodies of Unidentified Dead," *Corpus Christi Caller*, September 1919, file 34, Kilgore Papers, SCR.

49. Biel, "Introduction," *American Disasters*, 5; Russell R. Dynes and E. L. Quarantelli, "Miscellaneous Report #46: Behavior in Disaster and Implications for the Insurance Industry," 10 (Newark, Delaware: Disaster Research Center at University of Delaware), http://www.udel.edu/DRC/main.html (accessed 6/21/02); Dodson interview, July 9, 2001; Patton, "Visiting Nun Recalls Storm in Old Spohn;" "Destruction of Spohn Sanitarium."

50. Patton, "Visiting Nun Recalls Storm in Old Spohn;" Nelson, "Hurricane of 1919 a Vivid Memory to Nun at Spohn;" Finck, *The Congregation of the Sisters of Charity*, 199; "Officially Revised list of the Dead and Missing Shows Only 357 Names."

51. Givens, "Old courthouse stories;" Paula Campbell, "Witness to Disaster," *Corpus Christi Caller-Times*, June 3, 2001; Dodson interview, July 9, 2001; Walraven, *Corpus Christi*, 80.

52. Slattery, *Promises to Keep*, 2:172; "A Touching Appeal," *The Southern Messenger*,

September 25, 1919, 1, Cal.ofSA; Givens, "The Streets of the City"; Fuller, *When the Century and I*, 248, 260–61.

53. "Facts About the Storm," "Brownsville Sends Relief," *Corpus Christi Caller*, Sept. 16, 1919; "Rehabilitation of Corpus Christi Is Assured by Nation through Red Cross," *Corpus Christi Caller*, September 23, 1919; Brigadier General W. D. Cope to Gordon Boone, October 2, 1919, box 23, file 1.03, #60, Cities—Corpus Christi, LHR; Dodson interview, July 9, 2001.

54. The American Red Cross, *Disaster Relief Work in 1919* (Geneva, Switzerland: Printing Office of the *Tribune de Geneve*, 1920), 24–26; "American Red Cross Issues Statement of Nearly One-Half Million Expenditures in Storm Relief Service," *Corpus Christi Caller*, June 6, 1920.

55. Crutchfield interview; Barbee, "Service brings families together after deadly hurricane severed ties."

56. Givens, "Letter describes city's worst disaster."

57. "History of Spohn Hospital," n.d., AMCIW, 2, 3; Slattery, *Promises to Keep*, 2:167; "Destruction of Spohn Sanitarium," CaofSA; Finck, *Congregation of the Sisters of Charity*, 199.

58. "Card of Thanks," *Corpus Christi Caller*, Sept. 27, 1919.

59. Conversation with Sister Francesca Eiken, CCVI, Archivist, August 19, 2002, San Antonio, Texas. The statue is preserved in the private collection of the Motherhouse of the Congregation of the Incarnate Word in San Antonio, Texas. "From Corpus Christi, Texas: City Recovering from Recent Disaster," *The Southern Messenger*, October 9, 1919, Cal.ofSA; Nelson, "Hurricane of 1919 a Vivid Memory to Nun at Spohn;" Patton, "Visiting Nun Recalls Storm in Old Spohn"; Finck, *Congregation of the Sisters of Charity*, 199.

60. For information about military aid, see these articles in the *Caller*: "Brownsville Sends Relief," September 16, 1919, and "Colonel Porter in Charge," September 17, 1919. The following are in General Correspondence, A.G.O., 1917–1925, Corpus Christi, Box 1269, 370/79/23/06, RG407, NA: E. C. Marshal, Brigadier General to Adjutant General of the Army, September 17, 1919; Major General J. T. Dickman to Adjutant General of the Army, Washington, D.C., September 19, 1919; John A Porter, Lieutenant Colonel to Commanding General, Southern Department, February 27, 1920.

61. The following in General Correspondence, A.G.O., 1917–1925, Corpus Christi, Box 1269, 370/79/23/06, RG407, NA: Major General J. T. Dickman to Adjutant General of the Army, Washington, D.C., September 17, September 18, 1919; John A. Porter to Adjutant General of the Army, Washington, D.C., Sept. 20,

1919, Sept. 21, 1919. Fuller, *When the Century and I*, 249–52; "Terrible Toll of Life In Very Prominent Family By Storm," *Corpus Christi Caller*, Sept. 25, 1919; "Dickman Praises Men Who Helped in Rescue Work," *Corpus Christi Caller*, Sept. 27, 1919; "Storm Survivor Anxious That Her Rescuer Be rewarded," *Corpus Christi Caller*, March 14, 1920; "Many Corpus Christians Demonstrated Their Stamina On September 14," *Corpus Christi Caller*, Nov. 27, 1919; Adjutant General to Joe Kielpinski/Lula Carter/Rosa Kurfirst, Sept. 22,1919, General Correspondence, A.G.O., 1917–1925, Corpus Christi, Box 1269, 370/79/23/06, RG407, NA.

62. "Rehabilitation of Corpus Christi Is Assured by Nation through Red Cross," *Corpus Christi Caller*, September 23, 1919; O. O. Woodman to S. S. Perry, October 15, 1919, file 58.3, W. E. Pope Papers, SCR. The following are in Cities—Corpus Christi, LHR: Chief of Police to Police Department, September 18, 1919, and to Gus Grimm, September 19, 1919, Box 23, file 1.06, #96; Proclamations by the Mayor, n.d., Box 23, file 1.05, # 74; Maggie Meuley by J. T. Clarkson, September 17, 1919, Box 23, file 1.09, #246; Gordon Boone to J. C. Houts, September 19, 1919, Box 23, file 1.04, #69. W. E. Pope to Central Relief Committee, November 27, 1919, file 58.11, W. E. Pope Papers, SCR.

63. All in Box 23, Cities—Corpus Christi, LHR: Roy Miller to O. O. Woodman, n.d., file 1.06, #131; Ralph Soape to Colonel W. E. Cope, September 27, 1919, file 1.02, #37; Miss Willi Casey to Roy Miller, September 17, 1919, file 1.01, #11; Colonel Porter to Roy Miller, n.d., file 1.01, #2; Maxwell Dunne to Roy Miller, n.d. file 1.01, #4; List of Dead, n.d., file 1.01, #23; Judge Childress to Roy Miller, White Point Report, n.d,, file 1.06, #131; List of Identified Dead, Corpus Christi, Texas, n.d., file 1.01, #28.

64. House of Representatives, Carlos Bee of Texas speaking to the hearing before the Committee on Agriculture, House of Representatives, 66th Congress, first Session, on H. R. Bill 9978, October 30, 1919, file 81.7, W. E. Pope Papers, SCR; O. O. Woodman to W. E. Pope, October 15, 1919, file 58.3, W. E. Pope Papers, SCR; Major General J. T. Dickman to Adjutant General of the Army, Washington, D.C., Sept. 19, 1919; "Death and Destruction Follow in Storm's Wake"; "Colonel Porter Says State and City Co-operated," *Corpus Christi Caller*, September 24, 1919; "State Takes Charge," *Corpus Christi Caller*, September 19, 1919; "Business Men Plan to Rebuild City," *Corpus Christi Caller*, September 26, 1919.

CHAPTER ELEVEN

1. Ellis, *Hurricane Almanac*, 73; Cox interview; "Wreckage Is Fast Disappearing Here," *Corpus Christi Caller*, September 25, 1919; "Business Men Plan to Rebuild City."

2. D. B. South, "The Corpus Christi Storm," box 34, Kilgore Papers, SCR; *Best's*

City Directory of Corpus Christi: 1919, inset page; "Credit Men Will Extend Help to Local Business," *Corpus Christi Caller*, September 25, 1919; Crutchfield interview.

3. Recent state redrawing had moved John Garner's district inland and created a new one for the Corpus Christi-San Antonio area, Congressional District 14, represented by San Antonio lawyer, Carlos Bee. Although no longer representing that part of South Texas, Garner continued to push coastal projects, including the future Gulf Intracoastal Waterway. See Fisher, *Cactus Jack*, 25.

4. For information about the rebuilding of Corpus Christi, see these articles in the *Caller*: "Sound Financial Condition of Corpus Christi Set Forth By Local Bankers," "Products of the Soil Contribute to the Greatness of the Texas Coast Section of which Corpus Christi is the Center," "Rail Lines Were Quick to Restore Usual Service," November 27, 1919; "Government Asked to Finance Loans Here," September 29, 1919; "City Schools, Open Again," September 30, 1919; "Tented City Plans Given More Fully," May 12, 1920; "Community Service Proposes Runway," June 6, 1920. In spite of the fact that the total of Corpus Christi inhabitants increased by 2,300 from 1910 to 1920, the percentage of growth (30 percent) compared with the years from 1900 to 1910 (75 percent) was much less. See *13th Census of the United States: 1910 Population*; *14th Census of the United States: 1920*; "Population of City and County Decreased But Little," *Corpus Christi Caller*, May 20, 1920.

5. "Carlos Bee Will Introduce Bill for a Loan," *Corpus Christi Caller*, October 1, 1919.

6. Ibid., emphasis added.

7. Sociological studies of disaster-hit cities have discovered that, rather than collapse, in many cases the community not only resumed its previous course but intensified it, just as Corpus Christi redoubled its fight for a port. Having especially energetic leadership often helped the recovery. See "A City Forever Changed? Maybe Not," *New York Times*, October 7, 2001; Kevin Rozario, "What Comes Down Must Go Up: Why Disasters Have Been Good for American Capitalism," in *American Disasters*, 72–74, 94; Rosen, *Limits of Power*, 140, 200–206, 252, 317. Loraine M. Long to W. E. Pope, September 16, 1919, file 57.7, W. E. Pope Papers, SCR; "New Beach Better than Previous Ones," *Corpus Christi Caller*, September 25, 1919; "Mechanics By the Hundreds Are Finding Employment Rebuilding Corpus Christi;" Clark Pease to Pope, November 27, 1919, file 58.10, W. E. Pope Papers, SCR.

8. "Carlos Bee Will Introduce Bill for a Loan;" Carlos Bee to W. E. Pope, October 24, 1919, file 58.2, W. E. Pope Papers, SCR; Morris Sheppard to W. E. Pope, October 25, 1919, file 58.12, W. E. Pope Papers, SCR; *A Bill Authorizing the Secretary of War to appoint a special board of engineers to make immediate examination*

and report of harbor facilities on the Texas coast, 66th Congress, 1st sess., H.R. 10139, file 81.7, Pope Papers, SCR; "Committee for Developing of a Far Greater City is Formed," *Corpus Christi Caller*, October 26, 1919; Roy Miller, "The Legislative History of the Port of Corpus Christi," file 2.05, Cities/Counties Collection One: Port of Corpus Christi, LHR, 6.

9. Roy Miller, "The Corpus Christi Port Project," in *Statements Regarding a Safe and Adequate Harbor at Corpus Christi, Texas*, frontispiece, PofCCal.

10. Roy Miller, *Statements*, 2; Corpus Christi Commercial Club to Seaboard Transport and Shipping Company, August 28, 1919, file 57.3, W. E. Pope Papers, SCR.

11. Miller, *Statements*, 2; Statistician, interview by Taylor, Houston, Tex., December 4, 1926, 12:28, Taylor Papers, Bancroft MSS; *The Javelin*, January 27, 1906, June 19, 1909, 12:27, Taylor Papers, Bancroft MSS; "Joseph Hirsch to the Bankers at Corsicana: Need of Another Port."

12. Sibley, *The Port of Houston: A History*, 166; C. M. Fish to Roy Miller, January 1, 1922, in *Statements*, 2.

13. A. Brown to Roy Miller, December 30, 1921, *Statements*, 4.

14. "Ranchmen Give a Wealthy Empire."

15. Roy Miller to Colonel H. C. Newcomer, January 3, 1922, *Statements*, 17.

16. Miller to Newcomer, *Statements*, 5.

17. Miller, *Statements*, 2–3.

18. Miller to Newcomer, *Statements*, 5.

19. Miller, *Statements*, 3.

20. Miller to Newcomer, *Statements*, 5.

21. Ibid.

22. Miller to Newcomer, *Statements*, 8–9.

23. Miller to Newcomer, *Statements*, 10.

24. Miller, *Statements*, 3.

25. Ibid.

26. Sibley, *Port of Houston*, 134–36.

27. Ibid.

28. Miller, *Statements*, 3.

29. Miller, *Statements*, 3; John N. Barnes to Richard King, "Greetings," n.d., PofCCal., 4–5.

30. "Carlos Bee will introduce Bill for a Loan;" Rosen, *Limits of Power*, 266–67, 289–92, 319, 335–36.

31. Riley, "The History of the Development of the Port of Corpus Christi," 103; Miller, "The Legislative History of the Port of Corpus Christi," 4–5; "Need of

Port Basis of Meet in Kingsville," *Corpus Christi Caller*, March 8, 1921; "Corpus Christi Deep Water Association Formed at Meeting of Land Owners, Bankers, and Business Leaders," *Corpus Christi Caller*, March 9, 1921; Roy Miller to W. E. Pope, April 16, 1921, file 81.7, W. E. Pope Papers, SCR; Lea, *King Ranch*, 2:601; Texas and Southwestern Cattle Raisers Association Resolution, March 15, 1921, Beaumont Chamber of Commerce Resolution, April 7, 1921, file 81.7, Pope Papers, SCR; "List of Endorsements of Corpus Christi as Location for Harbor," in *Statements*, 2.

32. C. W. Gibson to E. T. Merriman, September 17, 1936, file 9.1, E. T. Merriman Papers, SCR; Riley, "The History of the Development of the Port of Corpus Christi," 113, 116, 122; Miller, *Statements*, 2.

33. Gibson to Merriman; Riley, "The History of the Port of Corpus Christi," 118, 126; Barnes, "Greetings" 5.

34. Gordon Boone to W. E. Pope, January 11, 1921, file 81.7, Pope Papers, SCR.

35. "Breakwater Wins by Unanimous Vote," *Corpus Christi Caller*, March 11, 1921; Riley, "The History of the Port of Corpus Christi," 116; Miller, "The Legislative History of the Port of Corpus Christi," 8.

36. Russell Savage to W. E. Pope, April 8, 1920, file 60.2, Pope Papers, SCR.

37. Ibid.

38. Russell Savage to W. E. Pope, April 9, 1920, file 60.2, W. E. Pope Papers, SCR.

39. Ibid; Miller to Major I. Adams, November 5, 1921, *Statements*; Mrs. Elmer Noe to W. E. Pope, October 27, 1920, file 61.11, Pope Papers, SCR.

40. "Building of Seawall to Start at Once," *Corpus Christi Caller*, November 15, 1919.

41. "Construction Work on Seawall Expected to Start Here Within Next Three Months," *Corpus Christi Caller*, January 11, 1920.

42. "Substitution of Breakwater for Seawall Recommended by Citizens," *Corpus Christi Caller*, February 26, 1920.

43. "Council Approves Breakwater Plan," *Corpus Christi Caller*, March 13, 1920.

CHAPTER TWELVE

1. "Now Is the Time," *Corpus Christi Caller*, October 10, 1919; Barnes, "Greetings," 1.

2. Ibid., emphasis in original.

3. Ibid; "Now Is the Time," *Corpus Christi Caller*, October 12, 1919; "Now Is the Time," October 13, 1919, *Corpus Christi Caller*.

4. "Death List Now Exceeds 400 With More Than 100 Names on the List of Missing," *Corpus Christi Caller*, September 22, 1919; "Storm Victims Here Were 277," *Corpus Christi Caller*, March 31, 1920; "List of the Dead," *Corpus Christi Caller*,

September 17, 1919; Eleanor Mortensen, "Maps mute reminder of blackest day," *Corpus Christi Caller-Times*, November 1, 1975, SCR; Porter to Adjutant General of the Army, September 20, 1919, NA; Bluntzer interview.

5. Carl Smith, "Faith and Doubt: The Imaginative Dimensions of the Great Chicago Fire," *American Disasters*, 145; Ted Steinberg, "The San Francisco Earthquake and Cosmic Denial," *American Disasters*, 119–20; Patricia Bellis Bixel, "It Must Be Made Safe," *American Disasters*, 223, 240–41. The number of hurricane-related deaths is still uncertain. In his appeal for federal aid to devastated farmers, Representative Bee stated that over one thousand in the region had drowned. See Carlos Bee of Texas before the Committee on Agriculture, House of Representatives, 66th Congress, first Session, on H. R. Bill 9978, October 30, 1919, file 81.7, W. E. Pope Papers, SCR. Bill Walraven, in *Corpus Christi: The History of a Texas Seaport*, 81, states that estimates range up to six hundred, as does Michael Ellis in his *Hurricane Almanac, 1986: Texas Edition*, 73, and Vivienne Heines, in her Chamber of Commerce publication, *Historic Corpus Christi: a Sesquicentennial History* (San Antonio, Texas: Historical Publishing Network, 2002), 35. The Texas State Historical marker on North Beach, Corpus Christi, Texas, dedicated June 3, 2001, says 357 died from the surrounding area, of which 286 were from the city.

6. "'Excellent Business Conditions' Is Report of Corpus Christi Merchants," "Mechanics By the Hundreds Are Finding Employment Rebuilding Corpus Christi," and assorted ads, *Corpus Christi Caller*, November 27, 1919; "Corpus Christi, Texas: August 1919," *Sanford Map Company*.

7. Editorial drawing, *Corpus Christi Caller*, November 27, 1919; Smith, "Faith and Doubt," 131–32, 136–37.

8. "Substitution of Breakwater for Seawall Recommended by Citizens;" "Ten Million Dollars," June 26, 1921, *Corpus Christi Caller*; Riley, "The History of the Development of the Port of Corpus Christi," 127, 129, 132.

9. "Mob Threatens to Burn Texas Cow Kingdom," October 26, n.d., *San Francisco Chronicle*, 10:2, Taylor Papers, Bancroft MSS.

10. M. Harvey Weil, *A Brief History of the Port*, April 1986, PofCCal., 5.

11. Ibid.

12. "Engineering Board to Visit Coast Before Location of Port," *Corpus Christi Caller*, February 22, 1922; "Engineers Hear Aransas Pass Tell Why She Wants Deep Water Port Located There," *Corpus Christi Caller*, March 2, 1922.

13. "Engineers Now in San Antonio," *Corpus Christi Caller*, March 3, 1922; "Ku Klux Klan Initiation in Neighboring County Viewed by *Caller* Man," *Corpus Christi Caller*, March 11, 1922; Sullivan, *Our Times*, vol. 6, *The Twenties*, 569–70, 573–74;

"Corpus Christi Gets Designation," *Corpus Christi Caller*, May 25, 1922; U.S. House of Representatives, Letter from the Secretary of War from the Chief of Engineers, Doc. 321, 67th Congress, 2nd sess., Box 11, City of Corpus Christi Collection, LHR, 2, 67; Miller, *The Legislative History of the Port of Corpus Christi*, 8.

14. U.S. House of Representatives, Letter from the Secretary of War, 24–25; Gilbert McGloin, Commissioners Court Minutes, October 31, 1921, file 2:15, Collection 1, Section C, Port of Corpus Christi Collection 145, 1928, LHR; H.R. Sutherland, Document #10, November 28, 1921, file 2:15, Collection 1, Section C, Port of Corpus Christi Collection 1928, LHR; Riley, "The History of the Development of the Port of Corpus Christi," 125.

15. Gilbert McGloin, Minutes, January 12, 1922, September 29, 1922, file 2:15, Collection 1, Section C, Port of Corpus Christi Collection 1928, LHR; W. F. Timon to County Commissioners, Texas, February 17, 1923, file 2:15, Collection 1, Section C, Port of Corpus Christi Collection 1928, LHR; Harry Plomarity, "History of the Port of Corpus Christi," *Bulletin: Nueces County Historical Commission* (November 1997), 1; Riley, "The History of the Development of the Port of Corpus Christi," 127, 138.

16. Roy Miller to All Members, December 29, 1922, file 2:03, Correspondence, Collection 1, Section C, Port of Corpus Christi Collection, LHR; "Port the Fulfillment of Corpus Christi's Destiny," Port Edition-*Corpus Christi Caller*, September 4, 1926; Riley, "The History of the Development of the Port of Corpus Christi," 145.

17. "Vote is 16 to 1 for the Bond," October 31, 1922, *Corpus Christi Evening Times*; H. R. Sutherland et al., Return of Special Election Held in Nueces County, Texas, November, 1922, Collection 1, Section C, Port of Corpus Christi Collection 1928, LHR; Plomarity, "History of the Port of Corpus Christi," 15; Riley, "The History of the Development of the Port of Corpus Christi," 145.

18. Minutes of Special Term Meeting, January 2, 1923, file 2:15, Collection 1, Section C, Port of Corpus Christi Collection, LHR; Barnes, "Greetings," 8–9; Riley, "The History of the Development of the Port of Corpus Christi," 149, 151; McGloin, Statement of Bonded Indebtedness, March 23, 1923, file 2:15, Collection 1, Section C, Port of Corpus Christi Collection, LHR; "Port Specifications Will be Returned This Week" *Corpus Christi Caller*, February 13, 1924; "Specification of Port Plans Received Here," *Corpus Christi Caller*, April 8, 1924.

19. Pleasant interview, May 4, 2002; "Picton and Company and City Contract for Erection of Breakwater and Work Expected to Begin at Early Date," *Corpus Christi Caller*, June 29, 1920; First Breakwater Stone Placed Today," *Corpus Christi Caller*, October 22, 1920; "Would Amend Bill to Assure Completion of Breakwater,"

Corpus Christi Caller, July 18, 1921; "City's Breakwater Bond Issue Sold for Cash," *Corpus Christi Caller,* February 8, 1924; Eisenhauer and Starnes, *Corpus Christi, Texas: A Picture Postcard History,* 126, 127; "Port Stands as Monument to Engineering Skills," Port Edition—*Corpus Christi Caller,* September 4, 1926.

20. "Port Stands as Monument to Engineering Skills"; M. Harvey Weil and Port of Corpus Christi Staff, "The History of the Port of Corpus Christi," *The Port of Corpus Christi,* http://www.portofcorpuschristi.com/Chistory.html (accessed July 17, 2006).

21. "Port Stands as Monument to Engineering Skills;" Walraven, *Corpus Christi,* 82; Barnes, "Greetings," 9; Weil and staff, "The History of the Port of Corpus Christi."

22. "Port Stands as Monument to Engineering Skills;" Mary Morrow, *Brief History of the Port of Corpus Christi Since 1926,* January 1965, file 2.02(b), Collection 1, Section C, Port of Corpus Christi Collection, LHR, 1; Eisenhauer and Starnes, *Corpus Christi, Texas: A Picture Postcard History* 123, 142.

POSTSCRIPT

1. Weil and staff, "The History of the Port of Corpus Christi: 1926–2001"; *The History of Nueces County,* 95, 141–42; Tom Boyd to Robert Driscoll, November 30, 1927, file 2:03, Collection #1, Correspondence 1920s, Port of Corpus Christi Collection, LHR; "Praise for New Port, Optimistic Prediction of Future of City," *Corpus Christi Caller,* September 16, 1926.

2. "Celebration Crowd Pouring in Corpus Christi," *Corpus Christi Caller,* September 14, 1926; "Streets to be Decorated for Port Jubilee," *Corpus Christi Caller,* August 12, 1926; "Thousands Take Part in Parade," *Corpus Christi Caller,* September 15, 1926; *Centennial Journey: Corpus Christi Caller, Part One* (Corpus Christi, Tex.: The Caller-Times Publishing Company, 1983), 17; "Official Program of The Celebration of the Completion and Opening of The Port of Corpus Christi," September 14–15, 1926, Alan Lessoff Papers, SCR; Riley, "The History of the Development of the Port of Corpus Christi," 163.

3. Givens, *Old Corpus Christi,* 73; "Official Program;" "Praise for New Port, Optimistic Prediction of Future of City."

4. "Port Formally Opened Before Thousands of Visitors," *Corpus Christi Caller,* September 15, 1926; C. O. Hamlin to Mrs. Roy Miller, April 29, 1928, Roy Miller files, City Government Collection: Corpus Christi, Tex., LHR; "Roy Miller Dies in Baltimore Hospital"; *14th Census of the United States: 1920;* Davidson, *Race and Class in Texas Politics,* 104; Dallak, *Lone Star Rising,* 91–91, 108.

5. Archer Parr to W. E. Pope, October 19, 1919, file 58.10, W. E. Pope Papers, SCR;

"Pope Announces for Governor on No Tax Platform," *Corpus Christi Caller*, February 8, 1924; "When What is Sauce for the Goose Is Not Sauce for the Gander," *Corpus Christi Caller*, November 2, 1924; "Governor: Several residents have sought post," *Corpus Christi Caller*, February 14, 1972, sec. A; Law Offices of Pope, Pope, and Pope to W. E. Pope, July 7, 1924, file 66.6, W. E. Pope Papers, SCR.

6. Law Offices of Pope, Pope, and Pope to W. E. Pope.

7. Archie Parr to W. E. Pope, August 1, 1924, file 76.2, W. E. Pope Papers, SCR; "Port Formally Opened Before Thousands of Visitors;" James T. Moore, "Valuable Work in State House is Pope Record," *Corpus Christi Caller-Times*, 1938, n.p., Vertical Files: Biography: W. E. Pope, LHR.

8. "Robert J. Kleberg Is Chosen Honorary Celebration Head," *Corpus Christi Caller*, September 14, 1926; *Centennial Journey: Corpus Christi Caller*, Part One; Lea, *King Ranch*, 2:601–602, 624.

9. "Official Program of The Celebration of the Completion and Opening of The Port of Corpus Christi;" "Senator Parr Announces for Re-Election," *Corpus Christi Caller*, February 24, 1924; Archer Parr to W. E. Pope, March 2, 1922, file 82.3, Pope Papers, SCR; Archer Parr to W. E. Pope, December 17, 1921, file 64.13, Pope Papers, SCR. The Parr machine remained powerful in Duval County and environs until well into the twentieth century, its role in the Box Thirteen senatorial scandal of 1948 particularly infamous. Economic, cultural, and political changes eventually diminished Parr influence, however, with the suicide of Archie's son in 1974 effectively ending the family reign. Irregularities in Duval County elections still emerge with some frequency, even into the twenty-first century. See "BOSS RULE," *The Handbook of Texas Online*, http://www.tsha.utexas .edu/handbook/online/articles/print/BB/wmb 1.html (accessed June 22, 2004); Dallek, *Lone Star Rising*, 328–32; Murphy Givens, "The End of Boss Rule," *Corpus Christi Caller-Times*, September 6, 2002; "High Duval turnout attracts state's notice," *Corpus Christi Caller-Times*, March 16, 2006; "Voting fraud alleged in Duval," *Corpus Christi Caller-Times*, April 24, 2006.

10. Cumberland, "Border Raids in the Lower Rio Grande Valley, 1915," 302; Anders, *Boss Rule in South Texas*, 276; Douglas Foley et al., *From Péones to Politicos*, 82–83; Neil Foley, *White Scourge* 122, 127, 133, 137.

11. "White Man for Primary Bill is Passed," *Corpus Christi Times*, March 2, 1923, 1; "Negro Seeks Primary Vote," *Corpus Christi Times*, July 18, 1928; Chandler Davidson, *The Handbook of Texas Online*, s.v. "African Americans and Politics," www .tsha.utexas.edu/handbook/online/articles/view/AA/wmafr.htnl (accessed July 9, 2005); Pleasant interview, November 11, 2003.

12. Sutherland interview; Pleasant interview, November 11, 2003; Garza interview.

Three years after the port dedication, Garza and delegates from three different Mexican American organizations met in Corpus Christi to create the League of United Latin American Citizens, dedicated to "develop within the members of our race the best, purest, and most perfect type of a true and loyal citizen of the United States of America." See O. Douglas Weeks, "The League of United Latin-American Citizens,": A Texas-Mexican Civic Organization," *The Southwestern Political and Social Science Quarterly* (December 1929): 261–66.

13. Sanchéz interview; Blanton, *Strange Career of Bilingual Education*, 84–85; "Schools Open September 13," *Corpus Christi Caller*, September 2, 1926.

14. Dodson interviews, July 9, 2001, October 4, 2003; *The Official Catholic Directory, 1921* (New York: Kenedy, 1920), 287, 289, Cal.ofSA; "Official Program of The Celebration of the Completion and Opening of The Port of Corpus Christi;" Ledson, "Rise and Fall of the Texas KKK"; Alexander, *Ku Klux Klan*, 4–5, 14–19; "'Democratic Law and Gospel' As Practiced in Nueces County," *Corpus Christi Caller*, November 3, 1924; "Klan Parades Unmasked at Oklahoma City," *Corpus Christi Caller*, February 23, 1924; "The Klan's Latest Initiation," *Corpus Christi Caller*, March 2, 1922.

15. "Official Program of The Celebration of the Completion and Opening of The Port of Corpus Christi."

16. "Port Formally Opened Before Thousands of Visitors."

Bibliography

ARCHIVAL SOURCES

Catholic Archives at San Antonio. Periodicals. San Antonio, Texas.

City of Corpus Christi. Assessor's abstracts of city lots. Local History Room. Corpus Christi Public Library, Corpus Christi, Texas.

———. City directories. Local History Room. Corpus Christi Public Library, Corpus Christi, Texas.

———. Papers. Local History Room. Corpus Christi Public Library, Corpus Christi, Texas.

Coalson, George. Papers. South Texas Archives. Jernigan Library, Texas A&M University–Kingsville.

Givens, Murphy. Photographs. Private collection of Murphy Givens.

Kenedy Letters. Special Collections Room. Texas A&M University–Corpus Christi.

Kilgore, Dan. Papers. Special Collections Room. Texas A&M University–Corpus Christi.

Koch, Theodore. Papers. Special Collections Room. Texas A&M University–Corpus Christi.

McGloin, Geraldine. Letters. Private collection of Geraldine McGloin.

Merriman, Eli. Papers. Special Collections Room. Texas A&M University–Corpus Christi.

Moloney, Jim. Photographs and cards. Private collection of Jim Moloney.

Mooney, Larry. Papers. South Texas Archives. Jernigan Library, Texas A&M University–Kingsville.

Mozeney, Russell. Papers. Special Collections Room. Texas A&M University–Corpus Christi.

Nueces County. Tax rolls. Local History Room. Corpus Christi Public Library, Corpus Christi, Texas.

Parr, Archie. Papers. Local History Room. Corpus Christi Public Library, Corpus Christi, Texas.

Pope, W. E. Papers. Special Collections Room. Texas A&M University–Corpus Christi.

Port of Corpus Christi. Papers. Local History Room. Corpus Christi Public Library, Corpus Christi, Texas.

The Sisters of Charity of the Incarnate Word. Documents and congregation histories. Archives of the Mother House of the Mother House of the Sisters of Charity of the Incarnate Word, San Antonio, Texas.

Texas State Senate. Records. Texas State Archives. Austin, Texas.

U.S. Bureau of the Census. Records. Local History Room. Corpus Christi Public Library, Corpus Christi, Texas.

U.S. Coast and Geodetic Charts. University of Texas Institute of Marine Biology, Port Aransas, Texas.

U.S. Department of Justice. Papers. National Archives and Records Administration, Washington, D.C.

U.S. Military. General correspondence. National Archives and Records Administration, Washington, D.C.

U.S. Senate. Records. Bell Library, Texas A&M University–Corpus Christi.

Sanborn Maps. Local History Room. Corpus Christi Public Library, Corpus Christi, Texas.

Taylor, Paul Schuster. Papers. Bancroft Library, University of California at Berkeley.

Wagner, Frank. Research papers. Local History Room. Corpus Christi Public Library, Corpus Christi, Texas.

BOOKS, PERIODICALS, AND OTHER SOURCES

Adams, E. D. "British Correspondence Concerning Texas, Part XIII." *Southwestern Historical Quarterly* 18 (1915): 305–26.

Alexander, Charles C. *The Ku Klux Klan in the Southwest.* Lexington: University of Kentucky Press, 1966.

Almonte, Juan. "Statistical Report of Texas." Translated by C. E. Casteñada. *Southwestern Historical Quarterly* 28 (1925): 177–222.

Alonzo, Armando. *Tejano Legacy: Rancheros and Settlers in South Texas, 1734–1900.* Albuquerque: University of New Mexico Press, 1998.

Alperin, Lynn. *Custodians of the Coast: History of the U.S. Army Corps of Engineers at Galveston.* Galveston, Tex.: U.S. Army Corps of Engineers, 1977.

American Red Cross. *Disaster Relief Work in 1919.* Geneva: Printing Office of the *Tribune de Geneve*, 1920.

Anders, Evan. "Boss Rule and Constituent Interests: South Texas Politics during the Progressive Period." *Southwestern Historical Quarterly* 84 (1981): 269–92.

———. *Boss Rule in South Texas.* Austin: University of Texas Press, 1982.

Barnes, Donna A. *Farmers in Rebellion: The Rise and Fall of the Southern Farmers Alliance and People's Party in Texas.* Austin: University of Texas Press, 1984.

Baulch, Joe Robert. "James B. Wells: South Texas Economic and Political Leader." PhD diss., Texas Tech University, 1975.

Biel, Steven, ed. *American Disasters*. New York: New York University Press, 2001.

Bixel, Patricia, and Elizabeth Hayes Turner. *Galveston and the 1900 Storm: Catastrophe and Catalyst*. Austin: University of Texas Press, 2000.

Blanton, Carlos K. "Must Texas Educate Germans, Bohemians, or Mexicans?" Paper presented at the Borderlands in Transition Conference, Laredo, Tex., November 11, 2001.

———. *The Strange Career of Bilingual Education in Texas, 1836–1981*. College Station: Texas A&M University Press, 2004.

Blodgett, Terrell. *Texas Home Rule Charters*. Austin: Texas Municipal League, 1994.

"Blücher, Felix A." Available from "Old Bayview Cemetery," http://168.53 .172.250/oldbayview/blucherbiographicalinfo.htp (accessed November 17, 2002).

Boughman, J. P. "The Evolution of Rail-Water systems of Transportation in the Gulf Southwest, 1836–1890." *Journal of Southern History* 34 (1968): 357–81.

Brands, H. W. *T. R.: The Last Romantic*. New York: Basic Books, 1997.

Brown, L. F., and J. L. Brewton. *Environmental Geologic Atlas of the Texas Coastal Zone: Corpus Christi Area*. Austin: University of Texas Press, 1976.

Burke, James. *Connections*. Boston: Little, Brown, 1978.

Burr, Ramiro. *The Billboard Guide to Tejano and Regional Music*. New York: Billboard Books, 1999.

Calvert, Robert, and Arnoldo De León. *The History of Texas*. Wheeling, Ill.: Harlan Davidson, 1996.

Campbell, R. B. *Gone to Texas: A History of the Lone Star State*. New York: Oxford University Press, 2003.

———. *Grass-Roots Reconstruction in Texas, 1865–1880*. Baton Rouge: Louisiana State University Press, 1997.

Champagne, Anthony. "John Nance Garner, the New Deal." Paper presented at the annual meeting of the Texas State Historical Association, Ft. Worth, Tex., March 3, 2005.

Chipman, Donald. "In Search of Cabeza de Vaca's Route Across Texas." *Southwestern Historical Quarterly* 91 (1987): 127–48.

———. *Spanish Texas, 1519–1821*. Austin: University of Texas Press, 1992.

Chudacoff, Howard, and Judith E. Smith. *The Evolution of American Urban Society*. Upper Saddle River, N.J.: Prentice Hall, 2000.

Coalson, George. *The Development of the Migrating Farm Labor System in South Texas, 1900–1954*. San Francisco: R&E Research Associates, 1977.

Coffee, Phyllis. "Logs Reveal Texas Gulf Coast History, 1866–1900." *Southwestern Historical Quarterly* 65 (1958): 227–32.

Corbin, J. E. "Archeological Materials from the Northern Shores of Corpus Christi Bay, Texas." *Bulletin of the Texas Archeological and Paleontological Society* 18 (1947).

Corpus Christi Caller-Times. *Corpus Christi 100 Years*. Corpus Christi, Tex.: The Corpus Christi Caller-Times, 1951.

Crimm, Ana Carolina. *DeLeón: A Tejano Family History*. Austin: University of Texas Press, 2003.

Crimmins, M. O., ed. "Notes and Documents: W. G. Freeman's Report on the Eight Military Department." *Southwestern Historical Quarterly* 50 (1947): 350–57.

Crofford, Lena. *Pioneers on the Nueces*. San Antonio: Naylor, n.d.

Cumberland, Charles C. "Border Raids in the Lower Rio Grande Valley, 1915." *Southwestern Historical Quarterly* 57 (1954): 285–311.

Dallak, Robert. *Lone Star Rising: Lyndon Johnson and His Times*. New York: Oxford University Press, 1991.

Davidson, Chandler. *Race and Class in Texas Politics*. Princeton, N.J.: Princeton University Press, 1990.

Doughty, Robert. "Sea Turtles in Texas: A Forgotten Commerce." *Southwestern Historical Quarterly* 88 (1984): 43–70.

Doyle, Don H. *New Men, New Cities, New South: Atlanta, Nashville, Charleston, Mobile, 1860–1910*. Chapel Hill, N.C.: University of North Carolina Press, 1990.

Dynes, Russell R., and E. L. Quarantelli. "Miscellaneous Report #46: Behavior in Disaster and Implications for the Insurance Industry," Newark: Disaster Research Center at University of Delaware. http://www.udel.edu/DRC/main.html (accessed June 21, 2002).

Ellis, Michael J. *The Hurricane Almanac: 1986, Texas Edition*. Corpus Christi, Tex.: Caribbean Blue, 1986.

Ellis, L. T., J. W. Pohl, and Ron Tyler, eds. *The Handbook of Texas Online*. Texas State Historical Association. http://222.tsha.utexas.edu/handbook/online.html

Eisenhauer, Anita, and GiGi Starnes. *Corpus Christi: A Picture Postcard History*. Corpus Christi, Tex.: Anita's Antiques, 1987.

Fernández, Diana. *The Hill: Mexican-Americans in Corpus Christi, 1900–1950*. Class Project, Texas A&M University–Kingsville, 1974.

Fialka, John. *Sisters: Catholic Nuns and the Making of America*. New York: St. Martin's Press, 2003.

Finck, Mary Helen. *The Congregation of the Sisters of Charity of the Incarnate Word, San Antonio, Texas*. Washington, D.C.: The Catholic University of America, 1925.

Finley, John. "Tornadoes: What They Are and How to Observe Them." *The Insurance Monitor*. New York: 1887. http://www.lib.noaa.gov/edocs/tornado/tornado.html (accessed December 10, 2002).

Fisher, O. C. *Cactus Jack*. Waco, Tex.: Texian Press, 1982.

Flanney, John B. *The Irish Texans*. San Antonio: The University of Texas Institute of Cultures, 1995.

Foley, Douglas, et al. *From Peones to Politicos*. Austin: University of Texas Press, 1988.

Foley, Neil. *The White Scourge: Mexicans, Blacks, and Poor Whites in Texas Cotton Culture*. Berkeley: University of California Press. 1997.

Fuller, Theodore. *When the Century and I Were Young*. Sylva, N.C.: self-published, 1979.

Garraty, John A. and Mark C. Carnes. *The American Nation: A History of the United States since 1895*. New York: Longman, 2000.

Gibson, Robert A. "The Negro Holocaust: Lynching and Race Riots in the United States, 1880–1950." *Yale-New Haven Teachers Institute*. http://www.yale.edu/ynhti/curriculum/units/1979/2/79.02.04.x.html (accessed March 21, 2006).

Givens, Murphy, ed. *Old Corpus Christi: The Past in Photographs*. Corpus Christi, Tex.: Corpus Christi Caller-Times, 2002.

Golden Jubilee Souvenir of the Congregation of the Sisters of Charity of the Incarnate Word, 1869–1919. San Antonio: 1919.

González, Jovita. "Social Life in Cameron, Starr, and Zapata Counties." Master's thesis, University of Texas, 1930.

Goodwyn, Frank. *Life on the King Ranch*. New York: Crowell, 1951.

Gould, Lewis. *Progressives and Prohibitionists: Texas Democrats in the Wilson Era*. Austin: University of Texas Press, 1973.

———. "Progressives and Prohibitionists." In *Texas Vistas: Selections from the Southwestern Historical Quarterly*, edited by Ralph A. Wooster and Robert A. Calvert. Austin: The Texas State Historical Association, 1987.

Gower, Patricia Ellen. "Unintended Consequences: the Pecan Shellers Strike of 1938." Paper presented at the annual meeting of the Texas State Historical Association, Austin, Tex., March 5, 2004.

Graf, L. P. "Colonizing Projects in South Texas." *Southwestern Historical Quarterly* 50 (1947): 431–48.

Graham, Don. *Kings of Texas: The 150-Year Saga of an American Ranching Empire*. Hoboken, N.J.: Wiley, 2003.

Grantham, Dewey. *Southern Progressivism: The Reconciliation of Progress and Tradition*. Knoxville: University of Tennessee Press, 1983.

Griswold, Richard del Castillo. *La Familia: Chicano Families in the Urban Southwest, 1848 to the Present*. Notre Dame, Ind.: University of Notre Dame Press, 1984.

Haines, L. "Early Transportation History of South Texas." *Journal of Shortline Railroads and Transportation* 2 (1997–1998): 6–7.

Heines, Vivienne. *Historic Corpus Christi: A Sesquicentennial History*. San Antonio: Historical Publishing Network, 2002.

Huff, Millicent, and H. B. Carroll. "Hurricane Carla at Galveston." *Southwestern Historical Quarterly* 65 (1962): 293–308.

Jasinski, Laurie. "Memories of Early Sarita, 1905–1910." Paper presented at fall meeting of the South Texas Historical Association, Kingsville, Tex., November 1, 2003.

Johnson, Paul. *A History of the American People*. New York: Harper Collins, 1997.

Jordan, Edna. "Black Tracks to Texas." *Nueces County Historical Commission Bulletin* 2 (1989): 7–19.

Journals of the Convention Assembled at the City of Austin on the fourth of July, 1845, for the Purpose of Framing a Constitution for the State of Texas. 1845. A facsimile of the first edition with a new preface by Mary Bell Hart. Austin, Tex.: Shoal Creek, 1974.

Kilgore, Dan. "The 1919 Storm." *Nueces County Historical Commission Bulletin* 2 (1989): 51–55.

Kleberg County Historical Commission. *Kleberg County, Texas: A Collection of Historical Sketches and Family Histories*. Austin: The Kleberg County Historical Commission, 1979.

Laune, Richard. "Life of a Texas Shortline: The Riviera and Western Railway, 1912–1917." *The Journal of South Texas* 13 (2000): 78–93.

———. "Battle from Prominence: the Port of Corpus Christi." Master's thesis, Texas A&M University–Kingsville, 2002.

Lea, Tom. *The King Ranch*. 2 vols. Boston, Mass.: Little, Brown, 1957.

Ledson, Yvette. "The Rise and Fall of the Texas KKK, 1915–1950." Paper presented at the fall meeting of the East Texas Historical Association, Nacogdoches, Tex., September 16, 2005.

Lessoff, Alan. "Public Sculpture in Corpus Christi: A Tangled Struggle to Define the Character and Shape the Agenda of One Texas City." *Journal of Urban History* 26 (2000): 190–223.

Link, Arthur, and Richard L. McCormick. *Progressivism*. Wheeling, Ill.: Harlan Davidson, 1983.

McCampbell, C. *Texas Seaport: The Story of the Growth of Corpus Christi and the Coastal Bend Area*. New York: Exposition Press, 1952.

McClintock, W. A. "Journal of a Trip through Texas and Northern Mexico in 1845–1847." *Southwestern Historical Quarterly* 34 (1930): 141–58.

Montejano, David. *Anglos and Mexicans in the Making of Texas, 1836–1986*. Austin: University of Texas Press, 1987.

Morris, Edmund. *Theodore Rex.* New York: Random House, 2001.

Moseley, J. A. R. "The Citizens' White Primary of Marion County." *Southestern Historical Quarterly* 49 (1946): 524–31.

Neely, Lisa. "Henrietta Chamberlain King: Religious Influences in her Life and Work." *The Journal of South Texas* 14 (2001): 259–86.

Newcombe, W. W. "Indian Tribes of Texas." *Bulletin of the Texas Archeological Society* 29 (1958).

Nixon, Jay. *Stewards of a Vision: A History of King Ranch.* Hong Kong: King Ranch, 1986.

Nueces County Historical Society. *The History of Nueces County.* Austin, Tex.: Jenkins, 1972.

Nummedal, Dag, ed. *Sedimentary Processes and Environments along the Louisiana-Texas Coast.* Baton Rouge, La.: Geological Society of America Guidebook, 1982.

Painter, Nell Irvin. *Standing at Armageddon: The United States 1877–1919.* New York: Norton, 1987.

Payne, Darwin. "Camp Life in the Army of Occupation: Corpus Christi." *Southwestern Historical Quarterly* 73 (1970): 326–42.

Plomarity, Harry. "History of the Port of Corpus Christi." *Bulletin: Nueces County Historical Commission* 4 (1997): 14–17.

Price, W. A. *Reduction of Maintenance by Proper Orientation of Ship Channel through Tidal Inlets.* College Station: Texas A&M University Press, 1952.

Procheska, Alvin J. "Czechs in Nueces County." *Nueces County Historical Commission Bulletin* 2 (1989): 39–43.

Pycior, Julie Leininger. *LBJ and Mexican Americans: The Paradox of Power.* Austin: University of Texas Press, 1997.

Quinn, John F. Review of *Catholicism and American Freedom*, by John T. McGreevey. *Catholic Southwest* 16 (2005): 88–90.

Riley, Mary C. "The History of the Development of the Port of Corpus Christi." Master's thesis, University of Texas, 1951.

Rosen, Christine Meisner. *The Limits of Power: Great fires and the Process of City Growth in America.* Cambridge: Cambridge University Press, 1986.

Rosenbaum, Robert J. *Mexicano Resistance in the Southwest.* Dallas: Southern Methodist University Press, 1981.

Roth, David. "Texas Hurricane History." Unpublished manuscript in possession of author, National Weather Service, 2000.

Ruiz, Ramón Eduardo. *Triumphs and Tragedy: A History of the Mexican People.* New York: Norton, 1992.

Satel, Sally. "A Better Breed of American." Review of *Better for all the World*, by Harry Bruinuis. *The New York Times Book Review*, February 26, 2006.

Schneider, Dorothy, and Carl J. Schneider. *American Women in the Progressive Era,*
1900–1920. New York: Anchor, 1993.

Sibley, Marilyn McAdams. *The Port of Houston: A History.* Austin: University of Texas
Press, 1968.

Slattery, Margaret Patrice, CCVI. *Promises to Keep: A History of the Sisters of Charity of
the Incarnate Word.* 2 vols. San Antonio: Sisters of Charity of the Incarnate Word,
1995.

Steinberg, Ted. *Acts of God: The Unnatural History of Natural Disaster in America.* Oxford:
Oxford University Press, 2000.

Sullivan, Mark. *Our Times: The United States 1900–1925.* 6 Vols. New York: Scribner's,
1931.

Taylor, Alan. *American Colonies.* New York: Penguin, 2001.

Taylor, Paul Schuster. *An American-Mexican Frontier: Nueces County, Texas.* Chapel Hill:
University of North Carolina Press, 1934.

Thompson, Jerry. *Cortina: Defending the Mexican Name in Texas.* College Station: Texas
A&M Press, 2007.

Triplett, Henry, and Ferdinand A. Hauslein. *Civics: Texas and Federal.* Houston, Tex.:
Rein, 1912.

U.S. Department of Labor. Bureau of Labor Statistics. *Occupational Outlook Handbook,*
2006–07. http://www.bis.gov/oco/ocoso66.htm (accessed April 22, 2006).

Vera, Homero. "Cisneros Genealogy." *El Mesteño* 4 (2001): 16.

———. "Juan José de las Garza Montemayor." *El Mesteño* 4 (2001): 8.

Von Blücher, Maria. *Maria von Blücher's Corpus Christi: Letters from the South Texas Frontier.*
Edited by Bruce Cheeseman. College Station: Texas A&M University Press, 2002.

Wallace, E. S. "General William Jenkins Worth and Texas." *Southwestern Historical
Quarterly* 54 (1950): 159–68.

Walraven, Bill. *Corpus Christi: The History of a Seaport.* Sun Valley, Calif.: American
Historical Press, 1997.

Walraven, Bill, and Marjorie Walraven. *Gift of the Wind: The Story of the Corpus Christi
Bayfront.* Corpus Christi, Tex.: Javelina Press, 1997.

Ward, H. "The First State Fair in Texas." *Southwestern Historical Quarterly* 57 (1953):
163–74.

Webb, Walter P., and H. Bailey Carroll, eds. *The Handbook of Texas.* 3 Vols. Austin:
State Historical Association, 1952.

Weeks, O. Douglas. "The League of United Latin-American Citizens: A Texas-
Mexican Civic Organization." *The Southwestern Political and Social Science Quarterly* 10
(1929): 261–66.

Weil, Harvey, and Port of Corpus Christi Staff. "The History of the Port of Corpus

Christi." *The Port of Corpus Christi.* http://www.portofcorpuschristi.com/Chistory .html (accessed July 17, 2006).

Williams, Jack. *The Weather Book.* New York: Vintage, 1997.

Wynn, C. E., ed. "Lewis Harvie Blair: Texas Travels, 1851–1855." *Southwestern Historical Quarterly* 66 (1962): 262–70.

Zinn, Howard. *A People's History of the United States, 1492–Present.* New York: Perennial Classics, 2003.

Index

retail businesses, 22–25, 34, 35, 86–87
Riggs, Lee, 75–76
Rio Grande Valley Railroad, 117
Rivers and Harbors Committee, 2, 19, 89, 115, 128
Riviera Beach, 94
road construction, 24
Rockport, 105, 110
Ross, Tom, 75

Sammons, Anton, 35
San Antonio, 14, 15, 86, 114, 121
San Antonio, Uvalde and Gulf Railroad, 88, 105
San Antonio and Aransas Pass Railway, 16, 20, 88
Sánchez, Lorenza (born Mora), 35, 98, 99, 137
Sánchez, Manuel, 35, 64, 98, 99
Sánchez, María, 98, 99, 137
Sánchez, Ramón, 98, 99, 137
Sánchez, Roy, 98, 99, 137
San Diego, 16
San José Island, 7, 17, 102
Savage, H. A., 92
Savage, Russell, 122
schools, 34, 35, 46, 136–37
Scott, G. R., 68
Scott, John C., 63
sea turtles, 21
seawalls, 29, 89, 93, 115, 123
sheep ranching. See ranching/ranchers
Sheppard, Morris, 115
Shonk, Eukle, 112
Simpson, Robbie, 100
Sisters of Charity of the Incarnate Word. See Spohn Sanitarium
Slagt, Mildred, 113
Slattery, Sister Margaret Patrice, 153n11
slavery, 13, 140n11

Slayden, Jim, 89
smugglers, 11–12
Southern Pacific/San Antonio Aransas Pass Railroad, 86, 88
Spanish castaways, 11
Spohn, Arthur E., 85, 86, 102–103, 153n11
Spohn Sanitarium: during 1919 storm, 98–99, 102–103, 105; establishment, 85–86, 152n11; rescue/recovery, 108, 111
St. Joseph Island, 18
St. Louis, Brownsville, & Mexico Railway, 48, 67, 87
Stevens, Henry, 75–76
storms. See hurricanes entries
Sunset Central Railway, 59
surge levels, during hurricanes, 26–27, 95, 97, 101, 103
Sutherland, Hugh, 68, 112
Swatt, Mike, 112

taxes, 51, 70, 77, 79, 88, 119
Taylor, Zachary, 12
Tejanos: and Democratic Party, 46–47; displacements, 24, 41–42, 44, 49; early settlers, 14; electoral disenfranchisement, 55, 149n49; federal investigation, 74; hurricane deaths, 160n44; immigrants, 21–22, 24; mayoral election, 93; patrón/peón system, 42, 44–45; political activism, 169n12; population statistics, 144n27; prejudice against, 49–51, 63–64; segregation patterns, 34–35, 137; voting power, 61–62, 64
Tennessee Trust Company, 89
10th Virginia Regiment, 13–14
Terrell, Alexander W., 55, 56, 57
Texas Farmers' Alliance, 42

CPSIA information can be obtained
at www.ICGtesting.com
Printed in the USA
FSOW03n0235110517
34118FS